CAPITALISM OF HAPPINESS

AXEL BOUCHON

CAPITALISM OF HAPPINESS

INTRODUCING A NEW ECONOMIC WORLD ORDER THAT PUTS HAPPINESS AT ITS CORE

AXEL BOUCHON

:)$

Published by Axel Bouchon, Berlin, Germany

Edited and designed by Girl Friday Productions
girlfridayproductions.com

Cover design: Alban Fischer

Image credits: *Figures 11A, 12A-B, 16C*, and *17*, Helliwell, J., Layard,
R., & Sachs, J. (2017). World Happiness Report 2017, New York:
Sustainable Development Solutions Network; *Figure 11B*, Reprinted
from Journal of Affective Disorders, Volume 140/Issue 3, Brandon
H. Hidaka, "Depression as a disease of modernity: Explanations
for increasing prevalence", Page 10, © 2012, with permission from
Elsevier; *Figures 15B, 16B*, Helliwell, J., Layard, R., & Sachs, J. (2012).
World Happiness Report 2012, New York: Sustainable Development
Solutions Network; *Figures 25–27*, Shiota, M. N., Campos, B., Oveis,
C., Hertenstein, M. J., Simon-Thomas, E., & Keltner, D. (2017). Beyond
happiness: Building a science of discrete positive emotions. American
Psychologist, 72(7), 617-643. Reprinted with permission from APA

ISBN (paperback): 978-3-00-062774-3
ISBN (eBook): 978-3-00-062802-3

First edition

For Marie and Lisa

CONTENTS

PROLOGUE

I was born in a small village in Germany. My parents were teachers, just as my grandparents had been before them. Their jobs were very secure: I was raised in an essentially risk-free environment. We did not have a lot of money, but looking back, I realize now we had a lot of fun. I had the best childhood imaginable.

By the time I'd turned fifteen, I found this risk-free life boring, and any financial upside seemed very limited. So I came up with the ambition of becoming a millionaire before the age of forty. From then on, I focused on that one objective.

And twenty-five years later, finally, I was sitting in Boston with some investors who had just committed $25 million in seed funding for a biotech idea of mine. Great stock option package worth several million dollars and great salary.

Wow. I had made it.

I remember running back to my office and calling my wife, who was preparing to move from Berlin to Boston with our two kids. I was so excited when I told her the story.

Her response was: "Axel, I'm happy for you, but I won't be coming to Boston."

She wanted us to separate! She had fallen in love with someone else, and she planned to keep our kids and the house in Berlin, all because I had "chosen to work in Boston and get rich."

To this day my memories of that moment are precise and clear. I remember that I walked back to the room where the investors were sitting to tell them that I couldn't take the money or the CEO job because I had to go back to Berlin to save my family. An hour and a half later, I was on the plane back to Germany.

Of course, ultimately I couldn't save my family. But I didn't want to accept that. So I fought for months, all the while knowing that I would lose. During that time, my psychological and physiological erosion was dramatic: anxiety about losing my kids, anxiety about personal insolvency, panic about not finding a new job—I couldn't sleep anymore. Yet the most depressing thing was that I realized how big my own contribution to the failure of our marriage had been.

One summer night in Berlin eight months later, once again I couldn't sleep. At three in the morning I decided to go get myself the sausage we call a *Currywurst* in Berlin. It was a very hot night; thousands of people were out on the streets of downtown Berlin, having a good time. And in their midst was "Axel the Zombie," sitting on the sidewalk to eat his Currywurst and sweating like a man with malaria. While the sweat dripped into my Currywurst, a twenty-one-year-old girl came up to me and sat down. She was Lilly, from Amsterdam.

"Hey, old man," she said, "you look like you sell amphetamines and ecstasy—can I have some?"

What?! "No, I can't sell you amphetamines or ecstasy," I told her. "I am not doing drugs."

"Oh wow, I can hardly believe that," said Lilly. "You look so wasted. Well, I have one of these left and I think you should have it. You desperately need some fun, old man."

She gave me a small plastic token embossed with an enigmatic symbol. Then she walked away.

It took a few hours for this "old man" to realize that the symbol on the token could be found throughout Berlin: it guided people to underground techno parties. And the token was your entry ticket. I ended up in a former World War II bunker deep under the streets of Berlin. I had the most amazing time in my whole life—with 150 people I had never seen before—because we'd all had a single objective: having fun. And just to be clear—the old man was having all this fun without taking any drugs!

When I emerged thirty-six hours later, I was a changed man. Later that day, thinking back on the experience, I drew a graph on a piece of paper: a two-dimensional matrix with return on investment (ROI) on the y-axis and a new term on the x-axis, something I called **Return on Happiness (ROH)** (fig. 0).

FIGURE 0: BERLIN NIGHTLIFE "HAPPINESS TOKEN" (LEFT) AND FIRST DRAWING OF THE ROI/ROH MATRIX AS THE BASE FOR A HAPPINESS ECONOMY (RIGHT)

This graph contains the essence of that night, and the spark for this book.

Return on investment, or ROI, is one of the leading economic metrics. It measures how much money we get from a financial investment in a given year. We measure ROI in money, usually in US dollars. It's a quantitative metric that can be precisely compared with other similar metrics.

However, based on the experience of that night, there must be a second, complementary dimension that stands orthogonal to our economic metrics. That little plastic token—worth just ten cents—had given me a thousand times more happiness than anything else had ever done. By just opening a door for me to join a party perfectly suited to satisfy my needs in that night. And I can still feel that happiness when I think back on it today. That second dimension is Return on Happiness, or ROH.

It is not a revolutionary new insight that our economic system is insufficient to provide holistic happiness. Hundreds of brilliant brains in philosophy, psychology, and economics have elaborated on this topic. It is scientifically proven, and we all know it intuitively anyways: "Money can't buy happiness," as Freddie Mercury sang years ago. The reason is simple: our economic system focused on consumption is not fully aligned with our biology. We are wired on a molecular level to learn and progress. We definitely have to satisfy our lower needs, and our current economic system is perfectly suited to that. However, it does not work to provide satisfaction of higher needs such as emotional satisfaction, interpersonal satisfaction, friendship, family love, attachment love, or self-actualization. Money can't solve those needs. It is neuroscientifically impossible.

Therefore, using our happiness as the guiding compass for progress makes a lot of sense.

Just imagine if *Forbes* switched from ranking the richest people on the planet to ranking the people who provided the most happiness to others. . . . It would obviously change the world.

What actually is Return on Happiness?

Can we even measure Return on Happiness? Can we price it? To put a price on happiness would be essential to fill the ROI/ROH matrix, which is based on a mathematical correlation.

The conventional wisdom is that you can't put a price on happiness. It is believed that we simply can't quantify it. In addition, we all perceive happiness as something highly subjective, individual, and personal that can't be used as a universal metric.

But neuroscientifically, this is wrong.

We *can* measure happiness because we all use the same universal unit to quantify it: the molecular signals and electrical currents that make our neurons communicate. Each of us is equipped with the identical molecular detectors for happiness and the identical machinery to translate it into learning and growth. On that level, we are all the same.

Let me repeat this: Happiness is the ultimate driver of growth—on a molecular level and on a personal level. Happiness signals grow and shape our neuronal network in the brain, and grow our identity and personality. Connecting this neurobiological insight to our economic system has never been done, and that's where this book comes in.

I want to achieve two goals: one is to provide the first comprehensive educational guide on happiness, on a molecular and a psychological level. We desperately need a basic understanding of how our brain works and how our current environment, our economic system, is influencing its functionality. Such a guide is in particular missing as our schools and universities, our parents and friends, don't offer these lessons or do not understand the issue well enough. The impact of this missing knowledge is dramatic: we see an explosive increase in depression and associated mental illnesses across all income levels, all over the globe. By 2050, mental illnesses will be the primary cause of death on our planet. Not surprising, they are already the major cause of misery on our planet—surpassing poverty—as the global data of the World Happiness Report indicates. We simply don't understand enough about how our brain works and how we can proactively shape it toward more happiness. I want to change that.

Second, I want to provide a universal framework to overcome the limitation of our current economic system. I want to prove that we can and should put a price on happiness, and we should fundamentally change the focus of our economy from ROI to ROH. Such a "capitalism of happiness" would follow the only universal biological performance indicator relevant for human progress: happiness.

The remarkable result of such a shift would be that the less than optimally happy people at both ends of the economic spectrum—the very rich and the poor—would substantially benefit from each other. From a neuroscientific perspective, each side holds the key to happiness for the other side. Together we can achieve a radical new economy, one that will equally improve the lives of people in the poorest developing nations, people in the wealthiest corners of the globe, and everyone in between. Together we can unleash a new dimension of progress for mankind. Directed along traditional economic growth and happiness growth.

I promise you will adopt the concept of Return on Happiness after the moment you finish this book. You will understand how happiness works scientifically and that happiness is highly contagious in a positive sense. Your happiness will—neuroscientifically!—spread to others. Our brains have been built for that purpose.

CHAPTER ONE

LIFE

Imagine there is nothing but a clock in front of you. The clock has a Start button and the time set to 00:00:00. You don't know the future, but you still want to build a game that has one objective: to keep progressing for the better forever.

What do you do before pressing Start?

You take a deep breath first. And think very, very hard.

You realize that nothing could anticipate all potential scenarios in the unknown future. You conclude that the only answer to maximal *uncertainty* in the future is a game with maximal *optionality.*

I use the term "optionality" here in its broadest definition: having lots of options to freely choose from. With a range of options, you can thrive in spite of not knowing the future. A range of options allows you to wait and see what happens, and then freely exercise the most advantageous option.

In other words, in an environment of high uncertainty, optionality means freedom. Freedom of choice today and—even more importantly—in the unpredictable future.

You need a huge option space because the game is vulnerable to stopping or heading in the wrong direction, particularly at the

beginning. In addition, better options should be promoted over losing ones, in order to push faster toward progress. Next, you realize
the game has to be extremely adaptable in order to respond quickly to
unforeseen changes. To cover these requirements, the game needs two
essential features: *evolution* and *learning*.

And then you press Start and release a tremendous amount of
focused energy to play "the game of life."

As we know today, whoever or whatever pressed Start approximately
13.8 billion years ago and triggered the big bang did an amazing job in
thinking this through: the game of life is still on, and we can date life's
appearance on Earth to as early as 4.3 billion years ago.

Interestingly, life is heavily dependent on the environment in order
to exist at all. It took five billion years to get the environment ready. But
once the environment—our planet Earth—was formed, it took only a
quarter of a billion years for life to emerge—a ridiculously short time.
Starting from a few small molecules, life has survived and progressed
in all shapes and forms ever since. Meanwhile, a small group of living
organisms—called humans—are working on leaving Earth to populate
other planets and on using physical machines to help us learn better
and faster. A huge success, isn't it?

Of course you may argue that many organisms have been extin-
guished over the course of 4.3 billion years—through competition, natural disasters, and organisms killing each other for different reasons.
I totally agree with you. However, we should not forget the original
goal of the game: it aims only for the survival and progress of life *in its*
entirety. Not for the survival and progress of individual species or single living organisms. Not for the survival of a species called humans.
This is very unfair from an individual perspective—yet for life, it's
pretty effective. So, given the original objective, life is a resounding
success. So far at least; we have just started the game of life.

How do evolution and learning affect the range of options for life?

Evolution, first of all, provides one big chunk of our option space.
It is the perfect tool for preparing for uncertainty in the future and
ensuring the success of life overall by providing a huge range of possible

options. Charles Darwin, the father of the evolution theory, formed remarkably sharp conclusions from his observational studies of animals, plants, and humans. He introduced two fundamental features of evolution: mutation and natural selection.

Mutation means that the basis of life—our genes—is continuously facing small changes or larger exchanges. With these changes and exchanges, mutations provide variations or optionality. Unless immediately detrimental, most of these variations are silent. However, depending on the environment, the genetic variability may be exposed to natural selection, providing a benefit for survival or a disadvantage. With it, our environment together with the optionality of our genes creates a competition for survival (the "survival of the fittest"): those who survive until they reproduce inherit their genes from their ancestors and *can* pass to their offspring. This process is the ultimate survival mechanism for life as a whole: the vast genetic variations across all living organisms create a pool of optionality for life to react to the uncertainty provided by the environment—with the more beneficial options offering a higher likelihood to progress.

We as single individuals or as a particular species may not be equipped for what is coming in the future. However, some other living organism, another variant that already exists today, definitely will be. Thus, for life as a whole, this is the ultimate insurance policy for survival, for continuation and progress. Yet, from the perspective of the single individual with a limited life span, this is highly unfair: evolution does not act on individual organisms.

Fortunately, there *are* two ways individual organisms can overcome this limitation and not only survive, but actually thrive under pressure. It's something we humans excel at, along with species as diverse as whales and fire ants: *learning* and *cooperation*.

CHAPTER TWO

COOPERATION

Darwin's evolution theory related to cooperation seems counterintuitive at first. Based on the fundamental characteristics of mutation and natural selection, evolution should operate by way of fierce competition between individuals. As a consequence, individuals losing energy and focus in cooperating with one another ought to succumb to those who focus only on their own particular strengths. But in fact Darwin observed cooperation everywhere: between different groups within the same species, and also between individuals or groups of different species. Under certain circumstances, cooperation provides an evolutionary benefit to individuals. In other words, mutations happen only on an individual level, while selection happens on individual *and* group levels. On the individual level, selfishness is more successful, while on the group level, groups with more cooperative members are more successful.

Impressive examples of cooperative behavior can be seen in ant colonies; my favorite type is the fire ant. Under normal conditions, fire ants build highly cooperative organizations, housed in anthills that extend deep underground. These organizations are so sophisticated that fire ant colonies are sometimes referred to as "superorganisms."

Despite being composed of thousands of individuals, the colony acts like one big organism.

The sophistication of fire ant cooperation can particularly be seen under stress. Under specific weather conditions, such as a certain level of humidity and low air pressure, fire ants respond to the danger of flooding. A highly specialized group of fire ants leaves the anthill and forms a living raft to lay across a stretch of water. To do so, the ants produce a hydrophobic glue that enables them to stick to each other and float. Once the raft of fire ants is stably afloat, the colony's queen is brought onto the raft in order to protect her from drowning. Several fire ants die while serving as the living raft, and emerging holes during the raft trip are continuously filled with other fire ants. Only a specialized force of ants builds the raft, and only some of those die in maintaining it. Others serve as defense specialists against bird or fish attacks during the trip.

Once the raft hits dry land, the ants invade. The invasion is a highly unpleasant experience after a hurricane, when a fire ant raft lands in your flooded home, believing it should serve as the new dry land for the colony to build on. Fire ants attack in groups and are able to sting several times, releasing a cocktail of highly neurotoxic molecules that drive pain, skin irritations, and sometimes shock. The high firepower of such a raft with millions of ants is potentially life-threatening to any other organism that tries to invade the fire ants' territory.

The importance of cooperation for the progress of life is dramatic. From the beginning, combining certain unique features and leveraging joint benefits have driven every incremental change and every breakthrough advancement. Here is a list of the most remarkable collaboration advancements from the molecular level to the organism level:

- Single atoms to form molecules with distinct features that are essential building blocks for life
- Small molecules to form large, bioactive molecules, such as RNA, DNA, proteins, and lipids, the key macromolecules for building a cell
- Interaction of large bioactive molecules to form the first simple cells (prokaryotic cells)

- ◆ Cooperation of prokaryotes and eukaryotes on a cellular level to form higher cells, the basis for higher animals and plants
- ◆ Different cell types to form cell communities, specialized tissues, and higher, fully integrated organisms
- ◆ The fundamental foundation of ecology, with its cooperation and continuous exchange of metabolites between plants and animals. The essence of this cooperation couldn't be simpler: With light, carbon dioxide and water can be converted by plants into glucose (sugar). In turn, animals can metabolize sugar, turning it into carbon dioxide and water. The energy created is the basis for animal survival. Cooperation reduced—to the maximum! It's brilliant.

If we zoom in on a single species like humans, it becomes even more intriguing how powerful cooperation is for progress, for example:

- ◆ Community building, such as religions, cities, countries
- ◆ Any form of political or ethical alliances
- ◆ The basic idea of shareholding to jointly finance endeavors and enterprises with too-big-a-risk for an individual
- ◆ Global trade

Interestingly, if we stretch the term "cooperation" beyond biological interactions, entirely new dimensions emerge:

- ◆ The internet as a shared knowledge and memory platform
- ◆ Machines designed to support learning and execute certain tasks for us
- ◆ Machines designed to learn better than man
- ◆ Data storage designed to save—and potentially retrieve—all our biological and neural memories, and perhaps even identity beyond our individual life spans

The concept of cooperation—if we expand it to physical machines, such as computers and robots—is so successful that it may allow us to escape evolution on an individual basis.

Given the original objective of our game—the progress of life as a whole—it's not clear yet whether the collaboration of biological organisms and machines is truly beneficial to the game's continuation. However, the vastly expanded knowledge base of the internet, combined with artificial intelligence to help us learn, consolidate, and conclude, will definitely expand our possibilities for the future; this should indeed be a big advantage if we want to successfully keep playing the game of life.

Meanwhile, there is striking evidence from biologists and mathematicians that cooperation provides a key evolutionary benefit, even on a genetic level. Not a surprise, as cooperation adds another layer of possible directions to account for an uncertain future. Genes driving cooperation are not selected on the individual level but are prime-selected by group evolution: new levels of organization only evolve when the competing units on the lower level finally start to cooperate. Cooperation allows specialization and thereby promotes biological diversity (and massively more optionality).

Evolution is constructive only because of cooperation. Perhaps the most remarkable aspect of evolution is its ability to generate cooperation in a competitive world. As a consequence, cooperation—next to genetic mutation and natural selection—has been proposed as a third fundamental principle of evolution. Rightly so.

The biggest challenge of all characteristics of evolution is time. Evolution takes a very, very long time. And even if we as individuals could live for millions of years, we would not benefit—because the genetic information facilitating evolution is fixed for each of us. As individuals, we do not benefit at all from evolution—we are just its tools. For our personal optionality, that is pretty bad.

So where are the tools you and I can use to increase our ability to respond to changes that happen tomorrow, not in millions of years?

Thanks to the brilliance of evolution, two powerful features have been selected that work very effectively on our timescale: *learning* and *cultural cooperation*.

Cooperation occurs when an individual pays a cost while others receive the associated benefit. In evolution, this translates into reproductive success from a genetic perspective—it is the long-term driver of all our progress. In addition, cooperation drives cultural reproduction, involving the spread of knowledge, ideas, and joint learning. Such cultural cooperation is a key driver for short-term optionality and is relevant for our individual timescale. Interestingly, the underlying biological and mathematical concepts apply across all forms of cooperation, genetic or cultural.

In essence, competition provides the evolutionary drive for all living organisms, while cooperation is the best strategy for driving evolutionary progress on a higher level.

Effective cooperation requires a set of key capabilities. First and foremost is the ability to communicate, and even more importantly, to learn.

Learning is the secret to successful cooperation.

On a molecular level, the systems we use for learning are highly conserved throughout living organisms. Evolution has shaped our effectiveness in learning for millions of years. Or, in other words, whichever species deviated from the perfect design of learning died out very quickly because they could not compete with the others. In addition to the features of evolution, learning adds another new layer of substantial optionality for life.

Learning is a key tool for survival, and progress provides a very important philosophical aspect for us as well: as individuals, we are not just one option in this game based on evolutionary variability. Learning provides us with another mechanism to produce our own personal range of options and our personal identity. In addition, if we combine individual learning with cultural cooperation, we can tap into all the knowledge of our other *Homo sapiens* brothers and sisters and leverage it. For example, Scottish physician Alexander Fleming's 1928 discovery of antibiotics has helped billions of humans to survive longer, despite not having discovered antibiotics themselves. These billions of humans have added more optionality to our collective game of life by their genetic variability and their individual contributions to knowledge and cooperation.

Humans are very likely the first species who can leverage a network of present and historical knowledge for their progress and survival. The utilization of this network has led to a progress explosion in recent years. This may turn out to be irrelevant to the game of life in another few billion years, but still, our progress carries an impressive growth trajectory. Just one data point, for example: 94 percent of all data (knowledge) ever created and recorded, across all of human history, has been created in the past five years. It seems that human knowledge networks—comprising learning, memory, communication, and cooperation—are the ultimate driver to vastly increasing all our optionality, and, as such, the progress of life itself.

The conclusion for us as humans is actually pretty simple: evolution is cool, but cooperation and learning are awesome. The vast optionality created by learning is hugely relevant for us as individuals with a very limited life span; learning provides us with *freedom* vis-à-vis an uncertain future. By leveraging this freedom of choice, we indeed drive *progress*—for us and for life in its entirety.

CHAPTER THREE

OPTIMIZING OPTIONALITY

Let's look a little closer here. On an individual level, what are the key drivers that broaden our optionality? Genetic diversity does not play a role, because we can use only what we have been given at birth (unless we consider individual gene therapy). Thus, genetic diversity provides optionality only when we look at an entire species or all living organisms all together.

On an individual level, optionality—and progress—is a function of time, health, and drive; knowledge and creativity; and willingness to share and cooperate.

> **Time.** Optionality is a function of time. The longer we live, the more time we have to increase our optionality and potentially activate it as new situations come our way. If you die at birth, your optionality was essentially limited to your genetic base—and you had no time to activate it. Therefore, for every individual it is most important to live as long as possible. And there is the most fundamental dilemma of the game of life: How can life create the broadest optionality? By keeping

a set of genes for a longer period of time and trusting other levers, like learning and cooperation, to add optionality? Or by replacing and reshuffling genes rapidly in order to expand the range of options you begin with? Or is there an optimal balancing of the two forces? Looking at the various forms of life out there, it seems that there is not just one solution to balancing these powers. At one end of the scale, we have bacteria that replicate and mutate very rapidly but live a rather short life. At the other end, we have trees that can live almost ten thousand years and regenerate themselves very effectively.

Health and Drive. It does not help to live long if we are too sick or exhausted to make progress. If you have two broken legs, there is no option to run away from an unexpected threat. If you are depressed, you are not in a position to enjoy your genetic benefits—you miss the drive to build optionality and progress. Thus, it is also fundamental to be physically and mentally healthy.

Time, health, and drive are the basic individual activators for our genetic optionality. Without these three, the optionality we can create beyond our genes is very, very limited. Once we have sufficient time and we are healthy, we can leverage three additional factors for even more optionality, but only if we decide to interact with other organisms.

Knowledge and Creativity. On an isolated individual level, knowledge and creativity are functions of learning and applying what you learned only for yourself. This has a very limited benefit in comparison to leveraging historical and cultural knowledge collected within a species over a long period of time and shared; then optionality explodes. By recording, collecting, and memorizing knowledge over a longer period of time, we preserve all the optionality created in the past. In addition, we allow integration of new knowledge. All this together drives enormous creativity for more optionality for every one of us. That's why our progress as a species is dramatically more successful than that of so many other species: we have created another—nonbiological!—record beyond encoding genes and gene variants for optionality. We can access optionality by Googling it. Bacteria can't do that. Chimpanzees, dolphins, and trees can't do that.

Sharing and Cooperation. The final layer for even more optionality for each of us is to share, interact, and cooperate with other people. It's the ultimate layer, given that it is exponentially self-amplifying. A group of people will have a broader option space to leverage than an individual. Intriguingly, the way a group of people works together impacts optionality substantially: a team of people complementing and leveraging their individual strengths and weaknesses creates more optionality than a group of people acting the same way in parallel. In other words, a team of people working together in different ways will have a broader option space than a group of people who are all doing the same thing. Finally, a team of highly diverse people will have a broader option space than a group of similar people. All individuals benefit in diverse groups as their weaknesses are mitigated by others and their strengths are further amplified by those of others.

Thus, the broadest range of options can be achieved by living a long time and healthily, by learning a lot, and by cooperating with a lot of people. Or in short: *living a long and happy life is the ultimate progress.*

But even though our modern world has apparently made a long life possible thanks to these amazing features of life, I think it is a good time to assess how we humans are doing on that path to a happier life. Let's have a look.

Do we live a long time? Well, it depends on how we look at it. Average life expectancy has increased dramatically from an average of

30 years in the Middle Ages, to 58 years in 1970, to 65 years in 1990, to 72.5 years today. What is also dramatic is the spread between the countries on our planet: while Japan's average life expectancy is 84 years, the average life expectancy in Central Africa is just 50 years. Even more dramatic is the difference on an individual level, from a few minutes for babies who die at birth, to 122.5 years for the oldest person so far on our planet. Thus, a lot is still possible to improve and a lot of optionality to be gained by closing the gap between the extremes within our species, obviously. In absolute terms, we are just doing okay compared to other mammals, with bowhead whales in the lead at more than 210 years old. Compared to other living organisms, we are rather short-lived. Cypress trees, for example, can live more than four thousand years, and the *Scolymastra joubini* sponge is more than ten thousand years old. That is a massive improvement potential for us as human beings.

Do we live healthily? Clearly not. While healthy life spans have continuously improved over the past fifty years, 95 percent of all deaths are still caused by diseases. In essence, the major reason for the huge variability in life spans is the onset of diseases finally killing us. Thus, there is massive improvement potential. While most disease areas are declining or stable, there is a group of mental illnesses that has effectively exploded in recent years: depression, anxiety, and addiction disorders. For the creation of more optionality, these diseases are particularly problematic because they stop the drive and the enthusiasm for life, they block creativity, and they block social and interpersonal actions. Mental illness is the ultimate killer of optionality. Thus, given the skyrocketing increase in recent years of all kinds of mental illness, it seems that mankind has gotten stuck on the path to ultimate progress and happiness.

Do we learn a lot? If we look at the availability of knowledge for everyone, we have to highlight that the past ten to twenty years have been amazing. The internet has created the best knowledge base ever for almost everyone on this planet who can read and has access to the internet. In 2015, our planet had a literacy rate of 86 percent and an internet access rate of 45 percent. Thus we can assume that approximately half the population of our planet has access to the same high-level knowledge base. Four years later, in 2019, the internet access via mobile phones has increased to over 60 percent already. Almost everyone on the planet has a smartphone now—and with it access to a global knowledge base. That is remarkable. Unfortunately, the basic education rates and access to schools in poorer countries have not improved much in recent years. This is quite disappointing given the huge improvements in the past two hundred years. For example, the global literacy rate has improved from 12 percent in 1820 to 86 percent in 2015. Unfortunately we are stuck on that level. While access to basic education seems to be okay, access to high and very high education levels is reserved for only a small group within our global population. As with the previous parameters, it seems we have improved a lot on a one hundred–year time horizon but have gotten stuck recently. If we phrase it positively: there is still a lot of improvement potential left for mankind.

Do we share and cooperate enough? This one is very difficult to assess. On the one hand, we are connected to many more people than one hundred years ago—not only because there are many more people on the planet but also because the advent of social networks has created a true global platform for communication. On the other hand, anxiety and depression, driven by social isolation, dissolution of families, and loneliness, have emerged as major problems, especially in developed countries. It seems that the numerical increase of our social contacts comes with a reduced quality and depth of connections. In essence we have lost the ability to truly take care of other people, emotionally but also physically. From an optionality perspective, this development is very concerning because it takes away the amplifier for cultural coop-eration and replaces it with depression and anxiety.

Intuitively, it seems that in recent years nationalism, trade conflicts, other smaller conflicts, and cyberbullying have increased. However, compared to such atrocities of the twentieth century as World War II, it seems that we are improving. We should not forget that our current economic system was originally designed to allow and support col-laboration between parties. Yet, there is one data point contradicting that original design: 82 percent of the wealth created in 2017 went to the richest 1 percent of the global population, while almost four bil-lion people—half of our planet—got nothing. In 2018 and 2019 this discrepancy increased even further. Effectively, inequality has been continuously rising over the past 150 years and even accelerating in the past 25 years. Apparently, our economic system is systematically widening the gap between the few rich people and the many poor ones, and it seems that we have little if any ability to counteract it—even though we have full knowledge of its mechanisms. What seems to be just unfair for individuals economically is absolutely detrimental to the optionality of mankind as a species: the majority of ordinary people increase the wealth of a few without increasing their own wealth, their optionality, or their progress. The systematic loss of optionality by billions of people will obviously not be compensated for by the small increase of optionality for a few hundred billionaires. This is anti-sharing and anti-cooperation at their worst.

Looking at all this, we have to admit that over the past twenty-five years we have effectively reduced the range of options for mankind pretty dramatically. In particular the explosion of mental illnesses and inequality levels drastically impacts optionality on a global level. Living a little longer and having broader access to the internet can definitely not compensate for that. Intriguingly, this is happening despite the fact that we have more knowledge about the fundamentals than ever and that we have improved the healthy life spans to apply our knowledge substantially. However, it seems that the deficit in sharing and cooperation and the emerging pandemic of mental illness are stealing all the optionality. We are simply *not* living long and happy lives today. Our progress is halted. As individuals and as a species.

To be clear, the game of life will continue; of that I am absolutely convinced. If we all decide to go down a path of less optionality and less progress, we will simply be replaced. However, I would like us humans to stay in the game because I believe we are at the cusp of really driving progress exponentially in the coming years. All optionality we will build will truly benefit others on this planet, thanks to the reach we already have today. In addition, whatever we add today will benefit later generations, thanks to our shared, nonbiological knowledge base, the internet. Thus, if we work together, we can finally find a way to leverage nonbiological knowledge and intelligence in favor of a longer and happier life. In short, we should learn from the fire ants and the ten-thousand-year-old sponges.

Cooperation and learning are awesome when you use them to live a long and happy life, driving ultimate progress.

The book in front of you has the ambition of introducing a new economic world order that puts cooperation and happiness at its core. It merges our knowledge from philosophy, psychology, economics, evolutionary biology, and neuroscience into one universal concept that will equip us to continue the game of life. And to win it. For each of us. For our species. For life.

But before we get to the payoff, let us have a closer look at how learning—our central supporting partner—works in detail.

CHAPTER FOUR

THE BASIC SCIENCE OF LEARNING AND MEMORY

One promise of this book is the introduction of a new economy focused on happiness. A fundamental feature of such an economy would be a price tag on happiness. Intuitively, we might say that one can't put a price on happiness. Very interestingly, this perception is not correct: we can do so, and our brain is doing it all the time. To fully understand how our brain prices happiness, we must first understand some basics of how learning, memory, and the neuroscience of happiness work. So please bear with me as we learn about learning!

The frontline of neuroscience and cognitive psychology is moving very fast, with new observations about learning and memory appearing on a daily basis. As always in fast-moving scientific fields, data and perspectives are conflicting and debate is abundant. Despite all the action, we have to admit that on a detailed molecular and cellular level, we are far from understanding how real-world learning and memory work, either cognitively, molecularly, or computationally. Further, learning and memory can be studied from multiple angles. For example, we can focus on the dimension of time (when?), content (what in detail?), type (what in general?), process (how or in what sequence?), location (where on a physiological, cellular, molecular level?), or the behavioral implications. So terminology depends on the perspective and the expertise at hand.

We don't need to review all the different expert perspectives to gain an essential understanding of these concepts. Instead, I intend to provide a high-level overview of the scientific environment of learning and memory. Then I'll discuss reinforcement learning, reward systems, and neuromodulation—the key points we need to understand. Think of this chapter as a tour of how your brain works and how it influences your behavior.

Here are some basic definitions to get us started. *Learning* is the process by which we detect and, as such, acquire knowledge about the environment. *Memory* is the process by which the knowledge is encoded, consolidated, stored, and later retrieved. We are who we are largely because of what we learn and what we remember. Learning and memory enable communication and fill it with relevant content. These processes allow us to transmit cultures that can be maintained over generations. Importantly, when combined with communication and collaboration, learning enables us to drive progress in life very quickly, beyond the individual capacity and the individual life span without relying on evolution.

As confirmed by various brain imaging technologies in the last twenty-five years, learning comprises six components arranged in the *learning memory cycle* (fig. 1A): detection/input, encoding, consolidation, reconsolidation, storage, and retrieval.

FIGURE 1: LEARNING AND MEMORY TYPES

FIGURE 1A

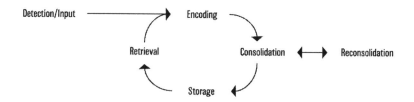

FIGURE 1B

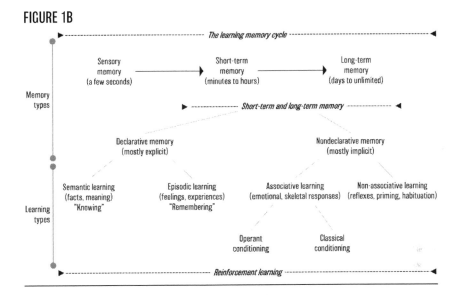

Learning is always initiated by the *detection* of an *input* signal, mostly by our primary senses. This may come from an event we detect through our eyes (vision), nose or tongue (odor, taste), ears (sound), or skin (touch), but also from other secondary senses that remain difficult to describe scientifically ("gut feeling"). Importantly, it is also possible to learn via imagination or retrieved memory—the brain can act as a self-amplifier or modulator under these circumstances. These input signals are then *encoded*—the brain's method of processing newly learned information—so that our neural systems are ready for the next steps on the way to forming a memory.

Encoding is critically influenced by attention to the information and association of meaningfulness. Encoding and memory storage are strongest when already known information can be combined with new information and when one is well motivated. (You will never forget the path to a hidden spring in the forest that you found when you were seriously thirsty.) The encoding process does not require the expression of novel biomolecules such as genes, transcripts, or proteins. Therefore, encoding is immediate and fast; it lasts only seconds on average. Our neurons, sensory neurons in particular, are fully equipped for input detection and immediate encoding.

The next phase of memory formation, *consolidation*, takes much longer. During this phase, newly stored and still labile information is refined and shaped in order to make it more stable and smaller for long-term storage. For example, if you see a red apple for the first time in your life, the novel shape and smell of the apple need to be stored. However, the color "red" does not need to be stored in connection with "apple" again because you know already what the color red is. As such, all information is segregated, stored at different sites in your brain to be most effective when re-aggregated later upon retrieval. Consolidation requires the synthesis of new proteins—a molecular process that takes eight to twenty-four hours. Memories can be enhanced or suppressed quantitatively and qualitatively in this phase. For example, we can enhance memory by repeating a certain task over and over again (positive impact of doing your piano finger exercises once a day). Or we can enhance it by consciously making ourselves aware of critical associations (you will never forget a bee sting after the first time). Based on the same concept, memories can be suppressed (negative impact of not doing your piano finger exercise) or even repressed (traumatic experiences can be effectively locked away in your brain so as not to recall them and continuously impair your daily life). With the mechanisms of memory recall, prompt and precise retrieval is prepared, as well as the transmission of particular memories from short-term to long-term memory. The time it takes to complete consolidation—several hours— is a critical hallmark (we return to this in Chapter Ten). *Reconsolidation* is a repeating consolidation that shuttles between existing knowledge, existing memory, and novel inputs in order to further optimize structured storage and retrieval. Reconsolidation is also dependent on new protein synthesis and thus takes some time. Reconsolidation can be stimulated actively by reflection and assessment of certain actions and memories. *Reflection*, a *conscious* neural activity, is another critical hallmark to be remembered.

Storage refers to the mechanism and physiological locations by which memory is retained over time. Different kinds of information are stored at different sites in the brain. It has become clear that short-term and long-term memories are not stored in just one part of the brain but are widely distributed throughout the cortex, the major part of our brain. Long-term storage has the remarkable feature of almost unlimited capacity, in contrast to the very limited short-term storage.

Retrieval comprises the processes that permit the recall, compilation, and use of stored information. Importantly, retrieval requires recollection of several pieces of information from different sites in the brain. But because the information was consolidated before being stored, the retrieval process may be subject to distortion. Retrieval is most effective when it occurs in the same context in which the initial learning occurred. For example, if you prepare for an exam by studying in the sun and drinking coffee, you can be sure that in a dark classroom with just water at hand your retrieval will be impaired. This feature reaches its extreme in managing drug addiction: as an alcoholic, it is almost impossible to avoid drinking with your friends in your preferred bar. The memories of all the good nights with alcohol and friends will come back—and with them the desire to drink again. This feature is called *state-dependency*, and it plays a major role later in this book.

Within the learning memory cycle, both short-term and long-term memory apply the same memory and learning types (fig. 1B), which all of us are intuitively familiar with even if we don't know the terminology. These types include declarative memory (facts and events that can be explicitly stored and retrieved; mostly conscious recall) and nondeclarative memory (past experiences prompt the remembrance of things, emotions, and actions without your necessarily thinking about them; mostly unconscious recall).

Declarative memory stores inputs primarily from semantic learning (the ability to recall facts and concepts, such as knowing that Christmas is on December 25) and episodic learning (feelings and experiences you remember as part of your personal history, such as recalling the events and emotions around Hurricane Katrina). Nondeclarative memory, on the other hand, stores inputs from associative learning (the association between two stimuli, such as a bee and a sting). Also stored in this type of memory is non-associative learning (permanent change of response based on repeated exposure to a single stimulus). Semantic, episodic, and associative learning can be subject to conditioning and reinforcement. Reinforcement learning is crucial to this book's big-picture vision to first understand what drives

our own happiness and then leverage it for our own progress and ultimately the progress of mankind. Without reinforcement learning, life
would not be able to progress.

CHAPTER FIVE

THE LEARNING TRIANGLE OF LIFE

Reinforcement learning is the process by which organisms learn to predict and obtain rewards; they do this by trial and error. Reinforcement learning is absolutely crucial for progress—most likely one of the most important processes we have as living organisms. It is not surprising that it has been a major focus for scientists to try to better understand the mechanisms and rules underlying reinforcement learning in order to apply these insights to enhance learning, memory, and the associated benefits for the health of our brain for improvements.

Unfortunately, the understanding of reinforcement learning is challenging from a neuroscientific perspective as well as a computational one because today's actions have long-term effects on future rewards. Further, these deferred consequences may depend critically on other subsequent events and, in particular, outcomes that occur later in a string of events. This sequential dependency greatly compounds the classical curse of dimensionality by extending it over time. In essence, all the variables and dependencies—only a few of them under our full control—leave us very uncertain about the ultimate outcome in the future when we make a single decision today. Let me draw an example here. You decide to launch a new business. However, when you launch it in 2008–2009 (in the middle of the financial crisis), it fails, despite all your other good decisions, because you simply cannot find any investors. The lesson should not be that the initial decision to develop the business was wrong, but rather that the timing of a business launch is critical. It is basically what we identified in the beginning when looking at the setup of the game of life: the future is uncertain—you still have to make decisions today in order to progress. It is therefore no surprise that we have no computational model so far that helps us to understand real-world reinforcement learning. Reinforcement learning is more than just computation; a central part of it is reflection. Sometimes such reflection requires considering your decisions over a very long period of time.

Fortunately for our current assessment, we have some simplified computational models that can help us to understand the essentials if not the entire universe of dependencies, options, and uncertainty. However, from a neuroscientific (and even philosophical) perspective, experimental testing is very challenging as well; as individuals, we can't embark on two options at the same time. Therefore, we will never be able to compare and prove which option was best in a proper scientific setting. We simply can't act as our own control "animal" in such an experiment. But perhaps in the end this is the ultimate fun part of life.

The underlying concepts of reinforcement learning were intensively studied in the past hundred years in two learning types that are pretty simple, clearly defined, and easy to test in experiments with animals and humans. These two learning processes are called *classical conditioning* and *operant conditioning*; both are types of associative learning, or trial-and-error learning.

The basic concept of conditioning can be best explained in sports and physical fitness: if you stimulate your body by an exercise, it adapts to the specific stimulus; for example, your biceps muscle grows (the response) if you do biceps curls with a heavy weight (the stimulus). Conditioning in learning means basically the same thing: learning happens by an association between a stimulus and a response. The famous psychologist John Watson proposed in 1924 that the process of conditioning would be able to explain all aspects of human psychology;

from speech to emotional responses, everything was simply a pattern of stimulus and response. Fortunately, it is not that simple, and our consciousness also plays a key role.

Nevertheless, conditioning is a fundamental component of learning. Recently, it has become clear that conditioning is also the key element in semantic learning and particularly in episodic learning. The conditioning in these learning types works on an ever-longer timescale but via the same mechanisms. Operant conditioning and episodic learning are the major learning types we are interested in.

In operant conditioning, the strength of a behavior is modified by reinforcement or punishment (fig. 2B). Importantly, stimuli that are present when a behavior is rewarded or punished come to control that respective behavior.

In essence, operant conditioning can have four outcomes: positive reinforcement, negative reinforcement, positive punishment, and negative punishment.

> *Positive reinforcement* (also called "reinforcement") occurs when a particular behavior or response is rewarding in itself (a primary reinforcer, like sweets), or the behavior or response is followed by an indirect stimulus that is rewarding because of its link to the primary reinforcer. This is called a secondary reinforcer, such as money that allows you to buy sweets. Positive reinforcement increases the frequency of the original behavior or response.

> *Negative reinforcement* ("escape") occurs when a behavior or response is followed by the removal of an aversive stimulus (like a reduction of strong lights when an exposed mouse presses a lever). Like positive reinforcement, negative reinforcement increases the frequency of the original behavior or response as well.

> *Positive punishment* ("punishment") occurs when a behavior or response is followed by an aversive stimulus (like electroshock or pain).

Negative punishment ("penalty") occurs when a behavior or response is followed by the removal of a positive stimulus (like taking away a child's toy upon an undesired behavior).

Over time and with significant research, four additional features have been identified that potentially alter the effectiveness of reinforcement and punishment. I will mention them here briefly in order to refer back to them when they become relevant for us later: satiation or deprivation; immediacy; contingency; and meaningfulness.

The principle of satiation and deprivation: The effectiveness of a positive stimulus will be reduced if the individual has obtained enough rewards to satisfy the associated needs. If someone is not hungry, food will not be an effective reinforcement of a behavior.

The principle of immediacy: an immediate reward/ aversion is more effective as reinforcement/punishment versus a delayed one.

The principle of contingency: the most effective reinforcement or punishment occurs when consistently applied after the behavior or response.

The principle of meaningfulness or cost-benefit principle: The size of a stimulus affects how strongly it works as a reinforcement or punishment. For example, a tiny amount of food may not be "worth" the effort to execute the behavior or response.

Reinforcers are the most important elements for us in the world of operant conditioning. As mentioned above, there are two basic types: primary and secondary reinforcers. They can work alone or together to reinforce a certain behavior positively or negatively (fig. 2).

FIGURE 2: REINFORCEMENT LEARNING AND NEURONAL IMPLICATIONS

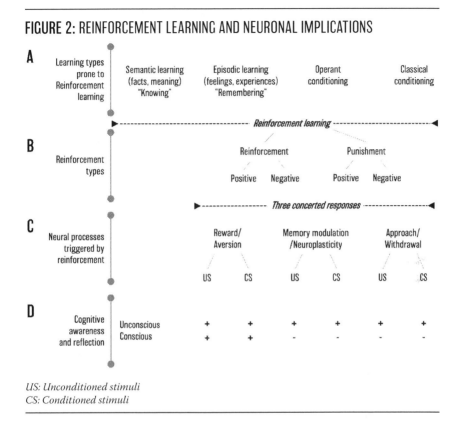

US: Unconditioned stimuli
CS: Conditioned stimuli

Primary reinforcers are unconditioned stimuli, meaning that no previous experience or learning is required to make them desirable. They are by themselves desirable and evoke unconditioned responses (figs. 2C and 3). Primary reinforcers occur naturally. As such, they possess characteristics that allow them to be of innate, biological value to the organism. In animal experiments, primary reinforcers are primarily selected to satisfy basic survival needs such as water, food, sleep, air, sex, and shelter—these have been proven to be the strongest primary reinforcers—in particular, when combined with deprivation (like providing water to thirsty rats as a reward for a certain behavior).

In human experiments, primary reinforcers are also highly effective and rewarding if higher human needs are satisfied. Thus, societal recognition, self-esteem, societal status, personal growth, or love can act as very powerful primary reinforcers. I will come back to these human primary reinforcers again later, but broadly speaking, when a behavior leads to a rewarding primary reinforcer, the reward in turn enhances and increases future frequency of the initial behavior. In other words, if you have a sweet tooth, you're likely going to reach for the candy jar again and again.

On the other hand, secondary, or conditioned, reinforcers are stimuli, objects, or even events that become reinforcing because they are associated with a primary reinforcer or grant access to primary reinforcers. That means in turn that previous experience or learning *is* required for them to be desirable. That is why secondary reinforcers are sometimes called learned reinforcers. They evoke conditioned responses (figs. 2C and 3). Secondary reinforcers do not have innate value to the organism. They are biologically useless. However, they can still be highly motivating and rewarding if they are associated with a primary reinforcer or provide access to a primary reinforcer. For example, a fake gold medal (secondary reinforcer) you win in a sports competition at school provides you with broad recognition and acceptance within your peer group or primary reinforcer (fig. 3).

Reinforcement learning by a secondary conditioned reinforcer associated with a primary unconditioned reinforcer is not limited to humans or mammals. Interestingly, such reinforcement learning is a general concept of neuronal activation and can be detected in insects and other invertebrates. Additionally, it is highly conserved throughout evolution.

In other words, we cannot run away and ignore the power of reinforcement on our human behavior. It has been selected as an obvious success factor for our survival and reproduction. No chance to escape. Instead, we should try to reflect on it and turn our knowledge about conditioning to our advantage.

One of the strongest secondary reinforcers for contemporary humans is money. To understand its power in today's culture and economy, briefly think about all the things people do to get money. Good and bad things. Legal and illegal. More than 50 percent of our lifetime is dedicated to getting or spending money. (Don't forget 30 percent of our lives during which we sleep, and the 40 percent of our lives during which we are too young, too old, or too sick to work.)

Unlike primary reinforcers such as food and clothing, money has zero innate biological value. However, because we have invented a whole economic system around money, one that is central to our lives, we learn at an early age to value money. Money can be used to reinforce behaviors because it can then be used to acquire primary reinforcers. If money were to lose its buying power through hyperinflation tomorrow, it would immediately lose its power as a secondary reinforcer while food, as a primary reinforcer, would not.

Most intriguingly, in modern human society, money's value as a secondary reinforcer goes way beyond food, clothing, and shelter. These basic needs are fully satisfied already in any developed country. Instead, money is used meanwhile to acquire or display societal recognition and status, satisfying higher unmet psychological needs in our societies. Perhaps we should all take a few minutes to reflect on how much of our existing, perceived societal status and recognition would remain if money were to lose its value. This gives us a good assessment of how much our societal status and recognition today are truly valuable as primary reinforcers—or whether they are instead pure *surrogates* (second-tier secondary reinforcers) created by money alone without any tangible biological value for us.

Here's how the learning cycle works with both primary and secondary reinforcers: one's behavior (working as a trader at the stock market) leads to a secondary reinforcer (money) that is indirectly rewarding by acquiring a primary reinforcer (food) or directly rewarding by experience (recognition by our neighbors when we park our Porsche in front of our house). The reward, in turn, enhances and increases future frequency of the initial behavior (working longer hours), just like in the primary reinforcer cycle (fig. 3).

FIGURE 3: REINFORCEMENT LEARNING CYCLE

FIGURE 3A

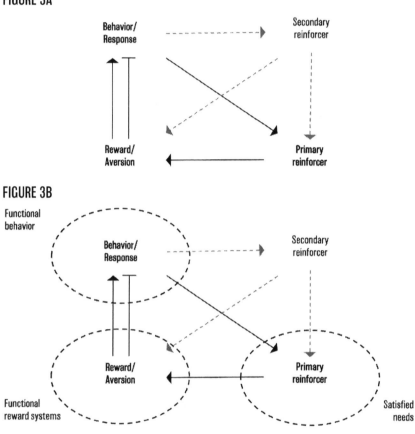

FIGURE 3B

Importantly, for a certain time, a secondary reinforcer can work well *even in the absence of a primary reinforcer*—but the effect lessens over time: a secondary reinforcer is not viable alone.

Since the groundbreaking work from Harvard psychologist B. F. Skinner in the 1950s, behavioral neuroscience has advanced further. Meanwhile, three processes have been characterized (fig. 2C) that are induced in parallel by reinforcement: approach/withdrawal, reward/ aversion, and memory modulation. I will not elaborate further on approach/withdrawal responses. However, reward/aversion and memory modulation are core to our understanding.

Reward and *aversion* are internal states. To be effective, they must be consciously experienced in order to influence behavior. This differentiates reward/aversion from the other two reinforcement processes—approach/withdrawal and memory modulation—that function unconsciously. In addition, the mere experience of a reward or aversion has no influence on behavior yet. It only affects behavior when the individual learns what to do to reinitiate or maintain the situation (in the case of a rewarding behavior). This kind of learning is necessarily a cognitive process that results in full conscious reflection of the link between a certain behavior or response and its consequences. Thus, behaviors in the future—despite not fixed in form—will remain oriented toward the desired outcome.

As with reward and aversion, *memory modulation* is an internal process. On the molecular level, when you consciously reflect on your behavior, your brain is hard at work. In molecular terms, that means that our protein and lipid structures are changing, building up and down. The ability of neurons in the brain to change and reorganize continuously to meet the dynamic demands of the internal and external environment is termed *neuronal plasticity* or *neuroplasticity*. We will use the term *neuromodulation* as an indicator that we are focusing exclusively on neuronal plasticity modulating learning and memory.

Neuromodulation acts in the brain to strengthen the neural representation of memories acquired at the same time and place as the reinforcer. So if you behave in a way that is rewarded, the neurons involved build stronger connections to each other. Over time, through reflection and repetition (whether actual repetition or recalled in memory), these connections become so strong that the memory involved can hardly be forgotten. One of the best examples is remembering the location and details of your first kiss. Such neuromodulation requires neuronal activation with subsequent synthesis of novel proteins. This process leads to morphological changes—more connections and with them a denser network between neurons—and changes to the neurons' sensitivity. These morphological changes can be measured by functional magnetic resonance imaging (fMRI), a noninvasive imaging technology that allows assessment of cellular structures in the brain. A very large portion of neuromodulation is the hard-wired support for optimal long-term memory storage and effective retrieval. It is important to remember that we can't consciously feel neuromodulation. The molecular changes to our neuronal network happens silently in the unconscious back. In contrast, reward/aversion is a conscious process.

All functional elements described so far interact to build the *reinforcement learning cycle* (fig. 3). Within the cycle, three elements—behavior, need satisfaction, and functional reward systems—constantly interact (fig. 3B).

We will call this universal model for learning *the learning triangle of life* (fig. 4).

FIGURE 4: LEARNING TRIANGLE OF LIFE (BSR TRIANGLE)

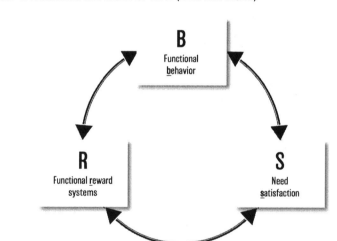

In the ideal case for learning, the three elements amplify one another positively:

+ functional behaviors
+ satisfied needs
+ functional reward systems

Most importantly, there are existing cause-effect relationships—six in total—between all three elements: each element is reinforced by the two other elements. This leads to an active reinforcement cycle that requires tight control for healthy and sustainable balance of reinforcers, rewards/aversions, and responses. Disturbance of the cause-and-effect relationships can lead to reversible or even irreversible mental illness. How is that possible?

CHAPTER SIX

REFLECTION VERSUS ADDICTION

We are fully aware now that rewarding stimuli—primary or secondary—function as reinforcers in operant conditioning. Importantly, the inverse also holds true: primary reinforcers and secondary reinforcers are rewarding. Sugar is an immediate happy-maker by itself in that it triggers one of our reward systems directly.

This reality allows for a "reward *perpetuum mobile*," a self-sustained, self-rewarding, self-amplifying cycle—a reward system that is "getting happy with itself," without a higher purpose or value for the organism. To see the full power of such a derailed reward system, we only have to look at a dramatic mental illness: addiction.

Broadly, addiction is defined by the National Institute on Drug Abuse as "a brain disorder characterized by compulsive engagement in rewarding stimuli despite adverse consequences for the organism." The two properties that characterize all addictive stimuli are that they are reinforcing and intrinsically rewarding.

The overall prevalence of addictions, in particular substance abuse, has been dramatically increasing in recent years. Looking at a broad range of addictions (nicotine, alcohol, illicit drugs, eating, gambling, internet/social media, love, sex, exercise, work, and shopping), it is currently estimated that 47 percent of the US adult population suffers from fully manifested addiction or addictive disorders. Before further examining the impact of addiction on today's society, let's understand better how addictions develop from healthy mental states and why they are so hard to break.

Driven by our underlying evolutionary objective of survival and progress, all people engage in self-regulating behaviors in response to their wants and needs. Many people use substances or engage in questionable behaviors to meet these needs. Some more, some less. Yet, not everybody develops a chronic or destructive pattern of use. Further, the ways people try to satisfy their wants and needs are individually very different. Indeed, the crossover from occasional substance abuse or dysfunctional behavior to a full manifestation of addiction is still completely unclear.

What we do know is that people's genetic and neurological make-ups differ greatly, as do their responses to their environments. Thus, the individual motivation, the neurological conditions, and the behavioral consequences for each person in a given environment need to be assessed to understand the drivers toward addiction. The initiation can come from each of the three elements (functional reward system, psychological needs, behavior) and each of the six relationships between the elements.

In contrast, scientific data clearly confirm that in a fully manifested and self-contained addiction, all three elements and all six relationships are derailed. Balance, self-regulation, and control are lost while reinforcement mechanisms are still fully active, driving the individual down the road toward the abyss.

FIGURE 5A: LEARNING TRIANGLE OF LIFE: OVERALL HEALTHY BEHAVIOR, NEED SATISFACTION, AND FUNCTIONAL REWARD SYSTEMS

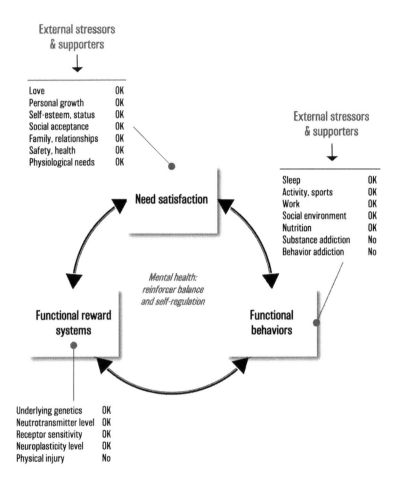

Now let's apply the model shown in figure 3 to two tangible examples. Remarkably, the underlying functional reward systems of chemical addictions (alcohol, nicotine, opioids, cocaine, amphetamine, food) and behavioral addictions (gambling, hand washing, work, sex, internet/social media) are highly similar on a molecular level. Thus, we don't need to distinguish between these addictive stimuli.

Nevertheless, I would like to describe two examples—cocaine addiction and work addiction—to put everything together that we have learned so far. Please remember that all relationships and elements are equally important. Thus, deviation from mental health can start at or between any elements. While we'll look at only two cases, it's possible to imagine thousands of others.

EXAMPLE 1: COCAINE ADDICTION

Let's start with an ideal situation of mental health (fig. 5A). I selected a short list of key drivers for each element. In our case, our test person—let's call him John—has all psychological needs satisfied (physiological, safety, health, family, relationships, social acceptance, self-esteem, status, personal growth opportunities, and love). He is neurologically healthy (no genetic defects; no physical injuries; normal levels of neurotransmitters, receptor sensitivity, and neuroplasticity). Finally, he displays functional behaviors across all activities in life (sleep, activity, sports, work, social environment, nutrition, uncritical substance abuse or behavior addictions).

Now, imagine that an external trigger disturbs this balanced system: John is actively excluded from a group of "cool party people" at school (fig. 5B, part 1), and this negatively affects his self-esteem, status, and perceived social acceptance. Such a trigger often comes from an external stressor, as in John's example. However, we also can imagine that a normal external trigger is enhanced by an internal situation, such as a mild autistic precondition.

To remedy this disturbance, John might decide to join the cool group by getting cocaine for everyone, leading to a phenomenal party weekend. Under the influence of cocaine, the level of inclusion for John would be significantly enhanced. He would become a fully accepted member of the group, thus correcting his unmet psychological need for social inclusion (fig. 5B, part 1).

FIGURE 5B: LEARNING TRIANGLE OF LIFE: REVERSIBLE COCAINE OVERUSE

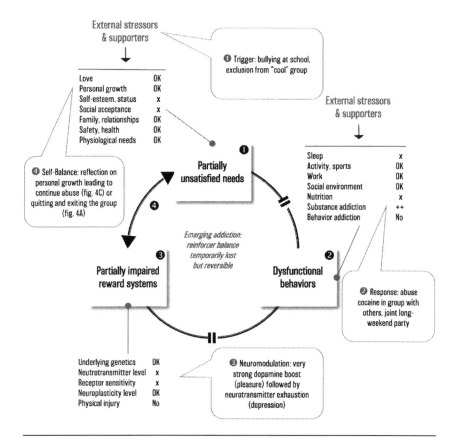

Cocaine acts here as a primary reinforcer for the behavior ("buy cocaine and have a great party weekend"). It even acts as a direct rewarding agent for John (it releases dopamine even if he is out partying alone), as well as for the other group members. In addition, cocaine acts as a secondary reinforcer because it indirectly enables the social inclusion that acts as a direct reward.

You see at this stage how powerful cocaine is as a reinforcer and reward, and how difficult it is to *not* repeat the same behavior again the next weekend. Importantly, the reinforcement model does still offer a mechanism to counterbalance the system at this stage. While the immediate neurological response is very rewarding, it is followed by a rebound effect that is driven by the exhaustion of the rewarding neurotransmitters and the desensitization of the reward receptors (the connected molecules that are stimulated by the neurotransmitters). In other words, John feels horribly depressed the next day (fig. 5B, part 3). Under normal balance, this leads to a conscious reflection about the entire sequence of activities (the reinforcement cycle) and should induce John to question whether this behavior is in line with his existing personal growth ambitions and values. Based on his reflection, he can consciously decide whether to change course and return to his ideal mental health state (fig. 5A).

As a consequence, John might decide the following weekend to party without cocaine, party with other people, or not at all. Alternatively, he could decide to repeat the behavior from the previous weekend and potentially take even more cocaine to further enhance it. Over time, this repeated behavior will not induce a conscious reflection anymore. John would then move very quickly toward a fully manifested cocaine addiction (fig. 5C). Such addiction is marked by impaired functional reward systems on all levels. His dysfunctional behavior would broadly impact his quality of life, leading to issues like chronic sleep deprivation, reduced fitness, and underperformance at work. And he would build up substantial unmet needs, such as health problems and impaired self-esteem in the absence of cocaine. The only remaining reward is now the reinforcer itself: cocaine.

FIGURE 5C: LEARNING TRIANGLE OF LIFE: FULLY MANIFESTED COCAINE ADDICTION

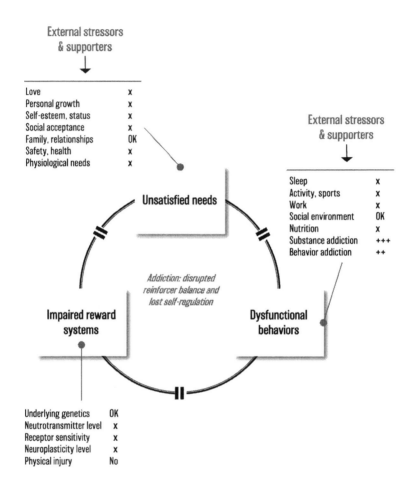

Unfortunately, uncontrolled and sustained cocaine abuse leads to massive neural damage and loss of neuroplasticity. As a consequence, very severe secondary mental illnesses can occur, including anxiety, depression, psychosis, and schizophrenia. If there is no intervention, John will reinforce and reward himself to death.

EXAMPLE 2: WORK

As in the previous case, we start with a test person, let's call her Jane, who displays ideal mental health. Importantly, work is one activity among others, and Jane's behavior at work is normal (fig. 6A).

FIGURE 6A: LEARNING TRIANGLE OF LIFE: HEALTHY WORK-LIFE BALANCE

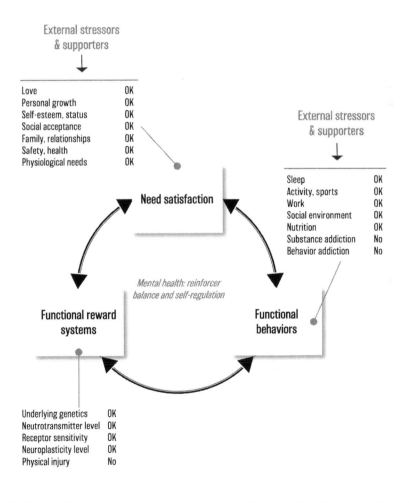

Love	OK
Personal growth	OK
Self-esteem, status	OK
Social acceptance	OK
Family, relationships	OK
Safety, health	OK
Physiological needs	OK

External stressors & supporters

Need satisfaction

External stressors & supporters

Sleep	OK
Activity, sports	OK
Work	OK
Social environment	OK
Nutrition	OK
Substance addiction	No
Behavior addiction	No

Mental health: reinforcer balance and self-regulation

Functional reward systems

Functional behaviors

Underlying genetics	OK
Neutrotransmitter level	OK
Receptor sensitivity	OK
Neuroplasticity level	OK
Physical injury	No

Let's anticipate now that Jane is motivated by the supervisor to take on a difficult project for eight weeks that will dramatically increase her workload temporarily but offers a potential promotion if she does a good job (fig. 6B, part 1).

The increased workload leads first of all to a reduced amount of sleep, mainly because the stress of the project drags on and Jane can't fall asleep very well anymore. Twelve weeks later (Jane needed an extension on the project's deadline), Jane successfully completes the project, and she receives the promised promotion, including a salary increase. This in turn strongly satisfies her self-esteem, because colleagues at work recognize the deserved promotion. With the salary increase, Jane buys a long-sought-after new car that provides her with a higher perceived recognition in her neighborhood. Money acts here as a secondary reinforcer that allows her to buy a new car, and through it, achieve a higher status and recognition in the direct neighborhood (primary reinforcer).

The promotion acts as a secondary reinforcer as well, because it drives the recognition at the job through the job title and positive announcement (primary reinforcer). The promotion, including salary increase, is the reinforcer, while the recognition acts as the reward. The supervisor's intention was to convince Jane to repeat the behavior and take on the next difficult project and perform again at a very high level. The combination of promotion and salary increase has been identified as the most effective reinforcer for talent retention and performance on the job.

There are certain types (called "insecure overperformers"), however, who are not sufficiently motivated by a salary increase, but rather through a promotion and recognition in public through the granting of a special title. The mechanism is in particular apparent with PhD students. There is hardly any group of employees working harder than PhD students despite a lousy salary—the sole focus of achieving the PhD title is a sufficient driver.

FIGURE 6B: LEARNING TRIANGLE OF LIFE: REVERSIBLE WORK-LIFE IMBALANCE

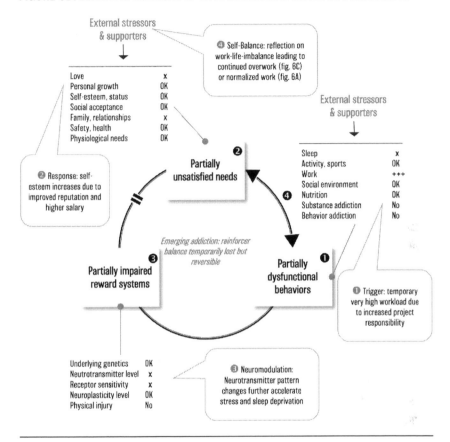

At the molecular level, the neurological response triggers dopamine and therefore works in a very similar fashion to cocaine. While the immediate neurological response is very rewarding, it is followed by a rebound effect. The rebound period allows for a conscious reflection on the past twelve weeks. During this time, Jane realizes that her family and relationship activities have been significantly impaired by her burdensome workload. Upon reflection, she should be equipped to decide whether she wants to take on the next project or focus instead on other areas she has been neglecting, such as her family (fig. 6A).

Contemporary work is highly demanding; people take on—or are forced to take on—project after project after project. It is critical for any supervisor to announce the next project before the current one is finished. In order to keep high-performing, smart employees going, one has to avoid allowing time for reflection. So most of the Janes in the world will accept the next project before completing the current one. They will work more and more (fig. 6C).

In the extreme case, Jane will give up all other activities in her life, aside from work. Usually this leads to a behavioral addiction to work. Normally, physiological needs are still satisfied, as well as self-esteem and social acceptance. In most of the cases, this balances the unmet needs on all other psychological levels for a period of time. However, the impact on our reward system functionality is basically identical to a serious cocaine addiction.

Ultimately, addiction to work ends up leading to burnout, with secondary mental illness similar to those seen in end-stage cocaine abuse, such as severe depression and anxiety. In addition, substance addiction is a frequently observed compensation mechanism for work addiction, given that other needs are not satisfied anymore; for example, increased cannabis consumption to compensate for missing time with friends and family. There is one very interesting difference, however. In contrast to cocaine use, salary increases and promotions have no upper limit. There is a clearly defined biological limit to how much cocaine you can use to stimulate your dopamine system. But there is no limit on how much money you can make or how many "rewarding" job titles you can collect. There is no limit on the perceived reward you may gain through recognition by others. Salary increases and promotions work on all levels of income, from the very, very poor to the middle class to the super-rich. At the university, you may be the perceived "king" by just having a twenty-five-year-old Fiat. On the C-level parking lot at your company, you may be nothing with a $200,000 Porsche.

That's why we observe, throughout our society, signs of early yet balanced addiction as well as fully manifested addictions to money and recognition. Money as a secondary reinforcer is much broader than cocaine, and the system built around money is much smarter than the one built around cocaine. This allows you to drive your addiction to money much, much longer before you crash—despite the identically pernicious manifestation on a neurological level.

FIGURE 6C: LEARNING TRIANGLE OF LIFE: FULLY MANIFESTED BURNOUT

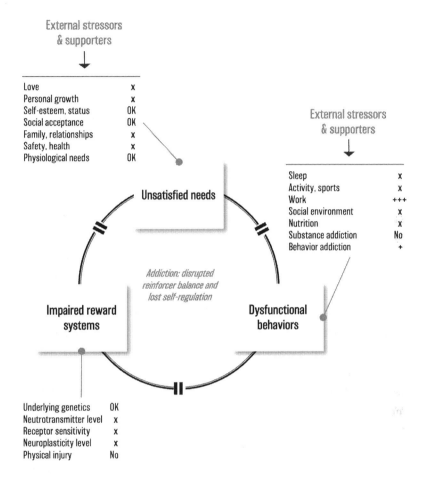

Note that any genetic defect or physical injury impairing the functional reward systems can have severe immediate consequences on mental health and addiction. Indeed, starting from impaired functional reward systems can lead very quickly to a fully manifested mental illness.

One additional key driver building up during an addiction is impairment of neuromodulation and neuroplasticity. In essence, ongoing addiction leads to a neurological state that is similar to physical injury or genetic defect. There are several reasons for reduced neuroplasticity, such as malnutrition, social isolation, insufficient mental activity, and chronic inflammation. One can't repeat enough how important it is to feed your brain well and avoid chronic inflammation in your body—in particular, inflammation driven by negative stress—in the first place.

Two additional features of healthy neuroplasticity are sustained long-term memory and efficient retrieval. It is important to note here that neuroplasticity and the associated long-term memory and retrieval are much strong under reinforcement learning than under punishment. In other words, rewarding stimuli drive deeper long-term memory better than aversive stimuli. These findings are a key concept for learning and motivation: providing a reinforcing/rewarding environment drives much faster learning and a stronger memory of a desired behavior. In contrast, punishment drives significantly less learning and associated memory—in particular if punishment is delayed in response to misbehavior. Indeed, when we look at good schools (reinforcement) and at prisons (punishment) and then compare their successes at driving certain positive behaviors, we can confirm these scientific observations.

I promised to spare you (almost) all the molecular details. However it is necessary to say a few words about the molecular basis of our reward systems here. Reward systems and associated neurotransmitters play a major role in the communication between neurons and stimulate and inhibit various molecular signaling pathways. We have one hundred billion neurons and over one trillion support cells. So we better make sure the communication works properly; otherwise, we have a mess.

The key neural reward systems are named in figure 7. It is not a surprise that for almost every reward system there is a known agent that is abused as a drug. And most of them have been out there for hundreds of years already. Humans were always on the hunt for reinforcing and rewarding agents, mainly to shortcut the path to natural happiness. Even more intriguing is the level of evolutionary conservation of these systems, down to the deepest molecular level. For example, our current dopamine system is highly similar to that of insects and other invertebrates. Thus, the underlying reward system seems to be a fundamental success factor of life, or we would have lost it over the years. Different species apply the same system in different settings, depending on the environment, obviously. However, when looking at the reward systems supporting pleasure, we can confirm even identical physiological responses between species. Even more remarkable, the genetic variability of the key molecules active in reward systems is minimal between different human cultures. Feeling rewarded holds a very high and very similar importance for all humans. This will be a key point as we work toward the big-picture vision—how to create a whole new economy powered by human happiness.

FIGURE 7: HUMAN REWARD SYSTEMS

REWARD SYSTEM	NEUROTRANSMITTER	MEDICATIONS	DRUGS	ASSOCIATED EMOTIONS
Dopamine	Dopamine	Levodopa	Cocaine, Amphetamine	Enthusiasm
Testosterone	Testosterone	Testosterone		Sexual desire
Serotonin	Serotonin	SSRI antidepressants	Ecstasy	Recognition, status, pride
Oxytocin	Oxytocin	Oxytocin		Nurturant love, contentment
Opioid	Enkephalins, endorphins	Morphine, Fentanyl	Heroin	Pleasure, amusement
Cannabinoid	Endocannabinoids	CB1/2 agonists	Marijuana	Attachment love

We have learned a lot now about how learning, memory, and reinforcement work, both functionally and dysfunctionally. So far, we have been focusing solely on the learning mechanisms of an individual. The power and speed to learn, to amplify or reinforce, and to store massive capacities of memory is remarkable and the ultimate lever for an individual to survive and progress.

The evolutionary conservation of the reward and reinforcer systems across species down to a molecular level further confirms how important these systems are. Evolution provides the basic, long-term protection for progress of life by offering a vast variability to deal with uncertainty in the future. Learning provides the short-term mechanism for progress on an individual basis, but more importantly also on a community basis: individual learning can be applied and further advanced by others—as long as it's shared.

There is strong evidence that individual learning (competitive learning) and knowledge sharing can be further advanced when people learn together (collaborative learning). Meta-analysis estimates provide evidence that students in cooperative learning situations score, on average across many studies, almost two-thirds of a standard deviation higher than their peers in a competitive learning situation. The path for achieving this success is based on five elements: positive interdependence, face-to-face promotive interaction, individual and group accountability, interpersonal and small-group skills, and group processing.

The success rate can be further maximized if top-level, complementary expertise is available. However, most important is jointly setting clear objectives—and reflecting on the goal, both jointly and singly. Again, reflection is fundamental to keeping our active reinforcement model in balance (fig. 4).

In conclusion, learning, communication, and collaboration work like a knowledge network. All contributing people can even be seen as part of a mental superorganism. Together with global digital communication, artificial intelligence, and low-cost data storage, it seems that the speed and dimension of human progress is unlimited.

Let's have a look at what tangible things humans have produced and created in our world in the past one hundred to one hundred fifty years. Indeed, progress can be seen everywhere.

CHAPTER SEVEN

OUR GLOBAL CHALLENGE

Even though the media bombards us daily with negative news and short-term trends, we have to recognize that mankind has progressed impressively since the 1800s. For example, on a global scale, health care, life span, and education have all improved and extreme poverty has been mitigated (fig. 8).

FIGURE 8: GLOBAL DEVELOPMENT OF SELECTED PROGRESS INDICATORS FROM 1800 UNTIL TODAY. *All data from www.ourworldindata.org*

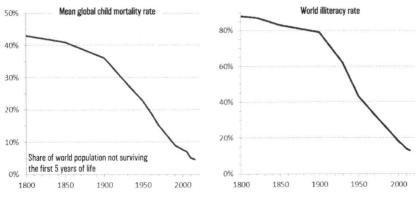

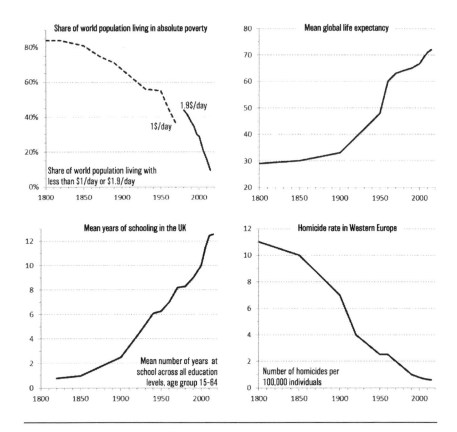

Similarly, markers for economic wealth and growth show very positive developments. Gross domestic product (GDP) and growth of GDP per capita are the leading metrics for global economic progress today. These statistics also represent a quantitative measure of modernization and human advancement. GDP is measured in a numerical amount of *money*, in US dollars or other local currency units, allowing for accurate comparison on a global scale and in real time. Growth of GDP per capita is a success story, with continuous growth over the past one hundred years on average on a global level (fig. 9), as well as on a local level for most countries.

FIGURE 9: DEVELOPMENT OF GLOBAL GROSS DOMESTIC PRODUCT FROM 1960 TO TODAY

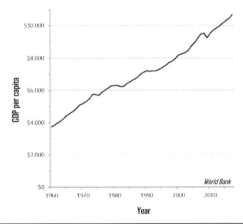

Originally, money was developed with a rather narrow focus on mediating the exchange of goods and services. Only later did money evolve as a standard measure of trade. It is the basis for the pricing of goods and services. Thus, money's most important use is for comparing the values of dissimilar objects. So it seems actually rather counterintuitive to use money as the key measure of global progress, the way it is done today. This system does not reflect any other driver of progress, such as social and environmental sustainability, freedom, health, life expectancy, or quality of life. While we would agree that these parameters are more critical indicators of progress than money, we have to recognize that all these are hard to quantify and are largely subjective in nature. In contrast, money is perceived as (and largely is) mathematically sound and objective.

In addition, as outlined in the previous chapter, money is the most effective and widely accepted secondary reinforcer. With money we can buy some of the primary reinforcers that are critically important for us as humans, such as food, clothes, a house or apartment, health (by paying for medication, a doctor, and health insurance). Thus, the original assumption to use money—the unit reflecting GDP—as a surrogate parameter for progress does not feel totally off. However, it seems obvious that other parameters also matter. Nevertheless,

GDP per capita has established itself over time as the first, leading, and sometimes even the *only* measure of progress by almost all countries on this planet—because it's so easy to numerically measure and compare.

Remember what we have learned so far: First, thanks to evolution, we love comparison and competition (like all organisms). Second, our learning mechanisms are so effective that we better make sure our goals are the right ones. Our brain is equipped to use any primary and secondary reinforcers to learn and adapt once we link them to certain behaviors. As long as we reflect on what we are doing and stay balanced, our progress is healthy. However, excessive reliance and loss of reflection upon and control over a given reinforcer can drive addiction and seriously damage mental health. In the last half century, such struggles have become all too prevalent: scientific data indicate a massive increase in depression, anxiety, and other mental illness around the world. Regarding depression over the past twenty to eighty years, almost all studies identify a significant increase. A lot of these studies do not adjust for potential experimental biases. However, even with most robust assessments (fig. 10), we find clear evidence for substantial increases.

FIGURE 10: INCREASE OF DEPRESSION DISORDERS OVER THE PAST 80 YEARS

COUNTRY	TARGET POPULATION	ANALYSIS PERIOD	PARTICIPANTS	KEY INDICATOR CHANGES	REFERENCE
United States	Adolescents age 12-17	2005-2014	172,495	8.7% to 11.3% (+30%)	R. Mojtabai 2016
United States	Young adults age 18-25	2005-2014	178,755	8.8% to 9.6%% (+9%)	R. Mojtabai 2017
United States	College students	1938-2007	63,706	+600-800%	J. M. Twenge 2010
United States	Depression patients treated outside hospitals	1998-2007	22,953- 29,370	2.37% to 2.88% (+22%)	S. C. Marcus 2010
Denmark	Random sample, age group 40-50	2000-2006	4,759	2.0% to 4.9% (+145%)	I. Andersen 2011
United States	Average adult population	1991/92- 2001/02	>42,000	3.33% to 7.06% (+112%)	W. Compton 2006
United States	Depression patients treated outside hospitals	1987-1997	34,459- 32,636	0.73% to 2.33% (+220%)	M. Olfson 2002
Sweden	Average adult population	1947, 1957, 1972	2612	sign. increase in all groups	O. Hagnell 1994

In one study, from 1938 to 2007 five to eight times more US college students scored high depression rates. In another example, a very large and well-controlled study covering 42,000 US citizens showed that depression increased from 3.3 percent of subjects in 1991–92 to 7.1 percent in 2001–02.

A similar conclusion can be drawn when looking at the rate of outpatient treatment for depression, from 0.7 percent of patients in 1987 to 2.3 percent in 1997 and 2.9 percent in 2007. There has also been an increase in antidepressant use, from 37.3 percent of patients in 1987 to 74.5 percent in 1997 and 75.3 percent in 2007 (not in fig. 10).

If we look at the leading studies assessing the increase of depression prevalence over time, we can say that retrospective studies (asking patients today about their history of depression) claim that depression in younger people is increasing and starting earlier in life. Longitudinal studies (asking the same person over time about his depression status) confirm a rising prevalence of depression as well. Some experts suggest that we are indeed in the middle of a depression epidemic.

Most interesting is the correlation between monetary wealth and depression: life risk of depression correlates with GDP growth per capita, and very strongly with income inequality.

To put it bluntly: on average, the rich are much more depressed than the poor (fig. 11).

FIGURE 11: INCOME INEQUALITY AND LIFETIME RISK OF MOOD DISORDERS

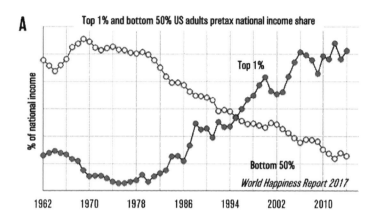

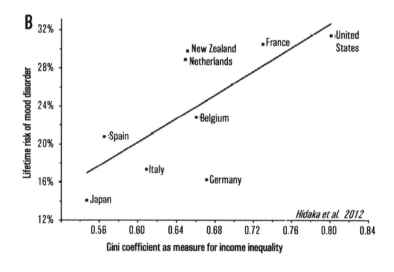

As explained in the previous chapter, any sustained impairment of functional reward systems is likely to lead to mental illness, such as depression. In turn, the abuse of rewarding drugs can be a directly triggered behavior to escape depression temporarily. It is therefore not a surprise that worldwide addiction rates are increasing in correlation with depression along several metrics.

It can be difficult to analyze the studies about behavioral addictions, given the various factors that influence the data, such as drug availability, legal situation, novel drugs, novel addictive stimuli, addiction identification, and general challenges in medical reporting. However, as with depression, addiction prevalence strongly correlates with income levels. So again, the rich are on average apparently more prone to addiction than the poor (fig. 12).

FIGURE 12: DRUG ABUSE IN RELATION TO NATIONAL INCOME AND GDP

FIGURE 12A: Prevalence of past-year use of drugs among persons aged 15-64, by drug category and national income, 2013

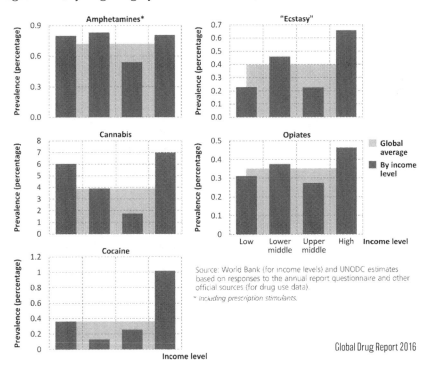

Source: World Bank (for income levels) and UNODC estimates based on responses to the annual report questionnaire and other official sources (for drug use data).

* Including prescription stimulants.

Global Drug Report 2016

FIGURE 12B: Prevalence of past-year use of opiates and cocaine versus per capita gross domestic product in countries with national data, 2013 or the latest year for which data are available

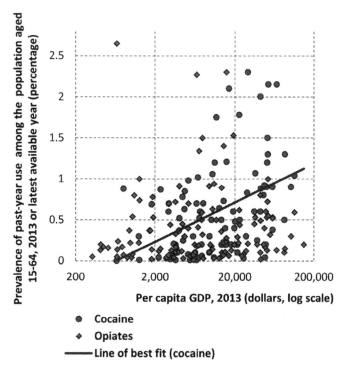

Source: World Bank (for per capital gross domestic product (GDP)) and national data and estimates based on responses to the annual report questionnaire and other official sources (for drug use data).

Global Drug Report 2016

All these correlations seem counterintuitive, given the proven positive relation between health, socioeconomic status, and reduction of depression. Yet, given our understanding of the reinforcement learning cycle, it is indeed not a surprise that wealth inequality in a given country strongly correlates with higher depression levels and a higher rate of addiction disorders. Meik Wiking from the World Happiness Research Institute in Copenhagen summarized it nicely in a recent TED Talk: in essence, the increase in depression is simply the "dark side of happiness." The whole point of economic growth originally was to improve well-being broadly. However, we have strong evidence now that for many, mental health is being left behind in the quest for prosperity. It even looks like mental health is at risk for all of us in the long run unless we find our way back to balance.

In recent years, consumption has been amplified by the utilization of the internet and social media in particular. Consumer behavior can be perfectly tracked online, content optimized to perfection by AI algorithms and ultimately leveraged to manipulate consumers and drive more revenue. The implications are dramatic. In the most recent World Happiness Report, Jean Twenge and Jeffrey Sachs have collected the latest scientific data correlating addiction, happiness, and digital media use for the US. They conclude that digital media makes a major contribution to unhappiness and that we exhibit all symptoms of a "mass-addiction society." Jeffrey Sachs elaborates in detail on various drivers for addiction. Interestingly, the most relevant ones all originate from dysregulated consumption behavior.

Can this really be true? Are we all driven by a stupid secondary reinforcer? One that we ourselves designed and yet have lost control over? Of course money is helpful for satisfying our basic needs, but beyond that it does not provide any value to us anymore. Are we simply all addicted to money, facing a fully manifested addiction with all the negative consequences for our neuronal mechanisms, our behaviors, and psychological needs? The easy answer is yes. And we've known it the whole time if we're being honest with ourselves.

With any other addiction, our immediate response would be to put the patient in a rehabilitation clinic; there are already clinics for shopping addictions. In addition, you would start an education campaign, printing unhappy faces on every hundred-dollar bill. Perhaps you would even try to erase our current economic system as the underlying theory that makes money so powerful. But what do you do if the entire "normal" world has legalized the addictive drug and is effectively run by it? And the most powerful people in the world even use the addictive drug as a performance metric to run companies and countries and pretend 24/7 that GDP growth drives all our well-being? You see, it's not so simple.

FIGURE 13: HAPPINESS AND GDP PER CAPITA IN SELECTED COUNTRIES

COUNTRY	HAPPINESS SCORE		GDP PER CAPITA		GDP TOTAL		
	#	Score	#	[USD]	#	[USD]	%world
Norway	1	7,54	2	90.344			
Denmark	2	7,52	6	60.637			
Iceland	3	7,50	16	48.614			
Switzerland	4	7,49	3	76.694			
Finland	5	7,47	19	45.825			
Netherlands	6	7,38	11	52.304			
Canada	7	7,32	15	50.232	10	1.529.760	2%
New Zealand	8	7,31	30	36.844			
Sweden	9	7,28	7	56.587			
Australia	10	7,28	8	55.671	14	1.204.616	2%
Israel	11	7,21	35	33.673			
Costa Rica	12	7,08	79	9.714			
Austria	13	7,01	17	47.909			
United States	14	6,99	12	52.263	1	18.624.475	25%
Ireland	15	6,98	4	69.632			
Germany	16	6,95	20	45.746	4	3.477.796	5%
Belgium	17	6,89	21	45.431			
Luxembourg	18	6,86	1	108.422			
United Kingdom	19	6,71	26	41.955	5	2.647.899	3%
Chile	20	6,65	57	15.020			
UAE	21	6,65	27	40.864			
Brazil	22	6,64	73	10.826	9	1.796.187	2%
Czech Republic	23	6,61	46	21.904			
Argentina	24	6,60	76	10.154			
Mexico	25	6,58	80	9.708	15	1.046.923	1%
France	31	6,44	33	38.720	6	2.465.454	3%
Spain	34	6,40	45	27.600	13	1.237.255	2%
Italy	48	5,96	42	31.730	8	1.858.913	2%
Russia	49	5,96	88	9.720	12	1.283.163	2%
Japan	51	5,92	34	37.930	3	4.840.159	6%
Korea, Rep.	55	5,84	45	27.600	11	1.411.246	2%
China	79	5,27	95	8.250	2	11.199.145	15%
India	122	4,32	171	1.670	7	2.263.792	3%
Top-15						56.886.783	75%
Total						75.845.109	

Thus, I believe we should not take this route and start treating ourselves like addicts and start a withdrawal from money addiction. I believe we should instead take a closer look at some fundamental data before we condemn our current economic system too quickly.

Material wealth reflected by GDP per capita growth seems to be one core factor for happiness (fig. 13), even though a consistent correlation cannot be drawn when comparing individual countries. The

World Happiness Report, an annual survey of the state of global happiness released by the United Nations, recently published an impressive deep-dive analysis of China over the past twenty-five years. It follows China's journey from a rural developing country in 1990 to a leading developed one today (fig. 14). On one hand, it shows a strong correlation between happiness and GDP growth from 2004 to today. On the other hand, it is intriguing to observe that the citizens' subjective well-being levels from the socialist era in 1990 have still not been reached. In 2016, China scored 5.27 on a happiness scale from 1 to 10—in the midfield. The leading country, Norway, scored 7.54.

FIGURE 14: HAPPINESS AND GDP PER CAPITA IN CHINA

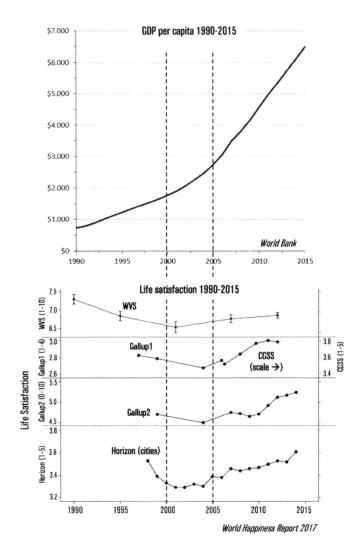

Three conclusions can be drawn from the World Happiness Report. First, since China turned toward a more capitalistic system, its happiness levels (measured as subjective well-being here) correlate strongly to GDP growth per capita. However, in absolute terms, China is still lagging behind the happiness levels observed in the end stages of socialism and is significantly behind countries leading the happiness ranking. Lastly, it seems that in the happiness midfield there is a high correlation between GDP per capita growth and happiness.

FIGURE 15: HAPPINESS AND GDP PER CAPITA IN GERMANY

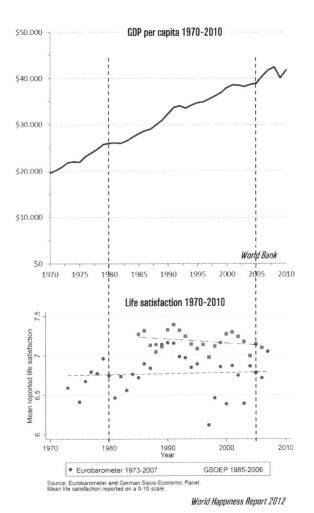

Source: Eurobarometer and German Socio-Economic Panel.
Mean life satisfaction reported on a 0-10 scale.

World Happiness Report 2012

Interestingly, when moving toward higher happiness scores, the correlation to GDP per capita growth gets lost in certain cases. For Germany, no happiness increase could be detected between 1970 and today, despite continuous GDP per capita growth (fig. 15). Most dramatic is the situation in the US, with a track record of decreasing happiness correlating with phenomenal GDP per capita growth for over sixty-five years now (fig. 16). There, the income inequality is continuously increasing and skyrocketing (fig. 11).

FIGURE 16: HAPPINESS AND GDP PER CAPITA IN THE US

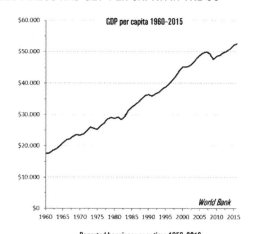

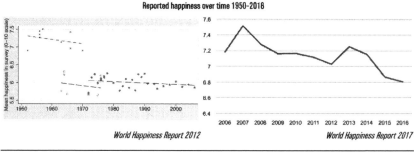

World Happiness Report 2012   *World Happiness Report 2017*

In contrast, in countries leading the world's happiness ranking, GDP per capita growth is still seen as important to a certain extent. However, social factors are the fundamental distinguishing drivers for ranking them at the top (fig. 17).

FIGURE 17: KEY HAPPINESS DRIVERS, NORDICS VERSUS US

COUNTRY	GDP	LADDER	FREEDOM	SUPP	LGDP	CORRUPT	HLE	DONATION
Finland	38901	7.66	0.95	0.95	10.57	0.25	71.38	-0.04
Norway	64124	7.60	0.95	0.96	11.07	0.41	70.78	0.11
Denmark	43613	7.56	0.95	0.95	10.68	0.21	70.92	0.13
Iceland	43872	7.51	0.95	0.98	10.69	0.72	72.05	0.27
Sweden	46365	7.37	0.92	0.91	10.74	0.25	71.96	0.13
Nordic Average	47375	7.54	0.94	0.95	10.75	0.37	71.42	0.12
United States	53088	6.80	0.76	0.90	10.88	0.74	70.13	0.13
DELTA	-5713	0.73	0.19	0.06	-0.13	-0.37	1.29	-0.01
Happiness Effect			0.20	0.13	-0.04	0.20	0.04	-0.01

World Happiness Report 2017: "America's happiness crisis is, in short, a social crisis, not an economic crisis. The combined effect of the four social variables (social support, freedom, donation, corruption) is a reduction of happiness of 0.31 points, implying that GDP (ldgp) would have to increase by 0.314/.341, or GDP would have to raise from $53,000 to around $133,000 to offset the combined deterioration of social capital assuming no further shift in inequality."

Key: GDP = Gross domestic product per capita; LADDER = Happiness score; FREEDOM = Freedom to make life choices; SUPP = Social support; LGDP = Logged GDP per capita; CORRUPT = Corruption Perception; HLE = Healthy life expectancy at birth; DONATION = Generosity.

So our easy answer ("We are all addicted to money!") was clearly not precise enough: money *is* correlated with happiness. But beyond a certain level, it apparently turns into a driver of unhappiness and potentially mental illness.

How can that be? To answer this question, Boston College conducted a research study in 2011 funded by the Bill & Melinda Gates Foundation surveying 160 very rich families in the US. In order to conduct a scientifically robust study, 160 families are most likely too small a sample size. Nevertheless, the findings were very interesting.

The study concluded that for almost all the families, their wealth has led to broad and general dissatisfaction, depressive symptoms, and deep anxieties about losing their social networks. The level of depression was higher for families with inherited wealth than for those from previously very low income levels who earned their wealth.

It seems reasonable that even within the group of very rich families, the drivers of dissatisfaction are different. Hypothetically, one would assume those with inherited wealth would lack any satisfaction of personal self-esteem, while those with earned wealth may carry a fear of losing it and returning to a "normal," poorer life. In addition, the perceived pressure to continuously drive returns on their wealth was a central element for the dissatisfaction across almost all families, in particular when comparing themselves to their peers.

We have seen how economic inequality has a particularly negative impact on those at low-income and middle-income levels. However, the other end of the spectrum, the high-income levels, also faces significant challenges, with a perceived pressure coming from inequality: they compare their material wealth in absolute terms to that of their peers. In addition, and even more importantly, they compare themselves on the success of further growing their wealth. The billionaires, the investment funds, and the big companies become disproportionately wealthier.

In contrast, the core metrics indicating investment success show that the financial performance of billionaires and big companies is rather poor, in particular at higher amounts of investment. Return on investment is a relative indicator that—in the investment world—assesses annualized returns. To sustainably increase return on investment levels from a very high level of absolute wealth can become mathematically extremely challenging. For example, if your net worth is $100,000 USD, you have to find an investment opportunity that can create a return of $10,000 USD to obtain a return on investment of 10 percent. To find such an investment opportunity is already tough. If your net worth is $10 billion, you have to find an investment opportunity that can create a return of $1 billion to show the same performance. There are very few, if any, investment opportunities that deliver a return of 1 billion dollars these days on an annualized basis.

In other words, rich people can scarcely find productive investment opportunities. Most rich people are actually dramatically underperforming on this key metric, one that is particularly relevant for them. From the perspective of the poor or middle-income people, this is sick and ridiculous, and it makes the average person's fight for survival much tougher because it drives substantial redistribution of money—and with it, inequality. From the perspective of the rich, it's simply "personal underperformance" against their peers, which is driving a desperate hunt for higher and faster return on investment opportunities, just to satisfy the individual needs that are psychologically most important for them.

The symptoms of this hunt are remarkable. Real estate prices are skyrocketing (just to own it; hardly anyone can afford to live in these houses and apartments). There is an investment rush into a cryptocurrency called Bitcoin, which does not have any underlying value in the classical sense associated with it. Other outrages abound, including $450 million for a Leonardo da Vinci painting, and CEO compensation packages beyond the $100 million range. In the end, everyone is less happy and everyone is potentially depressed, all due to the same secondary reinforcer: money. The ones who have too little are challenged to satisfy the basic needs for living, and the ones who have too much find there is no ceiling for money. Although you can always race for more money, the race hardly ever leads to a satisfying end. In addition, the rich also compete for a relative performance indicator that, to a large extent, simultaneously ignores the absolute amount while focusing on how much you can relatively increase it over time.

The response by our businesses, private or public, is even more concerning. Adam Smith, the "Father of Capitalism," said in 1776 that enterprises reinvest income and wealth into new activities in order to drive new growth. Ever since, this has been a cornerstone of the capitalistic concept. In recent years, however, this concept seems to have gotten weaker and weaker. Since 2008, the share buyback programs of the top global companies have exploded to $4 trillion in share buybacks. This means that instead of growing their businesses in the future by investing their returns today—in new research, development, manufacturing facilities, and people—companies are now giving their earnings back to their owners. The owners are the ones who already benefit from dividends and appreciating share prices.

In 2015 alone, $561 billion was invested in share buyback programs, $100 billion more than all investments in research and development. Company executives who own company stock and stock options love these programs because they increase existing wealth for themselves as well. In contrast, fewer new jobs are created that would create opportunities for middle-income and low-income people, opportunities that would allow at least some minor redistribution of wealth.

The latest round of this phenomenon can be observed in the impact of President Trump's recent tax reform. Announced as a stimulus for investment and employment, the reform has returned billions back to US companies. However, already more than 40 percent of the tax savings has been given back to shareholders via share buyback programs. As highlighted in August 2018 by David Kostin, the chief US equity strategist at Goldman Sachs, 2017 and in particular 2018 were the ultimate record years for share buybacks. Next, 10 to 15 percent of the tax savings was used for debt payback. Thus, no new opportunities for middle-income and low-income people were created. Finally, another 30 to 50 percent of these tax savings are expected to be used in merger and acquisition activities. These activities are enabled by convincing the shareholders of the acquired company to sell for a premium. These premiums are—depending on the industry—between 30 and 100 percent normally. For any investor, a sale in an acquisition is a very attractive way to obtain an above-average return on investment (30 percent of a basic acquisition premium is above the average expectations on return on investment, at least if you are a "normal" investor, not necessarily a hedge fund or a venture capital fund or a private equity fund).

Thus another win for shareholders—this time on the side of the selling company—one that increases shareholders' wealth. In contrast, acquisitions are mostly justified by potential "value synergies" that can be obtained for the acquirer by bringing two companies together. For the employees, "synergies" simply mean their jobs are cut. Employees are the most effective synergies once you fire them. Again, no win and no new opportunities for middle-income and low-income people. All this data just provides evidence that our current system obviously misses productive investment opportunities.

Economic inequality was identified very early on as a key risk and potential issue in classical capitalism. Already Adam Smith highlighted several times throughout his groundbreaking publications on philosophy and economy that "money can't buy happiness," and Smith was sincerely concerned about poverty and inequality leading to profound distortion of people's sympathies as a consequence. Basically, all big economists suggested ideas to correct or mitigate this issue, from Marx's more radical approach to eradicate capitalism in the first place to drastic increases of income and wealth taxes like in France. One major reason for taxes is a redistribution of value from the rich to the poor. Around the globe we consistently tax income at rates between 20 and 60 percent for individuals and 5 to 30 percent for businesses. Capital gains are taxed at consistently lower rates than income, and wealth—if not taxed at the time of inheritance—is actually hardly taxed at all (just silently sitting there increasing its value).

On the one hand, the idea of redistribution by taxes is a good one. On the other hand, the idea of taxes is horrible. First, it's obviously not successful, since the inequality on our planet is dramatically increasing (fig. 11). Second, the concept of taxes fulfills literally all parameters that work against positive conditioning and reinforcement: it's a punishment (a secondary reinforcer is taken away). The punishment is not linked to any behavior we should change. There is no clear objective or a clear rule for taxes. If there were, we would not need a tax department or tax advisors. No one equipped with the standard learning and memory systems will ever learn to change a behavior we all would like to see, such as donating more freely. No organism will ever like paying taxes, even if the underlying idea may be a good one. No organism will ever remember any detail associated with taxes. In turn, every organism hates taxes and will try to avoid them. This in turn triggers even more dramatic punishment (this time by law enforcement), punishment that is in most countries tougher than that for serious criminal actions.

In the 2017 World Happiness Report, renowned economist Jeffrey Sachs identified the US happiness crisis as "a social crisis and not an economic crisis." He further provided several ideas for how to increase happiness and decrease misery in the US by redistributing wealth and focusing wealth differently (fig. 16). His ideas are spot-on and get to the core of what needs to change in the US in order to resolve the happiness crisis. In a similar way, other nonprofit organizations are calling on policy makers to tackle the bizarre income inequality on a global level with a fundamental global tax reform. Even very large investors, such as BlackRock, KKR, and most sovereign wealth funds, urge company leaders to invest in a more long-term and purposeful manner.

Now let's pause here for a minute to reflect. In a widely distributed, autonomous system that is driven by the sole objective of increasing money and wealth, that controls the most relevant operating means, and heavily rewards the acting players, can any single player or event hold the power to change something?

Do we really believe we can still control our economic system? Or that we will be able to win back control in the future?

Obviously not. Capitalism, in combination with our biological reinforcement learning system, is perfect. It's the ultimate design. We lost control a long time ago.

To me, it feels awkward to blame any of the leaders of our current economic system for their success. They just did everything right according the metrics we all have given them—and ourselves!—in this game. We should call it an economic game to clearly distinguish it from the ultimate game, the game of life, introduced earlier. When we examine the fundamental mathematical core of our system, it's clear that there is no genuine reward for charity, no reward for paying taxes, no reward for taking care of this planet, no reward for increasing the quality of life, and no reward for making other people happy. The economic system we are running focuses only on making more money. Money, a token that can be counted so easily and allows for easy comparison. A token that allows us to identify winners and losers—that is, after all, our evolutionary foundation: "survival of the fittest."

Thus, the current outcry to significantly restrict our capitalistic system is the wrong approach. First and foremost, it would bring down the underlying order of global interactions, trade, and stability. Historically, such destabilization hits the middle-income and low-income levels much harder than the high-income levels. Secondly, we would lose capitalism's growth and wealth benefits for the less developed areas of our world.

I believe we require the opposite strategy.

We need an extension of the current economic system that would offer new pockets of hyper-growth for investors and drive growth in a direction that provides real progress for life. We have to extend our current economic game in order to make it truly beneficial for the game that really matters: the game of life.

We definitely should not change the economic game, because we are extremely successful at it. And the current rules have provided a certain level of progress for us on average. We just have to change the token—the purpose!—we're chasing. Money has been proven insufficient.

This time, we better make sure that we choose the right token, the right secondary reinforcer. Or even better: Let's forget about surrogates, let's forget about secondary reinforcers. This time, let's get the "real stuff." Let's find the ultimate *primary* reinforcer that is a core value for us and that's worth striving for.

As we've learned, there are several primary reinforcers. We have also learned that the very few reward systems that detect these reinforcers are highly conserved over millions of years of evolution.

So in theory, we can do the reverse experiment: What do we get if we switch all reward systems on and (very importantly!) keep them balanced over time?

We get happiness.

So let's extend the core value of our current successful economic system from money to happiness. We will create the next level to benefit not only investors, but all people. Because that's how our game should be played—it should be played for the progress of life, not for money.

We'll create the **Capitalism of Happiness.**

CHAPTER EIGHT

HAPPINESS

The biggest challenge when using the term "happiness" is actually the term itself.

We all may understand the meaning of the word a little differently. But "happiness" actually says it all for me, and here's why: Everybody immediately associates the term with positive emotions. Second, I leverage our deeply ingrained evolutionary foundation when combining happiness with economy. The reward systems in our brains are insensitive to money as a secondary reinforcer, but still can create plenty of happy emotions when triggered; thus, on a neurological level, happiness is astronomically more powerful than money.

Before starting to create an extension of our current economic system focused on happiness, we have to be crystal clear about which exact type of happiness we want to reward and encourage. Without such a clear understanding, we run the risk of installing another misguided reinforcer. This requires first a brief overview of the existing scientific understanding of happiness.

The term "happiness" is explored in various different disciplines and by various experts, namely philosophers, evolutionary biologists, geneticists, psychologists, socioeconomists, and neuroscientists. The challenge for us is the different definitions and perspectives each discipline applies.

Philosophy and religion first introduced the idea of happiness, and it has been at their center ever since. The philosophy of happiness can be best traced back to Aristotle, who described happiness as composed of two inseparable aspects: *hedonia* (pleasure of the senses) and *eudaemonia* (pleasure of reason: living well and doing well). It should be noted that the two are closely linked, which has been confirmed by studies recently. Questionnaire scores for *hedonia* and *eudaemonia* typically converge in the same individuals: if a person self-reports that they are hedonically happy, then that same person is very likely to report a high sense of positive meaningfulness in life. Thus, absent any addictive state in this person, there is a strong positive correlation between *hedonia* and *eudaemonia*.

From the perspective of psychology, the influential American psychologist Abraham Maslow opened a deeper discussion of happiness and need satisfaction in his landmark book *Motivation and Personality*, published in 1954.

Despite rarely using the term "happiness," he established a perspective on psychology that he termed positive, or humanistic, psychology. It is centered on the belief that humans have a positive potential first and foremost and that every person has the desire to realize their full, positive potential. To get there, it is critical to understand our basic needs before striving for higher-need satisfaction. On the highest level of need satisfaction—when all lower needs are satisfied—that potential can be reached.

FIGURE 18: NEEDS HIERARCHY MODELS FROM A. MASLOW AND C. ALDERFER

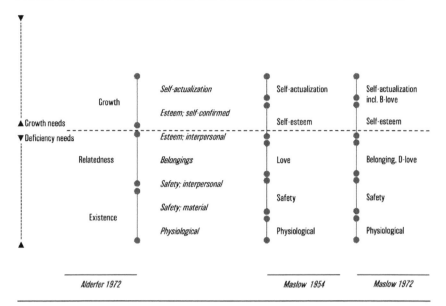

| | Alderfer 1972 | | Maslow 1954 | Maslow 1972 |

In support of the concept of potential, Maslow established a hierarchy of needs that comprises five levels: psychological needs, safety needs, love and belonging needs, self-esteem needs, and ultimately *self-actualization* (fig. 18, center column).

The first four base levels he termed *deficiency needs*, or *D-needs*. If a human being does not have enough satisfaction of such needs, you have the desire to fulfill them. Once such needs are satisfied, you feel content, but these needs alone are not fully satisfying. They are insufficient to fully realize our potential. The fifth level, self-actualization, Maslow termed *being needs*, or *B-needs*, which are holistic and accepting of people as they are, in contrast to D-needs. Self-actualized people accept that each person, simply by being, is inherently worthy and that the ultimate goal for each of us is to grow. Only through constant self-reflection, self-improvement, and taking responsibility for our actions can we become truly happy.

Interestingly, Maslow did not extensively use the terms "happiness" or "growth." To me, these two terms perfectly describe what

Maslow's positive psychology is all about. On a neurological level, neuroplasticity *grows* perfectly if you are happy.

Maslow described the characteristics of B-values and self-actualization by observing a small group of people around him whom he believed were self-actualized. They shared fourteen qualities: truth, goodness, beauty, wholeness/dichotomy, aliveness, uniqueness, perfection/necessity, completion, justice/order, simplicity, richness, effortlessness, playfulness, and self-sufficiency.

Maslow's focus always was on the individual; he described self-sufficiency as a key attribute of self-actualization. He never looked beyond that to groups or couples. From a psychological perspective this makes perfect sense, because the individual is in the center. However, from a neuroscientific perspective, we now have evidence that couples and groups of people who interact positively and grow together experience a mutually beneficial effect on their neuroplasticity. And the impact is huge. We will have a closer look at the psychological potential of groups later.

Yet Maslow made a very interesting observation when describing love in more detail. Maslow differentiated Deficiency-love, or D-love from Being-love, or B-love.

D-love is entirely focused on filling deficiency needs, mainly belonging and self-esteem needs but also safety needs sometimes. It is possessive love that sees the loved one as a means to fill a deficiency. In contrast, B-love, according to Maslow, can only be experienced by self-actualized people. B-love is based on the acceptance of the person we love. We simply love other persons for who they are and not what they can do for us and our need satisfaction. B-love is love of the essence of another person. It's unselfish love that is enjoyed, pleasure giving, and without limits. Thus, if our *B-loved* ones decide to leave us, it means that they move on to grow. The loss of love is regrettable but not devastating, and we wish our *B-loved* ones all the best for their future. In contrast, if our *D-loved* ones decide to leave us, we feel devastated because we feel insecure, incomplete, and rejected, which further increases our need for self-esteem.

Like Maslow, Erich Fromm, a leading social psychologist and humanistic philosopher, also described two love categories that are highly similar to D-love and B-love. In his landmark book *The Art of*

Loving, published in 1956, Fromm defined immature, or romantic, love as a potential escape from our loneliness. Whereas mature, or *true*, love is based on care, responsibility, respect for, and knowledge of the partner we love. The most comprehensive quote for me that describes the two love categories comes from Fromm: *"Immature love says, 'I love you because I need you.' Mature love says, 'I need you because I love you.'"* I like this differentiation a lot, and it nicely summarizes also the essence of B-love (mature love) and D-love (immature love).

For neuroplasticity, interpersonal relationships are crucial. Two is the smallest relational unit, so love and belonging become critical for us to understand. Thus, I apply here the ideas Maslow published in 1972 to a revised Maslow need hierarchy (fig. 18, right column) that differentiates love a little further. Note that Maslow himself never published an updated hierarchy like this. However, I would like to show these refinements here graphically for better understanding and to prepare ourselves for further refinements later. Maslow concluded that a psychological utopia (*"eupsychia"*) would result if all of an individual's needs on the hierarchy are met—a pretty complete framework for how to improve the general happiness of mankind.

Unfortunately, his framework for *eupsychia* was never recognized broadly and thus remained a theoretical concept instead of being implemented in real life. Instead, over the years Maslow's "need hierarchy" (inconsistently) morphed into a popularized "needs pyramid." Indeed, the term "needs pyramid" wrongly implies that the higher needs are available for fewer people or are less important than the lower needs, and that you have to build each level on the previous one. Maslow's original thoughts and manuscripts do not conclude that; they state that we can all evolve toward the highest levels and that, for an individual, starving for food is as dramatic and severe as "starving" for self-actualization. Remarkably, a large study of over fifty thousand people performed in 2011 basically confirmed Maslow's theory with solid observational data.

In the 1970s the American psychologist Clayton Alderfer refined Maslow's need hierarchy based on several studies to split it into three layers: existence needs, relatedness needs, and growth needs (fig. 18, left column). In particular the element of "growth" was a key advancement in comparison to Maslow's concept, in my opinion. Alderfer's description of growth needs is highly similar to the concept of human progress introduced in the beginning: satisfaction of growth needs depends on a person finding the opportunities to be what he is most fully and to become what he can. As we have learned, opportunities become more abundant with the more options a person can choose from. Thus, optionality is a key driver for opportunities that enable growth, based on Alderfer's concept. Further, Alderfer expands on Maslow's ideas by attributing growth not only to self-actualization, but also to interpersonal self-esteem. Most remarkable are Alderfer's observations on how frustration of higher-order needs affects lower-order desires. In essence, he demonstrated that the less growth needs are satisfied, the more relatedness needs will be focused on, and the less relatedness needs are satisfied, the more existence needs will be focused on.

The implications of Alderfer's theory can be observed all around us in the developed world. For example, if people lack a stable, positive social environment—relatedness—they start to overconsume. The clear symptom that can be observed is the dramatic obesity epidemic that particularly strikes the poorer population in the developed world. This has been confirmed by many clinical and sociological studies. In addition, the exploding success of social media has been shown to result in insufficient face-to-face relationships and missing growth opportunities for the younger generations. "Followers" and "likes" function as surrogates for missing hugs and personal growth.

From a neuroscientific perspective, it is not surprising. While the number and depth of your social contacts are directly correlated to your neuroplasticity and mental health, no correlation has been found between neuroplasticity and social media contacts. "Chatting" and posting online do not seem to have quite the same effect as experiencing things together physically.

Interestingly, there is another correlation that confirms Alderfer's theory: people highly active on social media are much more likely to be linked to behavioral addictions such as consumption and buying. That's why advertising on social media is so successful: the digital platforms are not sufficiently satisfying our relatedness needs, but they drive our desire to meet existence needs. Thus, flooding social media with advertising makes total economic sense: it hits the audience with the perfect desire on the spot.

To be clear, I am not claiming that social media is bad. I believe the democratization of information and education is amazing. However, we should reflect on our biology: deficiency needs are easy to instrumentalize. We are designed like this. But we are also designed to reflect on our needs and then make the best decision to maintain our real relationships and drive our growth. Indeed, I am sure that the coming generations will find a more balanced way to engage with social media and have a "life" on the internet, because the amount of happiness you can create by experiencing things together in real life is much greater. Digital applications will remain a secondary reinforcer. Primary reinforcers—the ultimate route to happiness—must be experienced in real life.

Remarkably, Maslow and Alderfer both performed a deep analysis on the disturbing impact of capitalism on the "need hierarchy" from a psychological perspective (Maslow 1972, Alderfer 1972). Starting in the late 1980s these analyzes were, in turn, the basis for socioeconomic discussions among experts about how to apply these insights to our economy.

New socioeconomic metrics emerged, comparing life satisfaction to the classical economic metric of return on investment. The most accepted surveys that use such metrics are Gallup World Poll, the World Values Survey, the European Values Study, and the European Social Survey.

Like the philosophers, the socioeconomists also placed Aristotle's *eudaemonia* at the center of their concepts and added certain aspects of Maslow's need hierarchy. With it they formed a novel scientific parameter called **subjective well-being**. In 2013 the Organization for Economic Cooperation and Development, a group of thirty-four democratic countries that create economic and social policies, published guidelines on measuring subjective well-being. Their recommendations include assessing "good mental states, including all of the various evaluations, positive and negative, that people make of their lives and the affective reactions of people to their experiences." The definition of subjective well-being hence encompasses three elements:

+ life evaluation—a reflective assessment of a person's life or some specific aspects of it
+ affect (close to Aristotle's *hedonia*)—a person's feelings or emotional states, typically measured with reference to a particular point in time
+ *eudaemonia*—a sense of meaning and purpose in life, or good psychological functioning.

The World Happiness Report, annually published since 2012 under the aegis of Jeffrey Sachs, is a central building block for discussions on global subjective well-being data. In addition to a robust analysis, the World Happiness Report makes a very smart move by using subjective well-being as its core scientific metric but paralleling it with the general term "happiness" when writing for a general readership. The authors of the World Happiness Report conclude that the term "happiness" helps to focus thinking and attracts attention more quickly than does "subjective well-being."

The annual guidance provided by the World Happiness Report uses a set of six parameters that are identified as driving happiness to a large extent (40 to 70 percent): GDP per capita, social support, healthy life expectancy at birth, freedom to make life choices, generosity, and perception of corruption. Based on the changes by country, country group, or globally, certain recommendations are suggested to policy makers in order to promote happiness ratings.

The journey to understanding happiness and in particular positive emotions from the perspective of biology and neuroscience was more challenging and took much longer. Darwin's discovery that humans have common origins with other animals has been widely acknowledged. However, his third book, *The Expression of the Emotions in Man and Animals*, which analyzes the relevance of emotions for evolutionary selection, received less public attention. Here Darwin provides strong observational evidence that emotions are key for survival of the fittest. He even demonstrates that defined physiological and physical expressions correlate with emotions and are highly conserved across species. He concluded that this was clear proof of the role emotions play as key positive drivers of survival and heritage of associated genes. This view was largely disregarded in philosophy and science for decades, but recently cognitive sciences have changed perspective.

One key view that initiated a lot of follow-up research was the broaden-and-build theory presented in 1998 by Barbara Fredrickson, a leading scholar in social psychology. The concept proposes that positive emotions help us acquire long-term informational, social, and material resources that are important for survival. Recent years have seen a focus on evolutionarily conserved pathways that drive pleasure, with impressive advancements by neuroscientists Morten L. Kringelbach and Kent C. Berridge and psychologist Michelle Shiota and her team.

Scientific data collected over the past five years strongly indicates that even defined, discrete, positive emotions can be identified by combining several noninvasive diagnostic readouts. These latest scientific advancements will be a centerpiece for us later.

It is very impressive how variable are the perspectives on the term "happiness." Yet all these different perspectives—the neuroscientific, the psychological, the evolutionary, and the philosophical—are critical for us to understand when applying it. Figure 19 summarizes the key differences between the perspectives in different fields. Most importantly, we have to recognize that philosophy, cognitive psychology, and socioeconomics focus on **Conscious happiness**, that is, the level of happiness that we are aware of and can reflect on. Consciousness is the final output we experience after consolidating information and memories from our subconscious and unconscious neuronal activities. Conscious happiness is the kind we should be really interested in. However, we have already agreed that measuring Conscious happiness is highly subjective, difficult to quantify in detail, and therefore difficult to compare among individuals. Thus Conscious happiness alone will be an insufficient parameter to look at if we want to scientifically understand the origin of happiness.

How can we make up for the missing objectivity and the missing quantification in Conscious happiness? Is there any way to measure the raw, scientific happiness our brain creates? The unbiased happiness signals before our mood, memory, attendance, disturbance, suppression, and negligence modulates it? We actually can. The parameter we would have to use is the immediate detection of an input at the moment of its being encoded in our rewarding neurons, but before consolidation starts. We will name this parameter **Unconscious happiness**.

Unconscious happiness is the primary focus of neuroscientists, while cognitive psychologists focus mainly on Conscious happiness. In particular, the former focus on the initial response our neurons deliver when a happy-making event hits us. The debate between the two groups is on, but it seems that both groups are right.

FIGURE 19: HAPPINESS: SAME TERM, DIFFERENT UNDERLYING SCIENCE AND PERSPECTIVES

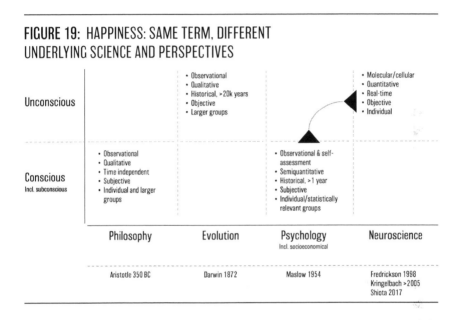

What finally counts for us as individuals is Conscious happiness. However, the raw, Unconscious happiness data would provide us with a scientific data set that gives additional insights about the moment when our brains create happiness signals. Having two complementary data sets would allow us to pause and reflect, just as Maslow has proposed in his positive, humanistic psychology.

We would understand how much happiness we actively repress or passively miss (Unconscious happiness > Conscious happiness). In addition, we would be able to understand how good we are at thinking positively (Unconscious happiness < Conscious happiness). Therefore, both data sets—Conscious happiness and Unconscious happiness—are crucial and would provide us with a different quality of cognition.

To reflect deeper, induce and reinforce learning, and create sustainable memories. First for ourselves, then for others.

As indicated by the arrows in figure 19, the only way to get this done is to combine existing psychological frameworks (individual, subjective, conscious) with deep neuroscientific data (individual, objective, unconscious).

Let's briefly conclude here with these insights:

- Yes, we can use happiness as a relevant and meaningful base value for an extended economic system. There is plenty of solid data and evidence.

- In order to leverage happiness as a universal indicator of our progress, we have to combine *Conscious happiness data* and *Unconscious happiness data* on an *individual level* that we acquire in *real time*. Unconscious happiness data provides us with the dimension, the size of happiness. Conscious happiness data provides us with its impact and true relevance.

I am aware that at first glance this proposal for a basis for good metrics seems pretty complex. However, with this proposal we have defined the first universal performance indicator of all our progress. And of the progress of life. To finally apply this ultimate indicator—happiness—in our real world today, let me show you in the coming chapters what is required to actualize happiness for all of us

We can utilize the beneficial situation to apply the wisdom of our current economic system, refine it, and expand the economic system so happiness is at its core.

CHAPTER NINE

THREE BUILDING BLOCKS

In the previous chapter, we laid the foundation of our concept by selecting *real-time, Conscious, and Unconscious happiness on an individual level* as the universal performance indicator in our extended economic system.

Happiness is directly beneficial for humans (and likely for animals, and perhaps even for plants). This has been proven by scientific evidence, from evolutionary conservation of key mechanisms to the benefits of learning and memory. Thus, any activity driving happiness will work as a primary reinforcer. Different people will respond to different ones; for example, the hungry respond to food. And the reinforcers likely vary in their perceived strength; food is a weak reinforcer if you are completely full. Neurologically, a person's response to a reinforcer is based on its ability to trigger one, few, or all reward systems, and on the number of hedonic centers it can stimulate in the brain.

What else do we need to put happiness at the core of a newly extended economy?

In our current system, the mixed economic framework provides a holistic basis for just about everything we do with respect to money, goods and services, and capital markets. Modern capitalism

developed certain variations of the mixed economy, with the US acting more laissez-faire and the Nordic states with a higher focus on
welfare. However, the fundamentals of our economic system are used
universally.

Unfortunately, such a universal framework is not available for happiness. So we have to define one.

We need a **Universal happiness hierarchy**.

Several brilliant minds have already worked on aspects of such a
hierarchy, and we directly benefit from this work. We just have to consolidate and adapt these available concepts to sufficiently cover the latest
significant changes and advancements in technology, science, and environment in the past five to ten years. I will do that in the next chapter.

We then need to mathematically quantify happiness in the same
way that economic prices provide numerical values for material goods
and services. The dynamics for "pricing" happiness seem bizarre at
first, but actually they are straightforward. In contrast to prices created
by economic market dynamics, happiness is "priced" instantly in our
brains (Unconscious happiness) and then potentially modulated and
translated into Conscious happiness by individual emotions, memories, and the associated environment. Measuring Conscious happiness
levels is easy: we can just ask people; they will tell us. But what they
tell us would be subjective and insufficiently precise because people
can only measure happiness in large, ambiguously defined buckets.
Consider trying to explain the last time you felt happiness. How happy
were you? "Very"? Or just "somewhat"? It is impossible to describe in
scientific terms.

In contrast, Unconscious happiness can be measured very precisely. Unconscious happiness is the molecular and cellular activation
level of our neural reward systems when they detect and encode an
incoming stimulus. In essence it's tiny, highly precise electrical currents flowing along and between neurons that we can measure.

Measuring these activation states, these tiny currents, is a different
level of complexity. It is really tough from a technological level to go
down to the molecular and physical level. Actually, it is the most ambitious frontline of neuroscientific research at the moment.

We need it for our concept, though. Even more challenging,
we would need real-time neural diagnostics to detect and value

Unconscious happiness levels. And we better find a way to do it non-invasively. We don't want to run around with needles sticking in our brains or wearing magnetic helmets.

Assuming we will be able to easily obtain this diagnostic brain data, we will also need a simple, objective, numerical measure translated from it so we can reference it on a daily basis—just as money provides us with a common measure of value for goods and services. And this measure should be as simple as money and should possess similar or identical features to money. We need a kind of *happiness currency*. There are three key reasons to introduce such a currency:

- All definitions applicable to fiat currency in our financial system can apply also to a currency that measures happiness. As happiness is created based on the same molecular system in the brains of all humans, such a currency would be universally accepted as a measure of value. If it is widely accepted, it can be assumed it would be widely accepted for transactions and exchange and perhaps even storage. Finally, we could keep transaction records to learn and remember. Thus, a happiness currency can operate just like any other currency based on the same monetary principles.

- Monetary wealth is and will remain a key driver for happiness. Thus, our current economic system based on fiat currency is an integral part. Likely, we will require exchanging different currencies along the way to happiness. Therefore, it is critical that the two concepts can communicate with—can exchange—into each other.

- In the absence of any direct value for an organism, the effectiveness of a secondary reinforcer entirely depends on how well its function is learned and memorized by the organism. Money has established itself as the strongest secondary reinforcer over the past hundreds of years by far, despite not offering any inherent life-sustaining value. Thus, all humans are extremely well-conditioned toward "money" as a concept: a token without any intrinsic value, but with significant buying power. So let's leverage these excellent "training results" for the expansion of our economy from just a market for goods and services, to a market for happiness as well.

Today, nothing like a happiness currency exists. We have to develop it from scratch.

I would like to reemphasize one aspect before we go down the road of measuring happiness: I do not intend to quantify our Conscious happiness. Conscious happiness is subjective, personal, and private, and, as such, it cannot and should not be measured, normalized, or made transparent. Otherwise we would influence our personalities and identities. This is not the idea presented here.

In contrast, quantifying Unconscious happiness means to read out the raw data our happiness centers in the brain produce in the split second after something positive hits us. It is important to take that data point before our consciousness modulates, suppresses, or ignores it, because it is the only time that point is unbiased. That's the data point we require for objective quantification.

More importantly, the raw data will allow us to consciously reflect on what or who makes us happy in the first place and what we miss by being too busy with other stuff. Reflection is the most critical aspect here: reflection enables us to recognize, learn, and potentially reward actions that drive our happiness consciously. Like the underlying transaction algorithms driving the trades on our stock markets every day, neurological data is not very convenient and consumer friendly. At the stock market, huge data sets and complex algorithms are finally consolidated in just one number representing the value of a share: a stock price at a given point in time, measured in US dollars or any other local currency.

FIGURE 20: CAPITALISM VERSUS CAPITALISM OF HAPPINESS

	DRIVING ROI	DRIVING ROH
FRAMEWORK	Capitalism / Global mixed economy	Universal happiness hierarchy[1]
PRICING	Supply & demand-based (driven by the market; illogical/emotional)	Need-based (driven by individual neural reward systems; scientific/non-emotional)
CURRENCY	Financial capital: medium to exchange, common measure of value and store of value	Happiness capital: medium to exchange, common measure of value and store of value[2]
FOCUS	Creating, producing, marketing and selling of goods and services to other people (at a profit)	Creating, sharing, and rewarding goods, services and actions driving happiness for other people

ROI—Return on investment; ROH—Return on Happiness

(1) The Universal happiness hierarchy contains capitalism but goes beyond it; (2) As has been scientifically shown, happiness can exist only in the present. Chapter Eleven explains how happiness can be stored.

In a similar fashion, we need to establish a happiness currency that provides a universal value based on all Unconscious happiness data recorded and consolidated per person at a given time. What we do with these data sets is our own free choice and will. It is therefore extremely critical that each person is the single owner of her/his data and that these data sets are secure.

In conclusion, we have to add three fundamental building blocks around happiness as our core value in order to expand our current economic system: a Universal happiness hierarchy, a pricing of happiness, and a happiness currency (fig. 20).

Let's get started with the first one, the Universal happiness hierarchy.

CHAPTER TEN

THE UNIVERSAL HAPPINESS HIERARCHY

The universal framework we build should deserve the term "universal"; have broad support from experts in science, sociology, economy, and psychology; and be simple enough to receive broad public acceptance.

Our framework will be universal as long as we measure Unconscious happiness through our neural reward systems, which have been evolutionarily conserved over millions of years. As introduced in the opening, we can feel pretty comfortable with the term "universal" as long as we systematically stay on the level of our conserved neural reward systems to measure happiness. These systems evolved millions of years ago and have been used ever since to drive positive reinforcement, learning, and long-term memory across the species. So it is highly likely that these established systems will stick around no matter which novel happiness triggers arise in the future.

From the available widely accepted models that are closest to these requirements, I've decided to start with the well-known need hierarchy from Maslow in its original and extended versions (fig. 18, center and right columns) and Alderfer's existence, relatedness, and growth (ERG) concept (fig. 18, left column).

We briefly introduced Maslow's need hierarchy in Chapter Eight. In 1954, Maslow focused exclusively on the individual and not on groups. In later publications, Maslow refined his views on interactions between individuals by looking closely into love, one of his need categories. A major advancement for his concept was the segregation of Deficiency-love or "D-love" from Being-love or "B-love" (fig. 18, right column). D-love is driven by insufficient satisfaction of certain individual needs like safety and self-esteem. D-love is egocentric. In contrast, B-love focuses primarily on the partner and his or her well-being. Maslow dedicated B-love only to people who have reached the level of self-actualization, the highest level in his hierarchy. As such, B-love is also egocentric in a way, as it is a key hallmark of the individual's self-actualization that accepts other people simply as they are. However, in contrast to D-love, it enables love on equal terms, with both partners not limited in personal growth.

In 1972, Alderfer published his "ERG theory" (fig. 18, left column). Interestingly, the D-love category of Maslow nicely corresponds to Alderfer's three relatedness categories: interpersonal safety needs and interpersonal esteem needs. In contrast, Alderfer's description of love and belonging stays rather undefined and is less well explained than Maslow's.

Thus, figure 21 provides a fusion of the two thinkers' concepts. It should be noted that Alderfer, like Maslow, still describes the growth category as individual focused. Both authors do not systematically expand growth beyond the individual, but I believe it is necessary to do so.

FIGURE 21: FUSION OF MASLOW'S AND ALDERFER'S NEED HIERARCHY MODELS

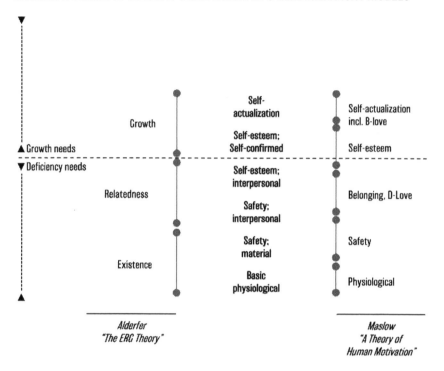

Alderfer's key contribution lies in the clear differentiation of certain need categories, particularly categories that require other people to satisfy you. Alderfer also added a social dimension: I am not the only one who is important. Situations that place *me against you* are important for existential needs, and situations of *me and you* are important for relatedness needs.

Given the huge importance of cooperation for our progress, it seems critically important to consider the interpersonal dimension of these concepts.

In the 1970s, when Maslow and Alderfer created their concepts, the future importance of the internet, global connectivity, and communication could not be foreseen. Social interactions and networks have since been accepted as some of the strongest drivers of happiness as well as depression. Recent advancements in neurological research, meanwhile, provide strong evidence that social influences are very powerful drivers of neuroplastic changes in our brain. As introduced in Chapter Five, neuroplasticity and neuromodulation are most important to learning and memory. Indeed, adapted and expanded neuroplasticity may be the core driver in cooperative learning, one that goes beyond the individual and drives community and cultural benefits.

Based on all these recent insights from behavioral biology, neurology, and genetics, I would like to expand the primary focus on the individual in the happiness hierarchy to add a new level of need satisfaction that can be achieved only through purposeful interaction with others, through collaboration. Alderfer started to expand toward the two nearest dimensions *me against you* and *me and you*. However, reflecting on the impact of relationships and social networks for brain neuroplasticity and mental health, I feel the urgent need to expand Alderfer's dimensions (*me, me against you, me and you*) toward a dimension I introduce here, **We-growth** (fig. 22).

FIGURE 22: G-LOVE AND WE-ACTUALIZATION, TWO INTERPERSONAL NEEDS CLOSING THE GROWTH GAP LEFT BY MASLOW AND ALDERFER

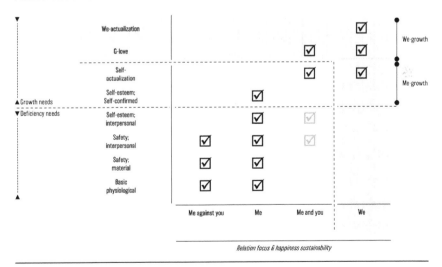

The importance of We-growth for happiness has been recently confirmed by neurological and psychological data that suggest happiness is more stable when more than one person is involved. Again, the main driver seems to be a dramatic increase in neuroplasticity, which provides longer-lasting happiness. In contrast, low levels of neuroplasticity are directly linked to loneliness and social isolation, with a significantly higher rate of depression. Loneliness was identified as one of the key problems for mental health by the World Health Organization (WHO) in 2017.

However, when we try to allocate the dimension of We-growth back to the need categories of Maslow or Alderfer, we quickly realize that a corresponding category is missing; their concepts stop at the level of self-actualization (Maslow) and personal growth (Alderfer). Consequently, I add two new need hierarchy levels here: **G-love** and **We-actualization** (fig. 22). These categories describe our need to grow together (We-growth), with a partner (G-love), or with a group, network, or community (We-actualization).

The concept of G-love I introduce here expands Maslow's B-love and Fromm's mature love into growing together and enjoying the growth of ourselves, our partner, and both partners together. In particular, growing together becomes the major objective in partnerships that have reached the level of G-love, which goes beyond Fromm's mature love and Maslow's B-love. While Fromm highlights genuine care, responsibility, and respect for a partner that is based on deep interest and knowledge of the partner, Maslow focuses on the acceptance of the being of our partner as such. The focus and joint push for growth is the central and unique attribute of G-love.

Neuroscientifically this can be indicated again in substantial and sustained neuroplasticity even in a very old age when couples act with a focus on growing together. I am sure that you have seen some relationships in which the joint focus is on growing together as partners. Such partners know that they are better suited to cope with any uncertainties of the future when they face life together as a growing team. The knowledge that there is a deeply caring, respectful partner who knows me well and accepts who I am and who I want to be opens the ultimate door for individual growth and also joint growth. G-love provides huge optionality for both partners in the face of almost any uncertainty that comes along in the future. Ultimately, this leads to increased personal security, no jealousy, deep trust, and full honesty between such partners. Joint learning, communication, collaboration, and progress are strong because there is a clear joint objective driving the two partners' lives on equal terms: to grow together to the max.

The reason for the deep trust in a G-love relationship is mathematically simple. Once the purpose is clear, totally reflected on, and accepted, growing together will always have an advantage over focusing on individual growth only, given the exponentially higher options a partnership enables, in particular when the partnership is built on G-love.

The only way to expand such optionality further is to involve more like-minded people, or a full network of people who share the same underlying objective: to work and grow together toward a clearly defined purpose.

I would like to emphasize that G-love can happen between any partners as long as the key parameters—care, respect, responsibility, knowledge, acceptance of being, focus on growth—are available. It also shows how detrimental any form of discrimination, arrogance, or attitude vis-à-vis your partner is: G-love can't be reached under such circumstances.

WE-ACTUALIZATION

We-actualization combines the emotional basis observed in G-love (honesty, care, respect, acceptance of being, focus on growing together) with a focus on specific goals and determined actions observed in self-actualization (a very high level of creativity, a pursuit of knowledge, a push toward enlightenment, and a desire to positively transform society). In contrast to self-actualization, which is primarily self-centered, and in contrast to G-love, which is focused on a couple, We-actualization is exponentially more powerful thanks to the joint emotional foundation of a larger group of people and a shared desire to progress and eventually positively transform society. From a neurological perspective, We-actualization exponentially drives collective neuroplastic expansion and maximum happiness. We-actualized people basically use a joint, integrated neurological network. The coolest characteristics of such integrated networks is that they are not just the sum of the individual brains but follow an exponential function. Interestingly, there is broad scientific evidence that physical interpersonal interaction, activities, and working with others on a joint task build substantial neuroplasticity. It seems that literally building something together is a key component of We-growth.

We-actualization transforms a group of organisms into a positively progressing superorganism. From an evolutionary perspective, such a group becomes very powerful compared to an individual or simple groups not linked by a purpose—pretty invincible.

Therefore, in any movement or revolution observed in the past, the formation of such a kind of superorganism with a critical mass was pretty much always successful in driving change in the long run.

Before the advent of the internet, We-actualization was very much limited to groups of people physically co-localizing. But now, worldwide connectivity allows for the faster formation of such groups around a clear joint objective. Initiations of such powerful movements on a global scale have been seen quite frequently in recent years (the #MeToo movement, the Occupy movement, the Umbrella revolution, and Bitcoin cryptocurrency). However, sustaining these movements seems to be significantly more difficult with only virtual We-actualized groups. For a full manifestation of We-actualization, it seems fundamental that people come together in person and work on a joint idea with a joint purpose.

In essence, what we observe on a daily basis confirms the scientific data on neuroplasticity: we have to get our hands dirty and work together to obtain full happiness. At the level of a single species, neurologically, there is no interpersonal competition anymore. Neuroplasticity and happiness explode when you unite in a group for a higher purpose, when you grow together, much more than when growing alone in competition against others. People in We-actualized groups are not motivated by competing. Real winners work together to tackle the true challenges for the species. Whoever has worked in a group of people that has reached We-actualization, at least for a certain period of time, will not accept going back to the "normal" level of group interactions.

We-actualization can be observed best in situations of collective positive excitement. For example, team sport victories, fanatic sport fans, entire countries during the World Cup, or start-up companies with a higher impact idea when they are very early in their life cycle. In these energized group situations, a joint target is normally provided by a clear competitor that is concentrating the group's effort and exponentially pushing the reward systems.

Under normal conditions, the competition stays friendly. However, the competition can be further enhanced by anxiety in situations like street-gang fights or football hooliganism. These situations are in a way a "soft" variant of what happens in war—normally people avoid killing each other and they follow a set of rules for the fight. The difference between normal football fans and football hooligans can easily be explained by the way the brain operates during normal behavior in contrast to the way it operates in addictive behavior. With normal behavior—excited but nonviolent support for your favorite football team—the underlying functional reward systems are entirely positive. In other words, these social activities strongly increase the neuroplasticity in this population. In hooligans, the adrenaline rush and potentially the injuries during fights significantly increase the chronic inflammation level in the body, leading to significant impairment of neuroplasticity over time. Yet, exiting these groups is neurologically very difficult, despite sustained damage to the person involved, because the entire social environment would instantly disappear, leaving a significant psychological need unmet.

Intriguingly, the level of We-actualization can be pushed even further in the absence of anxiety. In its extreme form, consider rock concert spectators—even more dramatically—participants in electronic dance music and techno raves. Music events are entirely absent of competitors and, as such, free from any aggression: everyone is focused on one objective (have a good party with your favorite band or your favorite DJ), enhanced by massive positive sound and light impact, a very tightly packed crowd (touch and feel), and long waiting times before the show (increased excitement). In these settings, the levels of both individual and group happiness soar to exponential heights. Theoretically, music events, but also large religious events and group meditation, are perfect examples of We-actualization. Indeed, it has been proven that an individual's level of neuroplasticity and mental health is very high after joining such groups.

Let me share my first moment when I literally felt We-actualization. It happened on July 13, 1985. The cool thing about We-actualization is that, even without knowing you, I am pretty sure that you've had a similar experience, especially if you are between forty-five- and fifty-five-years old today.

On that July day in 1985, I was playing in a handball tournament in the southern part of Germany with my team of friends the same age. I was thirteen years old. But older teams were also participating, so it was a bunch of thirteen- to sixteen-year-old boys and girls away from home, camping and having a lot of fun. The tournament included an overnight stay in tents on Saturday, while Sunday was reserved for semifinals and finals. It was a hot day, and the campground's grass was dry; I remember every single detail of the location, of the people, of the event. I can tell you the ridiculous detail of a guy explaining to me that he couldn't eat the delicious sausages because he had heartburn (very unusual for a young boy). I could go on for pages here telling you such details. Intriguingly, I cannot remember any other handball tournament in such detail, even though I attended dozens.

The handball tournament was one focus of the weekend. However, on that same day, the Live Aid festival happened. Live Aid was a charity music event that Irish musician and political activist Bob Geldof curated in order to collect money for the famine in Ethiopia. A great many famous musicians agreed to play short sets for free, in the hope that people listening would donate money to ship food to Ethiopia. The line-up Geldof put together was impressive—even more so was Geldof's personal involvement and passion driving the idea. In the months before the event, images of the starving kids in Ethiopia were on every news channel; the pictures were devastating and in contrast to today's internet coverage still unprecedented. It was "in your face": this planet is unfair; we have too much to eat while kids and babies are dying in Ethiopia. I have to admit that up to that point I was not deeply personally engaged, even though all schools in Germany had initiated a special educational project around the topic and my parents and I talked about it constantly.

To understand the situation on that evening fully, you need to know three additional things. First, Geldof intended to produce the first true global concert happening simultaneously in London and Philadelphia, one that was broadcasted worldwide live via satellite, so London's and Philadelphia's music programs were in sync. Apart from the satellite transmission delay of a few seconds, everyone on the planet would experience the same moment. Second, at that time punk rock was my favorite music, so the musicians lined up to play at Live Aid were not really exciting to me. Third, at that time cell phones, public viewing screens, and satellite TV weren't available in Germany, so we had to get a portable television, find and connect loudspeakers, and get a connection to the BBC channel.

I remember that basically all the people competing against each other in handball on the tournament were working together in the breaks to get the television going. And indeed, in the afternoon we had a stable connection and several hundred people staying around three televisions and a set of pretty amazing speakers, all of us listening to and watching the Live Aid concert while the sun set. That was already pretty cool. Then at 7:40 p.m. local German time, Queen and its lead singer, Freddie Mercury, went onstage in London. I did not like Queen, but the next twenty-three minutes would change my life forever.

Whoever experienced that performance (or watched on tape later) will not forget it. If you haven't seen Queen's Live Aid performance, please take a break here and watch it on YouTube before you continue to read. It's critical to have seen it at least once—for the fun of it and because I will use it as an example throughout the book.

When Freddie Mercury sang "Radio Ga Ga," the whole crowd in London's Wembley Stadium clapped in rhythm and sang along in perfect synchronization. The synchronization in London is so perfect that it truly looked like one connected organism was performing the song. Then, with a few seconds' delay due to satellite transmission phasing, the entire audience in Philadelphia started clapping and singing too. (I am not sure whether I truly saw that happen on screen or whether it was something I only learned later, when reading about the concert.)

And then, out of the blue, the same thing happened at our campground—everyone joined in. No exceptions. *All we hear is.* All arms went up. Then two claps in almost perfect synchronization. *Radio ga ga.* All arms went up again. Two claps. And so on. Somehow that was the trigger for all of us to understand that we were in this together. It was like an infection in one second. The next few minutes after the song we were awestruck and silent, trying to understand what had just happened. The feeling of *togetherness* was so strong, it was like we had all been vibrating together. I never again experienced anything like it.

Then Freddie Mercury started singing Queen's last song. "We are the champions (of the world)." And the whole world was singing— *we* were singing—and waving along with Freddie, with London, with Philadelphia, with the rest of the world. We could hear people singing along even in the distance downtown in the little village nearby. Everyone around me wept. Everyone. As I write these sentences, tears are dropping on my keyboard, as always when I watch this video. No chance—and actually no intention—of stopping them. The surge of feelings is so powerful and so awesome still that I sometimes wonder whether the real event was so epic. Whenever I meet anyone who was with me that evening, we clearly agree that these moments were among the most amazing of our lives. Almost two billion people watched Live Aid—at that time it was almost everyone with access to a television, 40 percent of the people on our planet. Before Queen's set the donations stood at just a few million dollars, ridiculously low, and Bob Geldof was upset. He used the epic Queen set to push one more time for more money on television. Donations exploded. By the end of the concert, Live Aid had collected $150 million, a huge amount for the 1980s.

This was more than just a global Queen concert. For one thing, the audience didn't consist solely of Queen fans (I myself, for example, preferred punk). It was Bob Geldof who had the idea of linking music with the purpose of helping starving children. It was the willingness of a hundred other artists, thousands of helpers, and big entertainment-industry players to work together for that positive purpose. For free. It was the London audience. It was the Philadelphia audience. It was just . . . everybody together. We-actualization.

You might say that a similar kind of group excitement has been seen before, particularly in situations of great fear like during preparation for war—for example, at the Nuremberg rallies of the Third Reich in Germany. I would disagree with that view: The ultimate power of Live Aid came from the global reach and the absence of aggression, which led to a feeling of belonging together. Nobody was excluded. Live Aid did not criticize the warlords ultimately responsible on the ground for the famine in Ethiopia. It just focused on the responsibility of the world to help with a positive attitude.

The day after the concert, on a Monday, I donated forty German marks to Live Aid, pretty much all I had in my savings account at that time. I had to ask a friend whose parents had a credit card to do it for me; my parents didn't have one.

The memory of that concert, along with other observations and experiences later in life, led me to develop the *Universal happiness hierarchy*, which is presented here for the first time. The Universal happiness hierarchy comprises *eight levels*, and it is the first framework that expands our need for individual growth to growth together, We-growth.

Based on today's scientific research, these eight levels cover all psychological needs and all associated neurological reward systems:

- ✦ **We-actualization:** A large group of people works together on a shared, positive, progressive objective, such as a start-up business that attempts to cure cancer.
- ✦ **G-love:** This is the experience of joint, superior growth with an intimate partner you respect, truly care about, and deeply accept as an individual.
- ✦ **Self-actualization:** You accept that each person is inherently worthy; drive your own growth by self-reflection and self-improvement; and take responsibility for your actions.
- ✦ **Self-confirmed self-esteem:** My esteem is self-confirmed; for example, I appreciate myself by being honest with myself about my strengths and weaknesses.
- ✦ **Interpersonal self-esteem:** This flows from a group—for example, appreciation of one's work by peers.
- ✦ **Interpersonal safety:** This safety is provided to you by others, such as police protecting your safety and rights, or your son driving you to the doctor in an emergency.
- ✦ **Material safety:** This is safety provided to you by material items, such as a power generator, or money (as a surrogate to buy whatever you need).
- ✦ **Basic physiological safety:** This includes the conditions for meeting essential biological needs such as water, food, sleep, and shelter.

FIGURE 23: THE UNIVERSAL HAPPINESS HIERARCHY

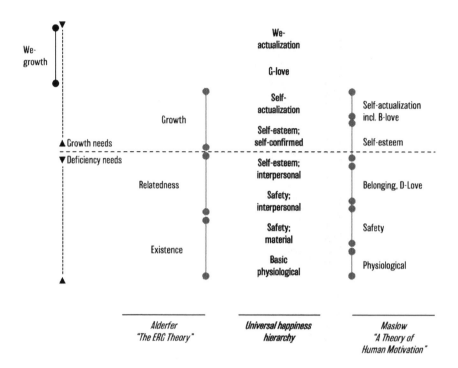

Alderfer "The ERG Theory"	Universal happiness hierarchy	Maslow "A Theory of Human Motivation"

In order to confirm whether our happiness hierarchy is truly universal, it is instructive to overlay all the introduced concepts driving us at this point (fig. 23).

Darwin's theory of evolution forms the basis for understanding our underlying biology and the essentials of capitalism, our current economic system. On lower need levels—up to material safety needs—all three frameworks overlay one another perfectly: Alderfer's, Maslow's, and my own. Indeed, we could easily confirm that on these levels, our capitalistic activities work by far the best. There is a perfect collaboration between evolution, capitalism, and happiness—up to a point. When capitalism was developed in its current form a few hundred years ago, the highest psychological needs to be satisfied were material and interpersonal safety needs. And today we still have areas in the world where these lower needs are not satisfied yet. The huge benefits of capitalism were seen after World War II, when substantial rebuilding had to be done and a new world order of interpersonal safety was required. Further, the harmony between capitalism and our most basic needs can be seen in the industries that operate in the lower need categories: the health care industry (supposed to provide health, the key material safety need), the food and beverage industry (satisfying basic physiological needs), the insurance industry (providing material safety for uncertain events in the future), and the security and weapons industries, just to name a few. Later, in the 1970s, '80s, and beyond, self-esteem needs became more and more the drivers of need satisfaction and happiness, with the emerging industries in entertainment, music, and media taking the lead as the most proliferating industry segments.

FIGURE 24: THE HOLISTIC HAPPINESS HIERARCHY FILLS THE GAPS LEFT FROM CAPITALISM, EVOLUTION THEORY, AND PSYCHOLOGY

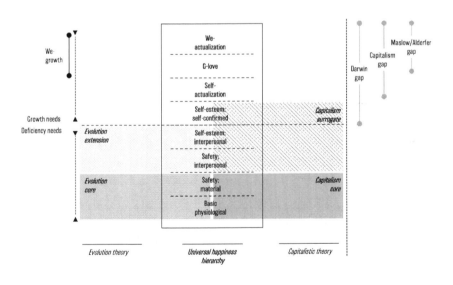

Intriguingly, beyond material safety needs, classical capitalism should actually not provide any additional needs satisfaction: it's designed for goods and services, so it should be basically useless to satisfy our higher social needs. But this is interestingly not the case. Capitalism has reached further up in the hierarchy despite not being designed for it. So how is this actually possible?

We observe on a daily basis a push toward "capitalistic surrogates," such as buying interpersonal safety through marriage or raising interpersonal esteem through buying status symbols. Already Maslow and Alderfer described nicely how missing interpersonal safety and self-esteem are replaced by exponential increases in consumption, a vicious cycle that weakens all sustainable interpersonal relationships. Alternatively, these missing interpersonal needs are simply purchased by offering money to obtain personal relationships in return, such as hiring a helper to take care of an elderly person at home or paying a fee to join an expensive, renowned, exclusive club. Thus, our capitalistic system is abused in order to satisfy our evolutionarily determined needs in these categories: relationships bought by money are the substitute for real relationships. Recognition bought by money is a substitute for real recognition for being a good person who provides happiness to others.

From an evolutionary perspective, however, we can accept these substitutions: interpersonal safety and self-esteem are key drivers for obtaining a reproductive benefit. However, they are not functional for obtaining happiness beyond a certain level. In addition, they cannot drive learning and memory in a balanced manner and drive progress to higher happiness levels. We will detail these flaws of our current system in later chapters.

A few industries today are focused on leveraging individual self-esteem and even trying to push consumers toward self-actualization. These are primarily sports, fashion, music, and entertainment companies, such as Apple, Adidas, Nike, Spotify, and Netflix. In addition, certain event management companies have optimized annual events toward a "We-growth" experience. Tomorrowland, an electronic dance music event, is one example. These companies and events combine material needs with a group association and group feeling. A few sports companies are even moving beyond selling products and are offering physical group activities driving brand loyalty and sustained product purchases. On a psychological level, these companies should theoretically be the ones most holistically driving the happiness of their customers.

Evolution theory, capitalistic theory, and also Maslow's and Alderfer's theories each lack some aspects of growth (fig. 24). Darwin's evolution theory reaches its limits for growth essentially at the level of interpersonal self-esteem. The personal growth potentially reached within the capitalistic theory attains a level just short of self-actualization. Indeed, psychological research done in the 1980s and '90s has demonstrated that being rich is the most effective inhibitor of self-actualization. The psychological theories of Maslow and Alderfer have expanded on individual growth potential, but they lack perspective on We-growth driven on a collective level (fig. 22). However, recent evidence in neuroscience has established the tremendous power of group experiences on substantially increasing group members' neuroplasticity. Such an increase correlates strongly with increased happiness reported by the group members. In order to fully cover all aspects of happiness, it is critical to introduce the Universal happiness hierarchy as a new order for all of us. Otherwise, when we strive for happiness, we might miss a significant opportunity in areas of We-growth and thereby miss powerful drivers for learning, memory, communication, and collaboration. In other words: progress for all of us.

Why are the We-growth levels so important for happiness growth and economic growth?

Based on the latest neurological data, the core for happiness, consciousness, intelligence, and long-term memory is neuroplasticity, which is the level of interconnection between our billions of neurons in the brain. Indeed, reduced neuroplasticity has been identified as the key factor for depression, anxiety, and social isolation. In particular, social isolation and limited learning activities drive loss of neuroplasticity. In contrast, strong social networks are identified as key drivers for neuroplasticity and mental health. We can see this correlation particularly in elderly people. The more social contact they have in their daily lives, the longer they live.

Thus, increasing neuroplasticity is an unlimited source for happiness and growth for us. In addition, we know that people interacting together with a joint objective see an exponential increase of neuroplasticity simply by growing together in a positive sense. Growing together becomes a healthy, self-fulfilling prophecy for happiness. And, as such, also for economic growth.

Like all growth opportunities, activation of We-growth requires substantial investments, both monetary and nonmonetary. Thus, We-growth opportunities drive significant economic growth opportunities directed toward real impact. Our neurological setup ensures that the growth opportunity is essentially unlimited as long as happiness is the driver: the more people involved and the more challenging the opportunity gets, the bigger the opportunity (more neuroplasticity in several brains) for returns on happiness and financial investments.

Let me give two high-level examples. First, imagine the amount of happiness created in a patient whose severe disease is cured. It is huge. Then imagine the amount of happiness created by the patient's family, and the nurses and doctors supporting the patient. Imagine all this happiness could be reinvested to kick-start more research and development to finally help other people with cancer. The investment most likely would not be sufficient, but it would attract other—financial— investors to join in. Second, imagine a young, no-name writer, artist, or musician who increases other people's happiness. In today's world, it is very difficult to earn enough money to make a living. As a consequence, almost all these writers, artists, and musicians have to stop their creative activities and look for a job that generates enough money for them to survive. This in turn eliminates all the future happy-making poems, artworks, and songs for other people. Only a few writers, artists, and musicians make it to the top and earn big money. A key requirement of our economic system is to "mainstream" your art, music, or writing in order to reach many people and get at least a small amount of attention. With this, we eliminate creativity, optionality, and much more intensive happiness for a lot of people. Just imagine, a writer, artist, or musician would be compensated by the true happiness she or he creates in the audience. First, the young artist would be able to continue to create more happy people. Second, a created surplus could be used to help finance the underlying infrastructure, like a music studio that benefits other young musicians in the future. As you realize, the famous artists would still be fine making a lot of people happy and making a lot of money. But we would have an entirely different investment concept in the beginning of new ideas: we would focus on happiness creation in the short and long term and not on making money.

In conclusion, the Universal happiness hierarchy introduced here adds a novel dimension of growth that has been largely neglected in the past: We-growth. The "total potential" for We-growth and associated happiness is essentially unlimited, and with it comes the potential for unlimited economic growth. We will see later in more detail how ideas, activities, and investments focusing on We-growth drive financial growth on the back of happiness and progress.

In the next chapter, we will focus on goods, services, and actions active within the Universal happiness hierarchy. We will zoom in closer on the mechanism of measuring and valuing happiness within this framework. I call it the "pricing of happiness." You will soon realize that the determination of price is fundamentally different from current economic pricing mechanisms.

CHAPTER ELEVEN

THE PRICING OF HAPPINESS

Developing, producing, and selling goods and services form the basis of our economy. Creating, sharing, and rewarding goods, services, and actions that drive happiness for other people is the basis of the Universal happiness hierarchy (figs. 22, 23).

In our economy, supply and demand determine the price and value of goods and services, which we can trade in a marketplace. Under normal conditions, the price floor for a product or service is defined by the cost of producing and selling it—unless you want to lose money and eventually go bankrupt.

But how can we measure the value of goods and—most importantly—actions that create happiness for other people?

At the center of this problem is the question of how to measure happiness in real time—Unconscious happiness (objectively measured) *and* Conscious happiness (subjectively measured). Measuring Conscious happiness is easy, but the low granularity and strong, continuous influence of our consciousness make it inappropriate as a base parameter. In contrast, measuring Unconscious happiness would provide the opportunity to obtain an unbiased, precise numerical dimension for the amount of happiness that is created precisely when a happiness-making event hits us. We therefore have to focus on Unconscious happiness as our base parameter. Using that measurement, we can then take stock of our Conscious happiness to reflect on what really matters for us.

How can we obtain a robust measurement of real-time Unconscious happiness levels?

On a cellular and molecular level, recent work by American psychologist and neuroscientist Kent Berridge and Danish neuroscientist Morten Kringelbach identified structures in the brain, the hedonic centers, which are primarily responsible for positive emotions and happiness. In these structures we could measure the small currents between activated neurons, currents that are produced when we encounter a happiness-making stimulus. Unfortunately, the invasive procedure associated with this measurement makes this option impractical for daily use in humans. There are other imaging technologies that could provide another activation readout. However, these approaches would mean wearing a helmet studded with electrodes. This is fine in a lab but impractical for everyday life; it likely even interferes with the happiness we are trying to detect. If we accept the fact that we technically cannot take our key measure at the site of origin, in the hedonic centers in the brain, we can look for a surrogate marker that is sufficiently correlated with what is happening in these neurons. Indeed, it is beneficial that the reward systems we would like to track for our Unconscious happiness measure are also the same underlying systems of our autonomous nervous system. One such response was briefly introduced already in the beginning of the book: unconscious approach/withdrawal responses (fig. 2). In other words, there are unconscious responses throughout our body that can be measured more easily, even noninvasively, and that still provide a direct numerical link to what is happening in the hedonic centers in the brain on a cellular level.

FIGURE 25: POSITIVE EMOTIONS CAN BE QUANTIFIED BY DIFFERENT FACIAL, VERBAL, AND PHYSIOLOGICAL INDICATORS

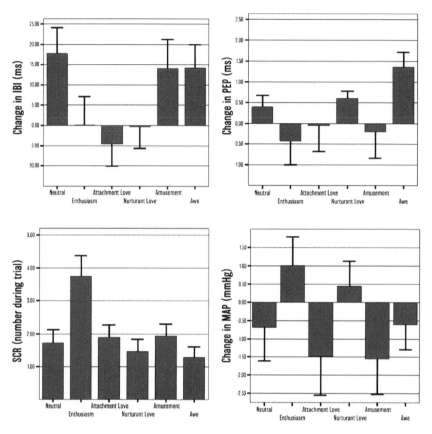

Baseline-to-trial changes in cardiac interbeat interval, preejection period, number of skin conductance responses, and mean arterial pressure during five positive emotions. Adapted from "Feeling Good: Autonomic Nervous System Responding in Five Positive Emotions," by M. N. Shiota, S. L. Neufeld, W. H. Yeung, S. E. Moser, & E. F. Perea, 2011, *Emotion, 11,* 1368–1378. Copyright, 2011 by American Psychological Association.

Shiota, M. et al. 2017. "Beyond Happiness: Building a Science of Discrete Positive Emotions." American Psychologist 72, no. 7: 617–643.

Fortunately, recent advances in neurological diagnostics and applied digital technology allow us to detect emotions and moods via wearables and smartphones based on these associated responses. Psychologists and neurologists are actively studying emotions such as pride, gratitude, amusement, love, sexual desire, and awe. Empirical studies have also begun to compare several positive emotions at once with respect to appraisals, expression, physiological responses, relation to personality traits, and implications for cognition (fig. 25).

In addition to scientific data, several technology companies offer mood trackers that integrate individual activities, geotracking, facial expression changes, and basic physiological data—such as heartbeat pattern, heartbeat intensity, and blood pressure or skin conductance—through artificial learning systems. These data sets provide further insights into positive and negative emotion states.

Based on all this data, in 2017 Shiota and her colleagues introduced a consistent framework called the positive emotion family tree.

FIGURE 26: THE POSITIVE EMOTION FAMILY TREE PROVIDES A FRAME TO LINK EMOTIONS AND UNDERLYING REWARD SYSTEMS

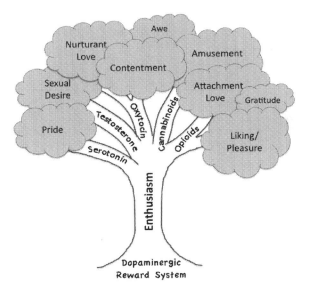

A proposed positive emotion "family tree." The trunk represents the ancient neural reward system giving rise to the positive emotions. Neurotransmitters shown at the base of new branches indicate the key, reward system-modulating roles they might have played at the beginning of each new positive emotion. Clusters of leaves represent proposed "discrete" emotions experienced by modern humans; at this level, each emotion is expected to involve complex profiles of activation across multiple neurotransmitter systems throughout the brain, and interactions with uniquely human cognitive capacities, as well as central roles of dopamine and the neurotransmitter associated with that branch. See the online article for the color version of this figure.

Shiota, M. et al. 2017. "Beyond Happiness: Building a Science of Discrete Positive Emotions." American Psychologist 72, no. 7: 617–643.

This framework links our key and most conserved neuronal reward systems to ten discrete positive emotions. In addition to the ancient dopamine reward system driving general enthusiasm, nine positive emotions have been isolated: liking/pleasure, contentment, pride, sexual desire, attachment love, nurturant love, amusement, gratitude, and awe These distinct positive emotions can be nicely linked to the well-characterized and highly conserved neuronal reward systems that we have already introduced (Chapter Six, fig. 7): the serotonin, testosterone, oxytocin, cannabinoid, opioid, and dopamine system . Most importantly, Shiota and colleagues provided a metadata analysis that indicated the current state of scientific evidence for the "positive emotion family tree" (fig. 26): some confirmatory science in detail still needs to be done, in particular on how to assess gratitude, but the essence of the concept is strongly supported already by existing peer-reviewed data (fig. 27).

FIGURE 27: CURRENT SCIENTIFIC EVIDENCE SUPPORTING THE CONCEPT UNDERLYING THE POSITIVE EMOTION FAMILY TREE

A Proposed Positive Emotion Taxonomy, With Current State of Evidence in Several Aspects of Emotional Responding

Emotion	Prototypical opportunity	Current status of evidence					
		Neural mechanism	Nonverbal expression	Peripheral physiology	Cognitive aspects	Motivation, behavior	Subjective experience
Enthusiasm	Food	✓	W	✓	IP	✓	W
Liking/Pleasure	Sweet (vs. bitter) taste	✓	✓	W	W	✓	✓
Contentment	Digestion	✓	IP	✓	IP	✓	W
Pride	Dominant social status	IP	✓	W	W	✓	IP
Sexual desire	Reproductive partner	✓	✓	✓	IP	✓	W
Attachment love	Affiliation, alliance	IP	IP	IP	W	✓	IP
Nurturant love	Altricial offspring, kin	IP	W	IP	W	✓	W
Amusement	Play; skill development	IP	✓	✓	IP	✓	W
Awe	Novel, complex information	W	✓	IP	IP	W	IP

Note. ✓ = evidence strong; IP = evidence preliminary or in progress; W = evidence limited or absent.

Shiota, M. et al. 2017. "Beyond Happiness: Building a Science of Discrete Positive Emotions." American Psychologist 72, no. 7: 617–643.

The large amount of data consolidated in the "positive emotions family tree" links neuroscience with our most relevant and well-described emotions. The same positive emotions have been described in all details by Alderfer, Maslow, Freud, Fromm, and other psychologists, on a behavioral level. Exactly these positive emotions were the basis for constructing the Universal happiness hierarchy: enthusiasm, sexual desire, pride, contentment, gratitude, nurturant love, attachment love, and amusement. That list is almost identical to the list in figure 26.

We just have to put everything together now in one consistent matrix (fig. 28: A happiness-making event activates our key reward systems and triggers defined positive emotions that can be linked to the levels in our Universal happiness hierarchy. The reward system activation can be indirectly detected and measured by a real-time, objective diagnostics application that provides us with a numerical value for positive emotions—a measure of our Unconscious happiness. From the detailed readout, we should even be able to delineate our satisfaction level with respect to the Universal happiness hierarchy. Please note that we require the activation of a more diverse set of reward systems the higher we climb on the Universal happiness hierarchy (fig. 28). It is intriguing that the three critical reward systems—oxytocin system, opioid system, and cannabinoid system—can be activated only by face-to-face social interaction and even more strongly with physical interaction. Without these systems—importantly, without other people—we cannot reach the highest three levels of the Universal happiness hierarchy.

FIGURE 28: OUR POSITIVE EMOTIONS PROVIDE A SYSTEMATIC LINK FROM REWARD SYSTEMS TO THE UNIVERSAL HAPPINESS HIERARCHY

UNIVERSAL HAPPINESS HIERARCHY	REWARD SYSTEMS					
	DOPAMINE	TESTOSTERONE	SEROTONIN	OXYTOCIN	OPIOIDS	CANNABINOIDS
WE-ACTUALIZATION	Enthusiasm			Contentment Nurturant Love	Gratitude Attachment love	Attachment love Amusement, pleasure
C-LOVE	Enthusiasm			Contentment Nurturant Love	Gratitude Attachment love	Attachment love Amusement, pleasure
SELF-ACTUALIZATION	Enthusiasm		Recognition, pride/status	Contentment	Gratitude	Amusement, pleasure
SELF-ESTEEM; SELF-CONFIRMED	Enthusiasm		Recognition, pride/status			Amusement, pleasure
SELF-ESTEEM; INTERPERSONAL	Enthusiasm	Sexual Desire	Recognition, pride/status			
SAFETY; INTERPERSONAL	Enthusiasm	Sexual Desire				
SAFETY; SELF-CONFIRMED	Enthusiasm					
PHYSIOLOGICAL	Enthusiasm					

The molecular mechanisms behind these reward systems' dependence on real (face-to-face or physical) interactions are still not fully clear. We know that oxytocin metabolism is largely dependent on physical touch, that the cannabinoid system requires face-to-face social interactions and can be enhanced by physical interactions, and that the serotonin system is strongly enhanced by face-to-face and physical interactions. Intriguingly, social interaction via a computer screen does not trigger the same reward system simulations—the positive emotions on a computer screen are mainly dopamine based and potentially testosterone based. In conclusion, face-to-face and, even more so, physical interaction massively drive neuroplasticity, and with it, happiness. Online activities cannot compensate for the lack of real, analog interactions. This is fundamental to remember, given today's digital movement.

To recapitulate, surrogate markers for these reward systems can be noninvasively measured because they also trigger other autonomous neural responses. For example, by simply looking at autonomic nervous system responses through changes in heartbeat characteristics, mean arterial pressure, and certain skin conduction responses, we should be able to quantify a certain set of positive emotions already today (fig. 25).

All this data can meanwhile be detected individually by wearable fitness tracker systems and by emerging basic emotion tracker systems. To add additional information from verbal and facial expressions or general activity data is a small gap to close in a world of smartphones. If we combine all this data, we can leverage AI to interpret it and draw increasingly accurate conclusions about what is influencing our pleasure and emotions. In addition, we can integrate updates from new scientific data as they come along.

In conclusion, it seems that we have all the elements to build an emotion tracker that provides us with all necessary information about our Unconscious happiness and—more importantly—to what extent our six reward systems are involved. It will require some additional tests and controlled trials to fill the missing gaps, but in essence we should be able to pull the necessary data sets together to measure Unconscious happiness with a very high scientific significance and robustness in real time. And—crucially—without sticking a needle into our hedonic centers in the brain. We will be able to detect this data noninvasively with our smartphones very soon.

CHAPTER TWELVE

HAPPINESS CURRENCY

If we were interested only in ourselves, in optimizing our own happiness, we would be totally fine at this point. We could just stop and enjoy all our primary data, reflecting on who and what truly makes us happy. We would have the ultimate emotion tracker in our hands. Neurologically, this would drive a simple learning cycle that optimizes *our* behaviors to obtain more happiness by satisfying our psychological needs. It is highly likely that such a tool would lead us straight into a severe addiction, the addiction to maximizing the Universal happiness hierarchy for *ourselves.*

We would get stuck in the same functional reward systems that are activated by our current consumption behavior, driving more and more material consumption and less and less purposeful and collaborative activities with other people. Consume in order to be happy . . . by yourself. Our predicament would be identical to that of rats that can decide to electrically stimulate the hedonic centers in their brains: these rats forget to eat or drink or nurse their pups. Like these rats, we would likely die "amusing ourselves to death," as Neil Postman already predicted in his 1985 book of that title.

That's why we don't stop here.

The underlying idea of the concept is not to measure *our* happiness but to reward *others* who have triggered our happiness. This creates another level of complexity. On top of getting our Unconscious happiness readout telling us how effective a given stimulus was at making us happy, we have to reflect consciously now on who or what triggered our happiness. Consequentially in a next step, we can decide to actively reward whoever was behind it—simply to trigger positive reinforcement so that person will be encouraged to repeat such happy-making behavior again for others.

It is critical at this point that we should reward them only if we want to. We are entirely free to make this choice. This nuance is important because we know that a forced push is not as effective as a free choice in making us learn faster and remember longer.

But what could we use to reward someone who is making us happy?

You may agree that it does not make a lot of sense to reward another person by forwarding a gigabyte of our private neurological data. First, we wouldn't like to share all this private and very sensitive data. Secondly, most people would not be interested in such data unless they were neuroscience nerds. Too complex, too much time to understand it and extract a reward for themselves. Lastly, this data would still consist of individual pieces of data that are not normalized or standardized. That means the receiver could hardly get a holistic view of the level of happiness he or she brought to others. So the raw data as a reward is a no-go.

Of course we could just use the old-school approach and simply say "thank you!" or send a "like" with our smartphone. Neurologically, "thanks" and "likes" should function as positive conditioning, as an appreciation. Unfortunately, saying "thank you" or giving "likes" is very easy (just say it or click it). It's so easy that these basic expressions of appreciation have become devalued. Perpetual overuse and dishonesty have undermined their credibility. We simply don't know any more whether the people who say it or click it really mean it.

At the same time, our society has developed into a rather isolated, distant, and disconnected community. We rarely even say "thank you" anymore, and when we do, it's more a matter of form. Very sad but true. So we should not use old-school "thank you" or digital "likes" as our means of positive reinforcement if we want to fundamentally improve the way humans interact and derive value from one another. (But as a side note, please say "thank you" to others more often—if you really mean it. It's priceless, and it drives behaviors that make a lot of people happier.)

What we need is a token of appreciation that is based on an *objective value that cannot be manipulated.*

This token should be:

+ A common measure of *value*—created based on our unbiased Unconscious happiness signals in the brain. Such value would be the purest way to quantify happiness without any chance to consciously manipulate it.

+ Easily *transacted or exchanged,* because we would like to send our token of appreciation to the person who induced our happiness.

+ Able to be *collected and stored* in order to *document* how much appreciation a person has received overall for creating happiness and why. Such a documentation library would provide a *transaction memory enabling us to learn and remember* which actions are responsible for our happiness—a huge data source to learn from—for each of us and for the societies around the world. For the first time, global policy makers and socioeconomists would have a holistic data bank from which to draw conclusions and recommendations. Just as the Human Genome Project provided the first insight into our genetic and evolutionary foundation, a global happiness data bank would provide the first real-time objective insights into how happy our planet really is and how effective certain measures are to improve our quality of life.

There is a slight problem, however: nothing like this exists yet. So we have to create it from scratch. Interestingly, "common measure of value," "medium of exchange," and "transact and medium to store" are precisely the three key characteristics for commodity money or fiat money, the standard currencies we currently use in our economic system. However, the only currencies available to date that also provide a "transaction memory" or transaction history on an individual level are *blockchain-based cryptocurrencies*.

Cryptocurrencies depend on two complementary technologies: tokens and blockchain. A token can be a digital coin, any kind of digital representation of a physical asset—or in our case, a biological one. A blockchain can serve as a shared, secure, irrevocable, and trusted ledger for any kind of transaction using the token associated with it. In addition—and in contrast to fiat money—cryptocurrencies can be a representation for a unit of utility; for example, the access to a certain network or storage capacity. Thus, a cryptocurrency is sometimes nothing more than a digital certificate that has a signature, rules, programs, and other attributes controlled cryptographically. In essence, we can create a digital version of everything, "tokenized" versions of some sort of product, service, or asset, or just a *promise*.

Bitcoin was the first blockchain-based cryptocurrency, and I would like to use it as an example to explain how cryptocurrencies work in general. Bitcoin was invented by a person or group under the pseudonym "Satoshi Nakamoto" and released as open-source software in 2009. The promise behind Bitcoin is based on a protocol that defines the underlying monetary policy. It is a huge success so far: Bitcoins can be exchanged for other currencies, products, or services, and meanwhile more than one hundred thousand vendors worldwide accept payments by Bitcoin.

Without going into too much detail here, the Bitcoin protocol comprises four essential pillars: decentralization, peer-to-peer transactions, privacy, and artificial scarcity.

Bitcoin is the first decentralized digital currency with no central bank controlling it. Bitcoins are created as a reward for a process called mining. Every existing and traded Bitcoin today has been created through that process. Mining is a record-keeping and maintenance service done through the use of computer processing power. As a consequence, miners keep the blockchain consistent, complete, and unalterable by repeatedly grouping newly broadcast transactions into a block, which is then transmitted to the entire network and verified by all other recipient nodes that make up the network. The reward is clearly defined until all Bitcoins have been mined or created.

From then on, the reward for adding a new block halves every 210,000 blocks. The miner finding the new block is rewarded with 12.5 newly created Bitcoins at the moment; this rate will drop to 6.25 in May 2020. Thus, the protocol confers mathematical certainty on how rewards for Bitcoin mining will develop in the future—the promise of the Bitcoin is a very sound and credible one.

The Bitcoin protocol is based on a peer-to-peer network. In other words, transactions are executed directly between users, without any middleman. Ownership and control of Bitcoins is the same thing. There is no need for an account; you can handle Bitcoins like physical notes in your pocket. Like notes, they can be lost or stolen, and the transactions are irrevocable. It is therefore of utmost importance that Bitcoin transactions are well verified.

The verification of transactions happens in the Bitcoin blockchain network. Again, the blockchain is a distributed database—to achieve independent verification of the chain of ownership of any and every Bitcoin amount, each network node stores its own copy of the entire blockchain. The network follows a simple rule that is also defined in the Bitcoin protocol: the network node carrying the longest chain is the one carrying the verified blockchain. Given the update frequency for novel transactions and the sheer number of transactions, the system is highly secure against any hacker attack. It simply does not pay out to hack the system; it makes more commercial sense to become a miner. So far, all attempts to hack the Bitcoin blockchain network have failed, demonstrating that the basic capitalistic rules also work very well in the Bitcoin universe.

Ownership and control are taken care of by the verification process in the blockchain. However, Bitcoins are not registered under our names. In the blockchain, Bitcoins are registered to Bitcoin addresses. If the private key is lost, the network will not recognize any other evidence of ownership. As such, Bitcoin transactions offer full anonymity. In contrast to all other pillars, one can imagine that the anonymity of such transactions is the key concern for government officials, in particular for tax departments, law enforcement, and central banks. Using Bitcoin brings back full independence to the people for transactions or savings. Not because it's illegal, but because it is the superior monetary system.

In that context, the Bitcoin has finally proven the Nobel Prize–winner Friedrich August von Hayek right. He said currency has no reason to be controlled by governments in the first place but should compete on a trust basis for stability alone and thus can be issued privately. On that score, Bitcoin is already outcompeting fiat currencies today.

A major intrinsic benefit of Bitcoin is its very limited inflation. Its monetary policy has set a limit of 21 million Bitcoins to be reached by 2140, and it defines the necessary mining activities and rewards. In contrast to fiat currency, this defined future policy removes uncertainty for the owners. Bitcoins don't have the risk of an inflation rate or interest rate determined by the central banks behind a fiat currency. In a world of massive public debt, this makes Bitcoin pretty attractive and drives its exchange rate higher than that of other major fiat currencies like the US dollar.

Intriguingly, Bitcoins have no underlying value other than the Bitcoin promise defined in the Bitcoin protocol. That's it. In contrast to other fiat currencies that have underlying, associated economies (the American economy for the US dollar) attached to them, this is actually very little.

So what is the value that Bitcoin—and all other cryptocurrencies—is actually creating, other than just providing another crazy tool for desperate investors?

Together, blockchain and digital tokens deliberately waste storage, which today is very cheap, in order to create something new and valuable. In the case of cryptocurrencies, such digital tokens waste storage in massively duplicative blockchains to create virtual continuity. Before the advent of blockchain technology, continuity was a universal property of the physical world only, not the virtual world. Continuity permits identity of both things and people. It permits property because a continuously identified thing can be owned by a continuously identified person. As such, continuity permits transactions: transfer of property. It permits trust. Continuity is a critical component in our economic system; without it, property, contracts, and even identities (passports, signatures) are worthless. Thus, blockchain and token technology create virtual continuity. Together they make the virtual real.

Taking all this together, for our needs, the features of block-chain-based cryptocurrencies are just perfect. It is crucial to have continuity when transferring tokens that represent a reward for happiness. Not only to provide a trusted framework for a single transaction, but also to provide longitudinal insight on who and what triggered happiness and who was involved in the transaction. That's the necessary data we need to reflect on, learn from, and use to reinforce behaviors that provide more happiness in the future.

In addition, this system provides total privacy (nobody should know your detailed personal happiness records unless you approve it!) because the user owns the data and can access it with their private key, while any transmission or transaction remains anonymous. Without knowing the "owners" behind the happiness data, any research organization, government, or the UN could access millions of pieces of detailed but anonymous data just through their cryptocurrency address. This would provide a huge set of real neuroscientific data to orient future global and country policies around more happiness on our planet.

With the hype around cryptocurrencies, a new way of company financing has appeared: initial coin offering (ICO). In ICOs, the companies encoding and creating the cryptocurrency sell a certain number of tokens for a certain monetary price. In essence, these companies record immediate revenues. However, with ICOs a lot of questionable sellers and originators have flooded the market. I am writing this at the end of 2018, when more than two thousand cryptocurrencies have been issued and we are just recovering slowly after the explosion of the largest cryptocurrency bubble at the beginning of 2018. Certain countries like China have prohibited any further ICOs because fraud on such offerings is increasing. As in any capitalistic gold rush, it's simply too easy to make a quick (American) buck if you are unscrupulous. However, the original idea of ICOs is a very good one. Blockchain technology could be used to issue new tokens or coins that are easy to transmit between transaction partners and are cryptographically secured. These tokens are the perfect vehicle for finance companies. They can be sold to fund activities, or they can function as a kind of share given to investors. Like investments in any IPO, investments in an ICO are only as valuable as the robustness of the underlying business plans or the underlying cryptocurrency.

Let's come back now to our—yet to be created—happiness currency. The token we have to create to complement our happiness concept is *a happiness cryptocurrency that rewards people for providing happiness to others.* The numerical value of such cryptocurrency is created by the unconscious, unbiased neurological activities of people receiving happiness. We call this currency the *Happiness dollar,* with the unit abbreviation :)$—very much like the abbreviation USD (or US$) for the leading currency in our economic world.

Before we continue to define the Happiness Dollar protocol, the rules and characteristics of our :)$, let us briefly reiterate the features of translating a neurological happiness signal into :)$. The numerical value of Happiness dollars created is directly proportional to the total Unconscious happiness created by our unbiased brain at the moment of happiness impact. Thus, the value of the :)$ is theoretically impossible to manipulate. Given the molecular identity of the underlying neuronal system, the :)$ value should be identical or at least highly similar between individuals. (At least when we anticipate stimuli of the same strength and assuming a similar baseline level of neuroscientific health of the respective individuals at impact.) As such, the :)$ has a common measure of value right at the beginning.

So what would our :)$ stand for? First of all, it's also not more than just a promise. It's the *happiness promise.* Sounds awesome. And actually it is.

It holds the promise to measure and value the true happiness we create in other people. It holds the promise to be the knowledge base for all humans to understand which investments make people truly happier (and likely richer) instead of just richer (and very likely less happy). It holds the promise to reward people who make others happier with an objectively valued token, not a conscious "Like" (perhaps produced by a bot). It holds the promise to create an upgraded economic system that is reinforced to direct investments into actions and goods that prioritize happiness.

Most importantly, this promise does not conflict with our current economic system. Given the nature of the :)$, it could be run entirely independently if we avoid any currency exchange. One system—dollars—focuses on our economy. The other system—:)$—focuses on our happiness. Neurologically, however, we know that on the lower psychological needs, the systems are heavily intertwined. Thus, the two systems are not really independent but rather act orthogonally to each other. I will go into further detail on this specific correlation later.

In essence, the :)$ is an extension in order to activate all our reward and learning capacity that is already available in our brains (!) but currently totally underutilized by just using money as our secondary reinforcer. As such, it is the ultimate promise to offer a token—the :)$—that can trigger the full capacity in our brilliant brains. Knowing how well our reinforcement learning cycle promotes repetition of behaviors when utilized in balance, the promise will further direct us to new pockets of economic growth. Whoever offers products and services that truly promote happiness will create a substantial market on the back of such happiness.

Examining the promise of the :)$ as one element of our expanded economic system, it is intriguing how well Aristotle described happiness thousands of years ago: the ultimate "good, complete without qualification, since we always choose it for itself and never for the sake of anything else." As clear as this description is, the key challenge in the past always was to measure it holistically and, as such, trigger our underlying neural mechanisms to learn and steer all of us properly. So far, all surrogates invented to help our brain to know where to go have been insufficient. I think the :)$ may have the potential to bridge the gap.

For a full Happiness Dollar protocol we must take a closer look at *value stability and inflation*. The :)$ will likely show very stable and consistent value at the moment of creation: the same neurological response should create the same amount of :)$ every time, given that the underlying neurological reward processes have been conserved for millions of years in every human being. This is very good information for investors: the intrinsic value of a :)$ is super stable and cannot be manipulated. Awesome!

However, there is a dramatic change when we take into account inflation rates over time. Our regular dollars can be stored for a long time in our savings account with limited devaluation driven by inflation (in a politically stable economy). In contrast, a :)$ devaluates to zero in a very short period of time, in theory, exactly in line with our emotional happiness, because a :)$ as we have defined it has no value for us as an individual if we keep it. It only creates a lasting value if we forward it as a reward to the person who triggered our happiness. Only in that person's account can it be stored for a longer period of time, together with its transaction and creation history.

Let's take a closer look at this interaction. Let's call the person who provides happiness to another person the *happiness giver* and the person receiving the happy-making action or product or service the *happiness receiver*. Upon impact, the happiness receiver creates a :)$ in his or her brain—so the happiness receiver is also the *:)$ creator*. Yet the token, the :)$, is basically useless for this person because it devaluates in a very short time. Only upon transmission to the person who provided the happiness, the happiness giver, does it convert into a real token of appreciation.

On the side of the happiness giver, the :)$ can be stored as a real reward, now with essentially no value loss. From a neurological perspective, this is already sufficient to achieve what we intended in the first place: to create a reward to give to someone who makes us happy. The process first of all triggers reflection on and learning about our own happiness. In addition, with the transmission of the :)$, we trigger reinforcement learning and reflection on the part of the person who provided our happiness—and perhaps we drive them to perform more such positive activities in the future, to benefit us and others.

You may be wondering what you will be able to do with an earned :)$ in your digital wallet. Stay tuned—we'll get there soon.

To recap, the :)$ is a super–high inflation currency if we keep it and a super–low inflation currency if we give it away. In our economic system, inflation has been a core lever to drive investments for growth today instead of to save our money in the bank. Because money we'd like to use for investment in the future has less value today. So it's better to invest your money now or in the short term. World-leading currencies show an inflation rate of 1 to 4 percent annually and are managed by central banks along those lines. The :)$ is intentionally designed to drive this concept to the extreme: you have to give a :)$ that you created away very quickly to activate it and make it work as a reward. If you wait too long, the entire value is gone. In economic terms: the inflation rate of the :)$ is 100 percent on a daily basis. Once the :)$ is activated by being invested, the inflation rate is close to zero in the hands of somebody else.

All this reaffirms the basic psychological rule of happiness: you have to enjoy and share your happiness *now*. The token of appreciation will stay forever, and given how it is minted, transmitted, and stored, will be recalled by our memory. With positively reinforced recall, we will likely repeat the activity that makes us happy. Given how the reinforcement cycle works, it is highly unlikely that people will stagnate with reflecting on memories of happiness. The neuroplasticity growth associated with action should stimulate continuous action and with it further neuroplasticity. In other words, the growth opportunities for dollar investments are limited by its going-in definition (goods and services and limitation on wealth). The growth opportunities in the :)$ universe are essentially unlimited, given that we have defined it with a very, very high ceiling: We-actualization.

Happiness cannot exist in the past or the future, but the memories of it can stay forever and can be actively recalled whenever we like. You can easily confirm it right now: just recall one of the happiest moments of your life. See how well you remember that moment and what the recall of such happy moments does to you instantly: it triggers the same reward systems that were triggered when the happy moment hit you the first time. Less intense, but it makes you . . . happy. Happy again. Amazing. As our neuroplasticity—our memory—is more and more robustly formed when we recall and in particular when we consciously reflect, our :)$ is actually the ultimate happiness memory recall trigger.

The definition of the :)$ as a single numerical representation for unconsciously created happiness takes advantage of another neurological feature of happiness. We can leverage different levels of happiness very effectively. With a single, consolidated number on a token, we eliminate information about where someone's happiness falls within the Universal happiness hierarchy. It would not matter anymore whether we were gaining a big chunk of happiness because we finally receive the Porsche sports car we dreamt of for twenty years or we find a bottle of water in the sand after getting lost in the desert without any water for ten hours. From an Unconscious happiness perspective, there is no difference—our neurons actually don't care and most likely they fire with the same neurotransmitter intensity because the brain uses the same or similar neural reward systems. The :)$ just represents the quantity of happiness.

As you can see, this feature opens a decoupling of the :)$ from the US dollar. The value of a :)$ is formed by our individual needs at a given point in time. It's independent of other people's forming a market with prices and status symbols. Regarding happiness alone, all humans on this planet are the same.

On the other hand, this feature creates a link between people at different levels of the Universal happiness hierarchy that can be leveraged for the benefit of everyone: if I buy a Porsche for $100,000, I will make myself happy. Depending on how I see the situation, I may transmit the created :)$ to the car dealer or to the Porsche company directly because they developed, produced, and sold the car to me. Or maybe I just don't transmit the :)$ to anyone, because I feel I deserve the credit for creating my own happiness by investing my money in the car. Most likely, when you buy your fifteenth Porsche, your brain will not even create any happiness—any :)$!—anymore. Your brain is used to it, so no happiness created. Not for you. Not for the car dealer. Not for Porsche. And the good thing is that you will see it immediately on your emotion tracker: ha, the fifteenth Porsche didn't make me happy at all! And hopefully it will make you reflect on why you spent $100,000 for it. In contrast, if you envision that the $100,000 would instead be distributed to ten homeless people whom you pass on the way to your Porsche dealer, you can be sure there is a lot of :)$ being created and coming your way. I will let you reflect on this metaphor for a little longer—I will go into further detail in later chapters.

The key properties and functions that define the :)$ are summarized in figure 29.

FIGURE 29: CURRENCY COMPARISON

Properties	Barter	Gold	US$	Bitcoin	:)$
Anonymous	◑	○	○	●	●
Decentralized	○	○	○	●	●
Government issued/controlled	◔	◑	○	●	●
Fungible	◔	◕	●	◑	◑
Divisible	○	◑	●	●	●
Globally transferable	○	◔	◑	●	●
Durable	◔	◕	◕	◕	●
Secure (counterfeiting)	◑	◕	◔	●	◑
Beyond-monetary use	○	◔	○	◔	●
Scarce (predictable supply)	◔	◕	◑	●	○
Portable	○	◔	◑	●	●
Transparency	◔	◑	●	●	●
Traceability	○	◔	◔	●	●
Intrinsically Valuable	◕	◕	◕	○	●
Functions					
Measure of financial value	○	○	●	◑	◑
Medium of exchange	○	◔	●	◑	◑
Store of value	◑	●	◑	●	●
Measure of happiness value	◔	◔	◑	◑	●

Value indicator: ○ (Poor), ● (Excellent)

In order to put it in perspective, I compare the :)$ to barter, gold, US dollars, and Bitcoin. I would like to highlight in particular three specifics. First, similar to Bitcoin, the :)$ is anonymous, decentralized, and not controlled by any government. Second, the :)$ is the only currency that is an objective measure of happiness, and it goes substantially beyond monetary use. Third, the amount of :)$ is unlimited; in other words, it is not scarce. I will later explain why this becomes even a benefit in monetary terms when the world moves to the higher levels of the Universal happiness hierarchy.

We are almost there. We know which happiness types we would like to look at, we have developed a universal framework guiding us, we know how to objectively price happiness, and we have condensed everything into a smart cryptocurrency.

However, before putting the whole system together in a smartphone app supplemented with a high-end wearable and a direct line to our bank account, I would like to briefly describe how the two currency systems—US$ and :)$—are intertwined neurologically and economically. As always, let's start with the neurological perspective.

CHAPTER THIRTEEN

HAPPINESS REINFORCEMENT LEARNING

Like the US dollar, the Happiness dollar, or :)$, we have introduced is a secondary reinforcer, so it holds no intrinsic benefit for us, the organism, but can be exchanged for primary reinforcers that do benefit us by satisfying certain psychological needs. A secondary reinforcer works only if the connection to the primary reinforcer is learned by the organism over time. For US dollars, this has been established for decades, while for the Happiness dollar, or :)$, it still needs to be established. We will detail the link between :)$ as a secondary reinforcer and other primary reinforcers in Chapter Nineteen.

Through evolution, the primary reinforcers and the associated neural reward systems became defined and pretty stable, at least in the time frame of our human life expectancy. So far, we have introduced the Universal happiness hierarchy as a framework that covers all levels relevant to make us happy, and then we linked our neuronal reward systems to these happiness levels. Preliminary evidence shows that these are not one-to-one connections, but rather a set of different reward systems acting together in order to move us between the hierarchy levels or satisfy us on a particular level.

How do US dollars or any other fiat currencies influence our reinforcement learning cycle (fig. 30)?

Given the underlying concept of our economy, we first and foremost focus on doing profitable business. We try to align our behaviors with this particular objective. The surrogate token that shows us how well we are on track is money, US dollars in our example. A dollar has no intrinsic value for us; we cannot eat, drink, or wear it. It is, therefore, just a secondary reinforcer. But because we're so familiar with how money can be exchanged for necessities like food, clothing, and shelter, our reward systems fire positive signals when we just see dollars that we have earned. The reward systems activated by money are primarily the dopamine system, the testosterone system, and to a certain extent, the serotonin system. Indeed, as with experiments in rats, people higher up in society (rich people) present with a significantly higher level of testosterone than poorer people. It should be noted here that the other reward systems—the oxytocin, cannabinoid, and opioid systems—are basically not activated; natural activation of these reward systems requires positive physical interactions with other people.

Now, over the years, the US dollar has emerged as a representation of other things that make us happy, such as interpersonal safety and self-esteem. You may agree that the link from dollars to self-esteem is a long one, but indeed our brain acts as if it's under a fully manifested addiction (Chapter Six, figure 5C and 6C) when we try to boost our confidence through our purchases. Intriguingly, self-confirmed self-esteem cannot be purchased with money. This can be best seen in people who are born very rich. Some of them are perceived as either insecure or arrogant, with the latter described in psychological terms as "overcompensating."

In contrast, people who earned their money have a robust level of self-confidence most of the time, in particular if it took them some time and effort to earn their wealth. Most importantly, our dopamine, testosterone, and serotonin systems can hardly support any higher levels on the happiness hierarchy beyond self-esteem. The next levels simply cannot be achieved by earning more money or accumulating wealth. You need true personal and interpersonal growth, societal connections, relationships, and—yes—love. In our Universal happiness hierarchy, these are the three levels defining growth: self-actualization, G-love, and We-actualization.

FIGURE 30: LEVERAGING OUR REINFORCEMENT LEARNING CYCLE ONLY FOR BUSINESS IS INSUFFICIENT TO DRIVE HOLISTIC HAPPINESS

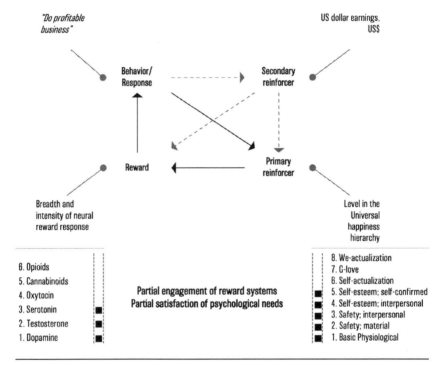

Early research has started to assess activities across all reward systems in people who potentially have reached these levels. Interestingly, all of them are people older than sixty, confirming Aristotle one more time—that full happiness needs an intensive and reflected life. Intriguingly, epidemiological and brain imaging data confirms that intensive social interactions and strong family networks drive substantial neuroplasticity, while loneliness drives significantly impaired neural structures and neuroplasticity and—with these—mental impairment and illness.

Obviously, this leads to a substantial level of frustration in those who have been taught that money provides well-being and happiness. It can be especially frustrating if your perceived happiness stagnates first and then—like in any other addiction—declines. There are essentially five behavioral responses that can arise in this difficult situation. Two are addictive and three are reflective. Unfortunately, only one can even partly address the ultimate deficit.

The addictive responses are, first, to work harder in order to make more money and subsequently increase consumption and accumulation of status symbols. In this route, we try to obtain more interpersonal self-esteem (status). Satisfying interpersonal self-esteem almost exclusively triggers the serotonin system and leads to a positive emotion we perceive as pride. A second addictive response frequently observed is the use of stimulants or drugs, particularly ones that trigger in particular the cannabinoid and opioid reward systems, which are chronically under-stimulated in our world due to a lack of social interactions. As discussed in Chapter Seven, these responses are by far the most frequently observed on our planet, with significant increases of drug and behavioral addictions in recent years, in particular in the high-income population. Given the long-lasting reduction of neuroplasticity caused by these addictive behaviors and the sustained dissatisfaction of key psychological needs, it is not surprising that depression levels are also skyrocketing. Again, with a major incidence in wealthier people.

In certain cases, however, we can observe a balanced response triggered by reflection (Chapter Six, fig. 6B) and the conclusion that accumulating more money will not lead us to more happiness. Reflection triggers three behavior responses. First, the primary behavioral change is that people start to donate money or, secondly, invest to build their own businesses. Both responses induce the feeling of pride by giving something back to society or people in need. So the key system activated is the serotonin system, which allows us to maximally satisfy the need for interpersonal self-esteem. We are stuck on the self-esteem level because we don't really take personal care of people—we don't actively, physically provide happiness to people in a way that would stimulate the upper three reward systems we so desperately need to activate. And even if we create our own businesses with our money,

we are stuck with money as the limit: you pay people monetary salaries and bonuses, your business is valued by its monetary performance,
your personal performance as an investor and entrepreneur is measured by return on investment, a parameter measured in money. In
other words, donating money or building economic businesses will—
again—only address unsatisfied needs on the lower level, basically
safety and—to a certain extent—interpersonal self-esteem. For the
receivers of the donation or the job opportunities, we are stuck with
the limitations of money again.

The third behavioral response to reflection leads a few people to
form foundations focusing on the greater good. Most of them are active
in these foundations hands-on in a way that can lead to true self-actualization and even beyond. Importantly, the action and interaction with
people in need is the strongest driver for happiness in these people—
not the monetary investment in the activity. While from a happiness
perspective such foundations indeed reach their goal for the happiness
donor and receiver, such concepts are most of the time unsustainable
from an economic perspective. Without a continuous infusion of capital, mostly through donations, these operations go bankrupt, as they
don't earn back their investments. In our world that is based on a capitalistic economy, it actually is unreasonable to run such operations,
and they can only be kept active based on reinvestments of existing
wealth—obtained from other economically viable businesses.

Just considering these five behavioral responses—work more, compensate with drugs, donate, invest in businesses, or create nonprofit
foundations—it becomes clear how big the challenge is to find happiness within our current monetary system. And it's even more difficult
to make a monetary return on providing happiness at the highest level
of psychological need satisfaction. All responses described above are
detours taken to overcome the intrinsic limitation of our economic
system: money alone is insufficient to trigger all six reward systems.
Money alone won't make us happy. In fact, it leaves our core psychological needs unsatisfied, particularly in the areas of personal and interpersonal growth.

Now let's have a brief look at how this would change with a novel
objective: provide happiness to others (fig. 31).

FIGURE 31: LEVERAGING OUR REINFORCEMENT LEARNING CYCLE TO PROVIDE HAPPINESS TO OTHERS IS SUFFICIENT TO DRIVE HOLISTIC HAPPINESS

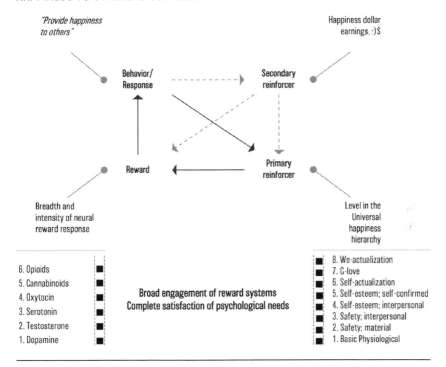

First of all, US$ cannot fulfill this objective, but :)$ could. To recap, :)$ are created from the unconscious, unbiased molecular reaction of our neural systems in the moment a happiness-making event hits us. Please realize that the :)$ is created in the receiver of happiness first of all. This part—the creation of the :)$—is not even shown in figure 30. We focused on the creation of the :)$ in Chapter Twelve. So let us assume for now that we receive the :)$ as a reward, a token of appreciation in transparent connection with an action or good we have provided to somebody else. The :)$ would act as a secondary reinforcer like dollars. However, because we can "earn" :)$ for everything we do to make people happy, the :)$ has a much broader application than dollars that drive a marketplace for goods and services alone. In the new economy, all six reward systems can be stimulated, satisfying the highest levels of individual needs. As a consequence, our reinforcement learning system in the brain would condition us toward more actions that make people genuinely happy.

From a learning perspective, this is the fundamental difference between US dollars and Happiness dollars, or between US\$ and :)\$.

All of a sudden, we can earn a reward for making other people happy, not only for enriching ourselves or making ourselves happier. There is one neural clue: learning is much more efficient with more reward systems triggered, in particular the opioid and oxytocin systems. Therefore, learning to provide happiness to others should be much faster and more effective than learning to do business profitably.

As the :)\$ are created from an unbiased, unconscious neural system, it would direct us toward actions that first of all trigger the cells in our hedonic centers in the brain in a balanced way. Manipulations would hardly be possible—you have to make people truly happy, not just pretend to do so. Otherwise, no :)\$ is produced. The shortcut of providing addictive actions (like video gaming) or goods (like sugary foods) wouldn't last long because neuroplasticity declines in the case of addiction, and, as such, the hurdle to creating :)\$ would increase very quickly.

FIGURE 32: LEVERAGING OUR REINFORCEMENT LEARNING CYCLE WITH TWO SYNERGISTIC SECONDARY REINFORCERS, US$ AND :)$, DRIVES PROFITABLE BUSINESS AND HAPPINESS

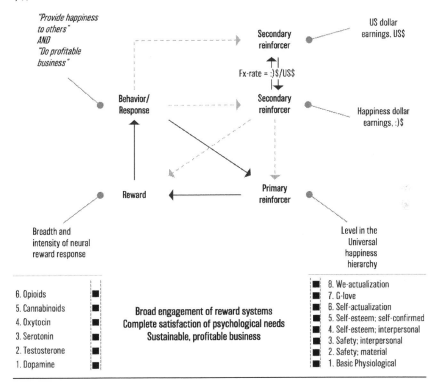

The US dollar system and the :)$ systems nicely overlap on the lower levels of the hierarchy. It would therefore seem obvious to use both currencies in parallel to link the two objectives and amplify them: "do profitable business" and "provide happiness to others" (fig. 32). Higher on the psychological need hierarchies, dollars and :)$ start to differentiate, with dollars unable to trigger the personal and interpersonal growth levels.

From a reinforcement learning perspective, it is straightforward to link the two secondary reinforcers on levels where they overlap and both trigger our reward systems. Especially because dollars are so well accepted and we are—on average—so successfully addicted to them, it makes a lot of sense to leverage this trigger. Applying the nomenclature of addiction, the :)$ is actually the perfect drug substitute. First, it should make us happier than the original drug (money) while not showing any detrimental effect as it triggers personal, interpersonal, and societal growth. Secondly, it would ensure that your brain does not display the degradation and loss of neuroplasticity seen in classical forms of addictions. Finally, it would ensure that the societal downsides of drug abuse are turned into the opposite: "You get more drug substitute if you make other people happy."

So far, so good from the neurological perspective. Seems to be straightforward. However, from an economic perspective, linking the two currency systems is slightly more challenging. I will address that in the next chapter.

In addition, we still have to establish how :)$ as a secondary reinforcer can be exchanged into a real, tangible primary reinforcer. Or, as I like to put it, will you ever be able to buy an ice cream cone with a :)$? You bet. We're almost ready to put all the concepts together into one grand experiment.

CHAPTER FOURTEEN

CAPITALISM MEETS HAPPINESS

Our economic system and the Universal happiness hierarchy do not act hand in hand along all eight levels of the hierarchy. On the lower levels, they are well aligned, but they decouple entirely on higher levels. The Happiness dollar, or :)$, will therefore not replace our monetary system, because the economic rules and key measures of success for running a business will stay unchanged. Instead, the :)$ provides an extension of our economic system toward goods and actions that money can't measure, detect, or even understand. The two frameworks ideally act orthogonally to each other (fig. 33).

FIGURE 33: CAPITALISM OF HAPPINESS: ROI VERSUS ROH

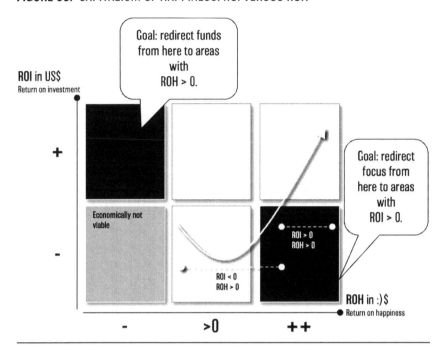

In the previous chapters, we set up the Universal happiness hierarchy alongside the definitions of our economic system (fig. 20). Whereas our core economic performance indicator—return on investment—focuses on profitable business over time, our core objective in the happiness dimension is providing sustainable happiness over time. Given the confirmed correlation between short-term and long-term happiness—as long as we avoid fully manifested addiction states—it seems neuroscientifically sufficient to measure unconscious reward system activity (Unconscious happiness) as a base parameter and ensure deep reflection and learning (Conscious happiness) on the receiving side.

I therefore define the core happiness performance indicator as: **return on (providing) happiness** or, in short, **Return on Happiness**. Our framework for happiness, however, is broader than the economic framework and essentially covers the whole matrix shown in figure 33.

I will call this extended economy the **Capitalism of Happiness.**

Both dimensions, return on investment and Return on Happiness, are treated similarly from the underlying mathematical parameters in that they have a dimension of time. Return on investment is primarily used on an annualized basis to reflect the annual financial reporting standards for businesses and allow comparison between different investments normalized over time. Thus, for comparison between return on investment and Return on Happiness, it is advisable to always cover the same time horizon. As human life across the world is organized around annual calendars, it seems reasonable to use annualization for happiness as well.

For both dimensions, the philosophical dilemma between short-term and long-term returns apply pretty much the same; for example, short-term satisfaction by chocolate eating versus potential long-term dissatisfaction because of weight gain, fitness loss, and potential health problems. Interestingly, on a purely scientific level, it seems that short-term and long-term returns are more correlated for Return on Happiness than for return on investment. Considering only short-term returns in the regular economy can be very successful (like hedge fund and venture capital investment tactics), while for happiness this strategy leads very quickly to addiction. The implications for long-term happiness are substantially harmed, as are the short-term and midterm prospects, since our reward systems face increasing hurdles to be stimulated. Ultimately, all data obtained for *hedonia* (pleasure of the senses, short-term) and *eudaemonia* (pleasure of reason: living well and doing well, long-term) show a tight link for a given individual: the more short-term happiness an individual accumulates, the more *eudaemonia* is reported. (This is the case with balanced short-term happiness, not the addictive kind.)

In the real-life economy, most importantly, return on investment and Return on Happiness turn into complementary vectors: Return on Happiness directs economic investments toward the objective and purpose of providing happiness. In addition, return on investment guides investments in happiness to stay profitable, show long-term economic growth, and be based on a sustainable business concept. The orthogonal nature of return on investment and Return on Happiness should drive investments away from business areas that don't create any happiness (fig. 33, upper left sector), simply by making areas that do and do not provide happiness transparent and quantifiable. In addition, pouring investments into high-need areas for happiness (for example, development aid) would have to confirm economic viability at least in a certain timeframe that is also economically relevant. Such transparency would push much smarter economic investments in contrast to what we do today. For example, investments that go beyond pure monetary donations, such as education and key technology transfers, would prove themselves much more sustainable and successful mid- to long-term from an economic perspective as well (fig. 33, lower right sector).

One of the best examples of such behavior is the investment strategy of Costa Rica in the 1960s and '70s, when all development aid and loan-based military investments were discontinued and put—together with all development aids—into education and environmental sustainability. Twenty years later, Costa Rica has been developed into an island of well-being and stability in Latin America, driving toward zero-emission status in a few years. In addition, Costa Rica ranks among the top countries in respect to all happiness metrics, and some of its communities have the lowest rate of middle-age mortality and the highest concentrations of centenarians.

Today, all standard marketing activities for products and services are designed to elicit behavioral addictions in consumers in order to ensure repeated purchases and sustained revenues. Neuroscientifically, brand loyalty is nothing more than brand dependency and potentially brand addiction. The best examples can be seen in digital applications or foods that all follow—openly—a regimen that triggers dependency, primarily by sustainably triggering the dopamine and serotonin reward systems. Economically, such product and service designs are highly unproductive. Companies have to continuously invest money in brand extension activities in order to avoid exhaustion of the consumer and discontinuation of purchases. Addictive behaviors drive unhappiness over time. In our extended economy, the demand on product and service development and design will be much more ambitious. Leading products and services will have to trigger real Unconscious happiness on a neural level without driving addiction, such as a music streaming service that offers the original version of Queen's Live Aid session, triggering an explosion of recall-happiness in me and millions of others, most likely. With such a service, the associated artists would continuously be rewarded for what they have created. I stayed with the Live Aid example introduced earlier, but you can easily imagine how other music or art events can create not only immediate happiness but also recalled happiness through a streaming service. The same can be achieved by certain products that trigger Unconscious happiness, such as the first Nike Air Jordan sport shoes when they were launched in 1984. In return for such a design, companies will enjoy significantly more repeated purchases, because we learn faster and better when we reflect on a behavior that made us happy. Therefore, return on investment should be the highest in areas of balanced and reflected-upon happiness.

Key performance indicators that are orthogonal to return on investment are not new. For example, if you replace Return on Happiness with "reduction of greenhouse gas emissions," you end up with the carbon dioxide certificates, which have been used widely in Europe for the fossil fuel industry. The objective for the introduction of carbon dioxide certificates was to create an incentive for the industry to develop energy types with lower or no carbon dioxide emission. In a pure capitalistic world, there is no incentive to drive the development of novel, low-emission types of energy.

In addition, there are other add-on metrics to return on investment that try to highlight certain desirable product features: fair trade, vegan, no genetically modified organisms, natural certificates, you name it. The main objective with all these features is to inform the consumer of additional benefits that justify higher prices. These price premiums are necessary in order to subsidize certain costly product features that are not supported in the initial phase of a new product in our current economic system. To really enable change with such features, it is necessary to apply them industry-wide, with no manufacturer able to shirk the responsibility for renewable energy sources or the like. Otherwise, the economic competitive advantage for the ones producing cheap products would be dramatic and would reinstall the player with the highest returns as the leader immediately. This can be best seen when examining the difference in behavior between US energy providers and consumers and their counterparts in Europe. The amount of sustainable energy produced and consumed in Europe is much higher than in the US, due to the power of carbon dioxide certificates. However, the economic returns are significantly higher for the energy and power industry in the US. If there were no Atlantic Ocean between the two markets, the European power industry players would be wiped out economically in no time.

In neurological terms, most special-feature certificates act as negative conditioning—economic punishment to force change. But people forget much faster when conditioned negatively rather than positively. This is the simple biological reason why a lot of punishment certificates introduced to our economic system are so inefficient. They harm our economic key performance indicator: making money. We don't like such negative conditioning on our most important secondary reinforcer, obviously.

To overcome the shortfall of negative conditioning, the Capitalism of Happiness is entirely designed and built on positive conditioning and reward learning. First, the core parameter we use is the ultimate biological originator of positive conditioning: happiness. Secondly, we intentionally avoid introducing the feature of negative :)$ or :)$ debt. Any punishment or negative conditioning would defeat the purpose of driving positive growth neurologically and thereafter economically. Thus, for happiness we focus exclusively on activities, products, and services that drive behaviors that make us happy. The wiring of our brain ensures by itself that we remember positively reinforced behaviors much more and thus will repeat them. Thirdly, the complete dimension of the Universal happiness hierarchy is—by nature—much broader than our current form of capitalism. Yet the lower levels of the hierarchy entirely include and cover our current capitalistic drivers. A lot of things money can buy do indeed make us and other people happier if certain needs are being met. As long as we don't get addicted, of course.

So we will keep the underlying mechanisms of our economic system—and evolution!—particularly on the lower levels of the psychological needs hierarchy (fig. 24). However, we will no longer need to accept our current economic system as the limit. We will step beyond it. The Universal happiness hierarchy extends the capitalistic foundation of our economy dramatically, and it creates economic growth on the back of happiness growth.

Already today, consumer products and services that trigger a broader range of reward systems and satisfy a broader range of psychological needs are the most successful. For example, the leading sports companies are more and more driving toward building real, real-life communities and movements around a certain sport on top of their products, such as Reebok in CrossFit, Adidas in soccer, Nike in group running. In a similar way, Spotify is trying to link its digital music streaming services to real, live music events, and Red Bull is linking its energy drink to real, live extreme sport events.

All these companies are already trying to move their products toward an experience that allows for self-actualization, and ultimately We-actualization, in order to create more economic returns on the back of providing more happiness—exactly as predicted. In the presence of the :)$, we can predict that these companies will remain at the top of the dollar valuation ranking. However, it would become transparent that they lead the :)$ valuation ranking with a very big margin over others that can't provide a similar level of happiness-making products and services.

You can see this with the struggle of companies that sell via the dopamine and serotonin routes, such as Coca-Cola (trying to exit sugar-based soft drinks), Nestlé (divesting itself of its chocolate brands), McDonald's (reducing trans fat and carbohydrates in their meals), and video game companies (trying to move gaming into the real, analog world). All of these companies are under massive pressure to produce products and services with more sustainable, less addictive value propositions. In other words, to broaden the reward systems their consumption triggers and thereby reduce addictive behavior. In the next chapter we will assess in more detail how the :)$ would influence the design and development of new products and services.

You can now imagine how an extension of our economy from goods and services toward all actions would unleash a new dimension of economic growth. As long as we focus on a broad range of reward system stimulation—without triggering addiction!

All this makes the :)$ very different from any other certificate trying to drive impact. Unfortunately, most certificates effectively impair economic returns for the industry they are meant to change. Or they reduce the buying power of people paying a higher price for products with special features. Both types of certificates accept capitalism as the ultimate framework. They accept the limitations but try to mitigate the shortcomings of a defined slice of capitalism, such as cheap but emission-creating energy or cheap but genetically modified food, by introducing an economic punishment (negative conditioning). Instead, from a biological perspective, economic pricing on the upper end should much more orient itself toward the level of Unconscious and Conscious happiness. So far, this has been impossible, given our inability to measure Unconscious happiness. Once real happiness is created by any good, service, or action, the economic price will immediately increase.

Most importantly, we would never force anyone to participate in this concept (forcing is negative conditioning). Actually, we would love to run this experiment totally openly and freely. If neurobiology and evolution theory are right, many people will join very quickly because they are attracted by reward and positive conditioning. Or they may want to participate in order to better understand what makes them happier. If today's version of capitalism is right, only a few will join at the beginning. However, after the first big industry players who succeed in both return on investment and Return on Happiness, positive conditioning will set in and many others will follow. Either way, the Universal happiness hierarchy will win. I just don't know how long it will take or which route it will take. The route could be, first, Return on Happiness, followed by return on investment (white curve in fig. 33). Or the route could be, first, return on investment, followed by Return on Happiness (not shown ☺).

After all these theoretical details, let's get started and run the experiment. Given the digital dimension we are all living in, we first need a kind of "**Happiness app.**"

CHAPTER FIFTEEN

THE HAPPINESS APP

Smartphone apps are perfectly suited to drive behavioral change. They have been developed to attract customers to selling or advertising platforms, and to drive dependency and addiction to video games, fitness trackers, and chat groups.

We actually intend the same thing, with the only difference that we would like to drive behavioral change toward providing more happiness to other people, and without creating addiction. The underlying concept is the learning triangle of life that was introduced in the first chapter. I repeat the figure here just as a brief reminder (fig. 34, which is identical to fig. 4). The learning triangle of life comprises functional behavior (B), need satisfaction (S), and functional reward systems (R).

FIGURE 34: LEARNING TRIANGLE OF LIFE (BSR TRIANGLE)

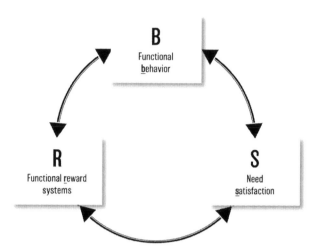

To recap, if these pillars are in balance, we induce sustained learning and substantial neuroplasticity, the underlying foundation of happiness. Now, the Happiness app goes beyond the individual. Instead, the objective is to link the learning triangle of life between people, first of all between two people interacting with each other. We anticipate this will drive behavioral change for both people, the *happiness giver* on the one side and the *happiness receiver* on the other side. An expansion toward group interactions is easy once we have understood and established the concept between two individuals.

Let's have a brief look at how reinforcement learning in favor of happy-making behaviors works today (fig. 35, left side). Say Sam is helping his friend Mary move into a new apartment on the seventh floor. On the day of the move, the elevator breaks, heavy rain is forecast for the entire day, and unless Sam is strong enough to carry all the heavy items, the move won't work out. Despite all these unforeseen limitations, Sam cancels all his other appointments for the day, pulls through, and completes the move for Mary.

This behavior of Sam, whom we'll call the happiness giver, leads to the satisfaction of certain psychological needs in Mary, our happiness receiver. This in turn triggers some of Mary's neuronal reward systems, primarily the dopamine system and the serotonin systems but also the opioid system. Up to this point, Mary was just lucky to have such a reliable friend in Sam. There are basically two options for how Mary can respond to the favor he's done her: she can say nothing, be privately glad the job is done, and make sure she finds a similar good friend for her next move—or as a normal response, she can feel deep gratitude, one of the most powerful positive emotions directly associated with happiness. Most likely Mary would respond with a genuine "thank you" and a facial expression that truly reflects her gratitude. Facial expressions are directly linked with positive emotions, and we have been trained over millions of years to recognize genuine facial expressions, so Mary's sincerity would not appear faked. Her heartfelt acknowledgment is the functional behavior in response to somebody helping her out.

The problem in our world today is that saying "thank you!" is a basic, standard response. In other words, we are used to it. Thus, the associated satisfaction on the happiness giver's side is very limited and disappears in the split second after the "thank you" is received. At best, we would see a very mild activation of the dopamine and serotonin systems, leading Sam to feel pride and perhaps also interpersonal self-esteem. The resulting reward is likely too weak to ever make Sam repeat this behavior a second time. That evening, sitting at home exhausted and suffering back pain, trying to justify all his canceled appointments, Sam would probably think twice about whether to help in such a move again. The learning result—repeat of a functional behavior leading to happiness of others—would likely be very disappointing, particularly when comparing the significant happiness created in Mary and the insufficient reward created in Sam.

There are three ways we could improve the situation.

First, Mary could just use her smartphone and book some cheap movers through a newly created moving app. Money as a secondary reinforcer is substituted for the "thank you." Regarding overall happiness levels, this is the poorest solution because Mary would lose the feeling of gratitude and there is likely very little happiness on the side of the movers doing the job, considering their low wages. With this solution, we have ensured that no happiness has been created on this planet.

Alternatively, Mary could enhance the power of her feedback to Sam. It needs some creativity; it's challenging to adequately reward someone for this task—an apartment move in the rain to the seventh floor without an elevator. Mary could combine the "thank you" with a big hug for Sam. We substantially underestimate the effect a genuine hug has on need satisfaction and activation of the reward systems in the person being hugged. Indeed, such a hug triggers strong satisfaction of interpersonal self-esteem and in turn a strong activation of the oxytocin system. Oxytocin is a general emotion amplifier but also provides the positive emotion of nurturant love, a very strong reward.

Finally, Mary could invite all her friends, have food and drinks, and associate a fun party with the otherwise dreary and arduous move. This basically turns a larger group into happiness givers and happiness receivers. Such a setup satisfies the higher levels of the need hierarchy and would trigger the opioid and cannabinoid reward systems that are primarily associated with the positive emotion of attachment love. The overall happiness created by such a moving party is substantial, and at the next move everybody will surely show up again. Indeed, such apartment moving parties are legendary—at least in Europe—and are events that are hardly forgotten for the rest of your life.

The popularity of these parties confirms a simple rule: *the best, most memorable moments in life are never purchased—they are shared.* These are the moments when we reach a form of We-actualization: a group of people working actively together to achieve and enjoy a joint objective. Because the joint objective of an apartment moving party is of limited meaning and purpose, the experienced We-actualization is limited in time to the event. Unless it is repeated.

FIGURE 35: REINFORCEMENT LEARNING WITHOUT (LEFT) AND WITH :)$ AMPLIFICATION (RIGHT)

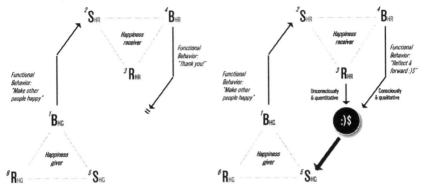

Key: R: Functional reward systems; B: Functional behavior; S: Need satisfaction; HG: Happiness giver; HR: Happiness receiver; 1-6: Sequence of interaction between happiness giver and happiness receiver

Unfortunately for the overall happiness levels created on this planet, we are turning increasingly into a so-called sharing economy in which all kinds of services can be purchased online. In our example, it was the moving app. In particular, the online platforms ensure that the price pressure is always on, and thus they minimize or even damage happiness levels on the service provider side (very low wage) as well as on the service receiver side (limited level of quality). We have all been accepting these downsides due to the perceived price reduction we enjoy. For all of us, however—suppliers, middlemen, and receivers—the overall effect on happiness is clearly negative.

In a sense, the term "sharing economy" is wrong from a neurological perspective. "Sharing" works effectively on a neurological basis only when money is not attached to it. In the moment when we purchase something, our need satisfaction is limited to the lower levels of the hierarchy. The secondary reinforcer that is money ensures that we achieve only insufficient happiness levels. If the quality of the received service is below our expectations, the sharing economy actually delivers unhappiness.

With the Happiness dollar, or :)$, we can resolve these limitations. The key feature of the :)$ is its objective creation in real time, based on the reward systems triggered on the side of the happiness receiver. It is an amplifier of the happiness sent by our biological facial expression when we genuinely say "thank you." It is a true representation of Unconscious happiness and a token of appreciation with a confirmed scientific value. It is not like a "thank you" someone says without really meaning it. In addition, the :)$ lasts in my digital wallet when I receive it as a happiness giver.

Therefore, let us repeat our apartment move story in the presence of our anticipated Happiness app (fig. 35, right side). As in the first scenario, Sam helps with the move and creates true gratitude in Mary. The firing of her reward systems—unconsciously—creates a number of :)$ that could be transferred—consciously—as a token of her appreciation to Sam. For two smartphones with geolocation, this can be executed with one click.

For now, it is important to understand that the :)$ is a substantial amplifier of our learning system. It is an amplifier of a "thank you," of a hug, or of an "apartment moving party," because we now know we truly created this happiness in others. We can also keep the :)$ as an amplifier for our memory, like a trophy. The value of such a trophy is something we will discuss a little later. One could even imagine groups of people trying to create fun competitions in order to achieve a maximum number of :)$ during a moving party. In a world of gaming and digital apps, I genuinely believe we would see several ideas for creating real joint happiness. And with it, :)$ would be created.

It is very important to note that the :)$ would not eliminate the need for moving companies.

We are ready to go for a deep dive now. Figure 36 provides us with a game plan for our experiment and has been designed to allow us to anticipate how the system could eventually work in a smartphone.

We anticipate that both people in the experiment have a smartphone (with all geolocation and connection services activated) and a wearable device that detects and reads certain neural signals and emotions through associated physiological responses, such as heartbeat pattern and skin conductivity.

As in our previous example, let us start with a happiness giver who provides happiness to another person (the happiness receiver). At a time point t0, the action hits our happiness receiver (impact t0) and is instantly detected by their wearable device. Most likely it will require a set of readouts, probably with cardio and skin conductivity data at the core. Based on an algorithm (figs. 25, 27), this data will be consolidated and may show a significant increase in Unconscious happiness in the happiness receiver's six reward systems. We are still at time point t0. Therefore, we refer to this value as ΔH_U^{t0}, with the Greek letter delta (Δ) indicating incremental change. Thus in the formula ΔH indicates the increase of happiness, the subscript U indicates that we are talking about Unconscious happiness data, and the superscript t0 indicates the time at the start.

Please note that ΔH_U^{t0} is consolidated from the raw data only if the data surpasses a predefined threshold of scientific relevance and significance. We are interested in measuring only the signals of real peaks of Unconscious happiness, not any noise in the brain. Thus, most likely more than 95 percent of actions hitting us in everyday life will be filtered out (as indicated by the little traffic light in the graph in figure 36). Up to this point, our smartphone is nothing more than a happiness tracker, similar to other emotion trackers and fitness trackers. It provides us with information about our own happiness.

In order to create the numerical basis for a potential reward, ΔH_U^{t0} will be automatically translated into $\Delta:)\$$ at a fixed rate.

You have created a :)$. Pretty cool.

FIGURE 36: HAPPINESS APP GAME PLAN

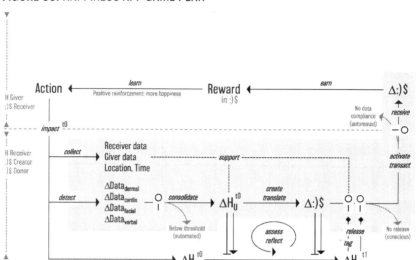

Key: t0: time at start/impact; t1: time after reflection/at release; ΔH_U: Quantitative, Unconscious happiness signal above threshold; ΔH_C^{t0}: Conscious happiness before reflection; ΔH_C^{t1}: Conscious happiness after reflection; $\Delta:)\$$: Created amount of Happiness dollars based on unconscious happiness signal.

Up to this point everything has happened unconsciously and totally automatically in a split second. Our smartphone would send us a notification now, or it could collect all notifications to show to us later, depending on how we have customized our Happiness app. The notification could read, for example: "Hey, Axel, at 4:16 p.m. you created one :)$! Congratulations! For neurological data, please see details."

From here, we have to continue consciously. The activation of our consciousness is critical at this point because we can induce learning effectively only if we reflect on the experience. If we like, we can dive deeply into the raw data ($\Delta data_{dermal}^{t0}$, $\Delta data_{cardio}^{t0}$, $\Delta data_{verbal}^{t0}$, $\Delta data_{facial}^{t0}$), the consolidated data (ΔH_U^{t0}), and the number of :)$ created. Then we can reflect on how much happiness we felt consciously (ΔH_C^{t0}) and who or what was likely responsible for it.

The moment of *reflection* is the most critical element of the whole process because it triggers learning and neuroplasticity.

That's why we need time for reflection before a :)$ can be activated and released. The release at the end is just a click, so it does not take much time. However, we know from the neurobiology of learning that memory formation and consolidation take time because active protein synthesis is required. In addition, reflection and the associated stimulation and build-up of neuroplasticity also take time. Based on the scientific data we have, such a build-up requires eight to twenty-four hours. So, in order to have enough time to reflect, we should reserve twenty-four hours before an unconsciously created :)$ is activated and released.

To be clear, the reflection itself ("Oh boy, it was amazing to have Sam helping me today") will usually take just seconds. If you enjoy fleshing out the details in your memory, perhaps it would take one minute. That is enough time to trigger the biological mechanisms that drive the build-up of neuroplasticity, and with it strong memory formation and consolidation. In total, for one day, it would mean spending a maximum of one minute and one click to say "thank you" to people who made us really happy. Given the time we spend on our cell phones every day (the average ranges between two and six hours!), this should be worth it. It would take a similar amount of time to answer a text message.

In addition, we will receive information about which reward systems ultimately have triggered our happiness. This information will be very interesting, as it would show us how the oxytocin, cannabinoid, and opioid system can amplify the underlying enthusiasm driven by dopamine. And how insufficient dopamine by itself is (in particular triggered by consumption) to drive sustained happiness. In addition, the reflection period allows us to really dive into the details of what made us happy. Was it the pride we felt when we managed to carry the fridge up the stairs by ourselves? Or was it the hug from Mary? Or was it the laughter at the end of the day when sitting together on the rooftop watching the sunset? This latter feature of the unconscious Happiness app will fundamentally revolutionize what we do and how we live our lives.

Why is the reflection period so important? Is it really necessary to wait for a day before we can transmit a created :)$ to our happiness giver? If we were to automatically release the created :)$ instantly, we would just be an unconscious :)$-distributing machine without any insights into what and who made us happy. The happiness that really matters is Conscious happiness, not the Unconscious happiness. Unconscious happiness gives us an indication on the dimension, the size. Our consciousness provides the quality—that's what really counts. Based on the notifications from the Unconscious happiness tracker, we will soon realize that we've been missing the biggest chunks of happiness that our brain is registering while our consciousness is filtering it out because we're too busy or too distracted to notice. That means we can't always appreciate someone having a positive impact on us. Our smartphone will support us with additional data from the impact moment (impact t0). For example, where did it hit us, when did it hit us, who was with us at the moment of impact, were any other digital apps running (music app, fitness app), which products or services were close by or purchased?

Based on our reflection, we can decide two things: First, do we want to activate and release the :)$ we created or not? Second, to whom do we want to tag the :)$ we created? Both questions should be answered in the spirit of positive conditioning: you have all the freedom of choice and decision to release your :)$ and tag it. Yet I recommend two general rules:

1. Release your :)$ only if you want to reward someone (other than yourself!) for the happiness you have received. This someone can be a person or an organization with a :)$ account. The more closely the person or organization is associated with the happiness you have received, the better.

2. Tagging and releasing are not limited to people or organizations that are physically close by when you create your :)$.

For example, if you feel that you made yourself happy, there is no case for tagging and releasing a created :)$ because—by definition—there is no receiver. Whenever you decide not to or forget to release the :)$, it will devaluate and disappear after twenty-four hours. That makes total sense because you enjoyed your happiness already, triggering your learning. Even if you know who made you happy, there is no obligation to tag and release—if you simply don't want to send a reward to a specific person (or company), just don't do it. It is up to you to consciously choose whether to release the unconsciously created :)$.

As Conscious happiness is highly dependent on our genetic background and experience, there should be no limitation on who you can tag your :)$ to. For example, if going running with a friend made us happy, we can tag and release the created :)$ to the friend who joined us, or to our youth coach who convinced us to seriously start running, or not at all if we think it was just us making us happy. Again, it is up to you to consciously choose.

Regardless of whether we release the :)$, the data in our happiness tracker will provide deep insights into the activities triggering our happiness—thus, we will learn for ourselves. The same thing happens if we cannot allocate the :)$ to a specific person, or if we simply don't want to release the :)$. All this is our conscious decision—we are entirely free to release a :)$. The time point of release we call t1. We have time to reflect and decide between t0 and t1. At time point t1, we should have some awareness about the happiness we have received (ΔH_C^{t1}), and to whom and whether we would like to release it. If we do, everything continues automatically: the created :)$ will be sent to the :)$ account of the person who made us happy, the happiness giver.

You have successfully donated a :)$. Very, very cool. You are a :)$ donor now!

Once the :)$ transaction is completed, the :)$ is activated with a constant and stable value. Transacting the :)$ via blockchain is critical. At this point there is true value in a :)$. Before that point it's just a piece of information for yourself that loses its value if you don't release it. In addition, without the features of a cryptocurrency, the route of transaction can't be tracked and documented. We would lose a critical part of the story behind the :)$: the positive connection between two people. And we would lose the necessary privacy we would like to have for such fragile, personal data.

To avoid intentionally or mistakenly mis-tagging or mis-releasing a :)$, there could be another automated consistency check between the two people involved in the transaction, based on personal account data and geolocation data. If there is a mismatch or logical nonsense, our smartphone app may then ask for a second active release or simply block the transaction, depending on how the Happiness app is customized.

On the :)$ receiver side, you will see a reward in your :)$ account, with all the necessary information about the transaction. In essence, you receive an unbiased, quantified "thank you" in the form of a :)$ reward that has been consciously transmitted to you. Like money, such a :)$ reward will act as a secondary reinforcer, driving our behavior toward more such actions in the future that provide happiness to others. In addition, once activated, the :)$ in the account of the :)$ receiver has a stable value.

To be clear about the valuation of the :)$, let us briefly reiterate this part: during the twenty-four-hour reflection period, the :)$ is stable; it will not gradually decline to zero during the reflection period. There should be no time pressure when you reflect on your happiness. However, the :)$ will devaluate to zero in a split second if you do not release it by the time twenty-four hours have passed. That means, after you have been alerted by your emotion tracker about a happy-event hitting your brain, you have twenty-four hours to reflect on your happiness *and* release the :)$.[1] So it is more a devaluation deadline than a period of devaluation. Once it reaches the wallet of the happiness giver, the value of the :)$ is stable, as discussed earlier.

Let's run a few tangible case studies to see how our Happiness app would work. These may help to illustrate the impact of the :)$ in real life.

---

1. The critical aspect still to be tested is the time between the alert and the start of active reflection. Imagine you collect your alerts and reflect on them every morning. For happiness-making events that happened just that morning, you have less time to reflect on them and release the :)$ if we stay with the total time window of twenty-four hours before devaluation. But we will figure that out. Perhaps thirty-six hours are needed, in order not to lose too many :)$ to devaluation.

CHAPTER SIXTEEN

:)$ IN REAL-WORLD SITUATIONS

I have spent hundreds of hours in different countries with almost a hundred friends, colleagues, and people I hardly know to discuss real-life examples and how they would change in the presence of a functional Happiness app and the Happiness dollar, or :)$. I tried to get a broad picture across different income and wealth levels and different kinds of expertise. From billionaires to people who have literally no money, from bankers, to artists, to full-time mothers. The youngest person who provided input was five years old, the oldest, eighty-seven.

Of course it is impossible to get a representative sample of the people on our planet. But at the end, I selected seventeen examples from over 150.

CASE 1: MAKING YOURSELF HAPPY

If we make ourselves happy by playing sports, listening to music we love, or going shopping, we would detect this as a normal notification that we have created :)$ by our Happiness app. Most importantly, tagging :)$ to ourselves is not supported by the concept, because we have had our slice of happiness and learning already—that is Commandment Number One. Now, let us jointly reflect for a moment. How often were you *alone* responsible for your happiness? I tell you, there are very few occasions, if you really think about it. If you created a :)$ during a run, forward it to the person who convinced you to start running, or the person who showed you the trail you ran the first time, or the running-shoe company. If you created a :)$ listening to music, forward it to the artist, or your friend who suggested the song to you, or the streaming provider. Just be creative! In almost all cases you can tag a :)$ to someone if you look at it more holistically and over a longer period of time. In the purest sense, you should at least tag and release a created :)$ to your parents. Without their decision to create you, bring you to life, and raise you, you would not be able to enjoy any amount of happiness. Think about it.

What seems unfair to you in the first place is a fundamental scientific concept behind creating happiness: First of all, we are already happy and the information on hand will help us to repeat *our* behavior attached to *our* happiness in the future. Yet making ourselves happy is less sustainable, neurologically, than making other people happy or—and this is the best—being happy together. This has been shown in scientific experiments: brain neuroplasticity in our brain and, therefore, sustainable happiness, are created primarily in social groups. Most importantly, it has been shown that making yourself happy is a prerequisite to making other people happy afterward. Or to use Maslow's words: "without self-esteem you can't reach self-actualization." The good thing is that your happiness tracker provides you with all the information about how to make yourself happy, which is a good basis for creating :)$ or (hopefully) receiving :)$ soon afterward.

Now of course you are free to choose to forward :)$ to anyone, even if the person is not related to the happiness you have created for yourself. Honestly, I don't care. But you should care, actually. Because the person can't relate it to any action, there will be no change in behavior triggered—you just forwarded your :)$ into a dead-end street. So neither you nor the receiver of the :)$ will learn anything. It will not happen often, given how our learning mechanism works, and it will be negligible in the greater scheme of things.

Now of course you could hold two accounts for yourself: one to create the :)$, and one to forward it to. Smart? Not really. Your brain obviously will recognize the fakeness on the receiving end, so no reward will be created for you. If you repeat it (or try to repeat it), you will realize that already the creation of a :)$ will become very difficult. Unconscious happiness is very sensitive to manipulation—very likely it will not even work anymore the second time. Of course you can start taking cocaine, ecstasy, or heroin to push yourself over the Unconscious happiness threshold by maximizing the dopamine, serotonin, and opioid systems. This will work for sure. For two or three times, if you are lucky. After that, you are in the region of addiction, and that means you will not reach the Unconscious happiness threshold needed to create a :)$ anyway. So our system is pretty tightly self-regulated. And you know this anyway, if you are honestly reflecting on your life.

Of course, if we move further toward organized criminality, there might be ideas that could trick the concept. Criminals always find ways . . .

CASE 2: CRIMINALITY

Overall the creation of :)$ in criminality should be rather low. Criminality will likely remain an ROI-focused business (fig. 33, upper left sector. In certain rare cases, like sadism, criminality might create self-induced :)$ for the criminal. But very clearly this would be rejected by the sadist's victim. If a criminal tried to allocate the :)$ to another criminal friend, it would become transparent where the :)$ was created, most likely leading to a higher risk of being caught by the police. Honestly, I don't believe criminals would use the Happiness app. At least I wouldn't recommend it for them. Unless they are in jail and would like to change their lives for the better.

CASE 3: RECREATIONAL DRUGS

An idea that jumps to mind easily is to boost :)$ by taking recreational drugs that massively activate our neural reward systems, such as cocaine (dopamine system), heroin (opioid system), or ecstasy (serotonin system). We would become a :)$-printing machine! Fortunately, the pattern created by such drugs would be easily detectable by the scientific data readout. So we could introduce an upper threshold or pattern-recognition filter into our Happiness app in order to exclude all such overshooting, artificial :)$ creation induced by drugs. However, I would rather not limit the system, as we immediately limit the opportunity to reflect. First, it is totally fine to create :)$ for yourself. But would a person taking cocaine really tag and release the created :)$ to his or her dealer? The moment the cocaine hits you, most likely yes. However, remember, between creation and release there is a mandatory time gap to allow reflection. Therefore, the moment one has to release the cocaine-induced :)$, the drug would not work anymore. Even worse, the moment you can finally consciously release your :)$, the drug user is in the middle of post-drug depression. So would you really release the :)$ to your dealer as a reward? If you would, the happiness rush was really worth it. I predict drug dealers will never receive a single :)$.

CASE 4: ONE-NIGHT STAND

Imagine you are cheating on your partner and you really think you had a great night. The next day, your Happiness app gives you a lot of great data to reflect on. Was it actually as good as you thought it was for you [amount of :)$ created] and for your date [:)$ released to you] Was it pure sexual desire satisfaction, or was there also an amount of nurturant or attachment love? Now that you have to release it, do you really still want to release it as reward? If you do want to immediately release it, you may want to think about the sustainability of your current relationship, or at least about whether you'd better move toward an open relationship model. The other good choice is always to simply not activate your Happiness app when you have a one-night stand. And avoid reflection. And personal progress.

CASE 5: RELATIONSHIP CRISIS

Most likely there will be very few :)$ created in a long-term relationship unless you move up to the level of G-love. This is not a problem at all; instead, it should lead to a good discussion of how to move forward before case four, the one-night stand, comes into play and potentially destroys your relationship. It could well be that the transparency of how happy the other person is in the relationship would lead to issues. What if disproportionate amounts of :)$ are created? Would that lead to jealousy or crisis, or would it just lead to a good discussion, followed by a solution? It's entirely up to you whether or how you use the Happiness app. Again, it is best to do so before case four, the one-night stand, hits both of you.

CASE 6: BULLYING AND DISCRIMINATION

Bullying and discrimination have become central drivers of unhappiness, amplified in recent years by the wide use of social media and global communication. As a positive reinforcer, the :)$ would not be able to influence these behaviors directly. However, the more powerful the :)$ becomes as a positive, secondary reinforcer—through wealth, public recognition, social advantages—the more it would also drive the reduction of bullying and discrimination. A very impressive confirmation of that hypothesis has been observed in the gaming industry. One of the largest online games, with over 100 million players per month, identified the unfair, noncollaborative, and destructive behavior of certain players as a major reason for other fairer players to leave the game and not come back. Once this was identified, the game developers tried to openly flag and discredit unfair players, under the assumption that such negative feedback would reduce unfair play. Interestingly, no real improvement occurred; the game even saw a slight increase in unfair and destructive behavior. However, when they implemented rewards for fair play instead (such as additional weapons, digital coins, or positive characteristics for the avatars), the game developers observed immediate behavior changes. It took only a short time, and most of the unfair players were removed or changed their behavior for the better. These observations fully confirm what we learned earlier: negative conditioning does not really change behavior, but positive conditioning does.

CASE 7: FREEDOM TO NOT BE HAPPY OR NOT ACTIVATE :)$

The easiest way to maintain the freedom of your happiness is just to not use the Happiness app. You would choose to live in a quantitative economic world and a rather qualitative emotional world. That is totally fine because evolution has provided you with all your biological senses to focus on Conscious happiness. It's entirely your choice. Collecting happiness, creating a lot of :)$ but not releasing them to others, is also totally fine. I would assume, though, that you might impair reward learning in other people by not providing feedback, so in the future you would most likely enjoy less happiness provided by others than if you had released your :)$. At least that should be the neurological consequence. If you are a reflective person, you should at least wonder whether you should change your behavior when looking at your happiness performance statistics—:)$ created versus :)$ released. From there, it is entirely your decision.

CASE 8: RECEIVING HAPPINESS THROUGH A PRODUCT WITH A DEEP VALUE CHAIN

Let's take the example of a gravely ill cancer patient who gets cured by a new medication. Who should the patient send the :)$ to? The doctor who selected the new medication? The pharmaceutical company that developed and manufactured the medication? The scientist who had the original idea for the medication ten years ago? Or the family who supported the patient during the difficult period of the disease? Or the nurse who gave her a smile when the chemotherapy was unbearable? Again, it is not possible to give advice about this choice. It remains an independent, free decision by the person who created the :)\$. The good thing is that, in the future, our smartphones very likely will provide us with all relevant information about a certain product and how it was developed and produced. So, before the patient tags and releases the :)\$, the patient would have full transparency about who really contributed to the cure and what the estimated US dollar investments behind each step were. One could also imagine the :)\$ being split and allocated to several parties.

CASE 9: SUSTAINABLE GLOBAL DEVELOPMENTS

Long-term changes associated with potential massive unhappiness in the future, such as global warming or microplastics pollution of the ocean, will be hardly visible for the :)\$ economy in time to induce change. However, certain potential impacts would become transparent in products sold directly to consumers. Imagine how much more quickly certain unsustainable products would be replaced in a world that has the :)\$ as an indicator of happiness: a supermarket that advertises only products that are packaged without plastic would very likely have higher :)\$ creation in their consumers—because their customers' brains are conditioned by the initial message. The :)\$ becomes an amplifier for other impact factors of consumer products. We will go into more details about this aspect in the next chapter.

CASE 10: EDUCATION

The deepest and largest impact the :)\$ would have is on our education system. The entire system would change. Just as we learn when very young that we have to pay money for our food in the supermarkets, and we learn in second grade to calculate with money, we would learn the basics of the :)\$ at a young age. In order to fully understand the concept, we would, early on—even before kindergarten—be educated in how happiness is created. And this education would be much more detailed and systematic than the way we teach children about money today. It is infuriating that the most important element of our lives—happiness—is not explained to us proactively, despite all the knowledge we have about it. Understanding your happiness when you are young guides you to strive for happiness, not blindly for any surrogate, like leveling up in a computer game or getting rich. Knowing how a computer game or a shopping spree influences your functional reward systems puts you in a position to reflect and finally make an educated decision about what you like to spend your time doing. As we move forward in our education—from preschool to school to university—we would systematically learn more about the psychological and neuroscientific fundamentals. Not because our teachers force us to learn about it. No, simply because we have to understand how to live and progress in our **Happiness economy**, which is—fully or partly—built on the :)$. Most importantly, everyone would go through such a basic education, like basic mathematics and basic economics. This would fundamentally change the world from scratch.

CASE 11: CREATING HAPPINESS AT THE EXPENSE OF OTHERS' UNHAPPINESS

There are many examples involving a chain of products, services, or actions in which one or a few participants are very happy while others pay with unhappiness. Energy providers make money using coal power plants at the expense of creating massive air pollution, impacting the health of millions of people and adding to the greenhouse gas emission driving climate change. Food production is made difficult by the very slim economic margins for the farmers. Therefore, chemical fertilizers creating higher yields have emerged, which make some downstream consumers unhappy by polluting their drinking water. The weapons industry produces goods that make its direct customers very happy, while the next-level "customers," or victims, further downstream suffer extreme unhappiness, namely death or severe injury.

In chains in which the consumer is involved at the end, we can anticipate that products that don't create any happiness will slowly but surely be replaced by ones that do. Because there is a clear incentive to replace these products, services, and actions. For weapons, unfortunately, the leverage of the :)$ is likely to be very limited. Weapons are mainly used in war, criminality, national defense, and personal defense. In war very little happiness is created—we are reduced to the lowest levels of the Universal happiness hierarchy, just saving our lives on a daily basis. The :)$ does not function effectively at such low levels of happiness—because only a very small number of :)$ are created, if any. We have highlighted the low impact of :)$ on criminality already in case two above.

These observations are actually pretty frustrating. It is likely the :)$ will have very little impact on the really bad things on our planet, the ones at the lower end of the Universal happiness hierarchy. Intuitively, these are the areas we would hope to change first. However, it is likely that "good old capitalism" is helping us out here. Actually, it has proven to be helpful. In the past 150 to 200 years, the number of wars and people killed by wars and criminality has continuously declined. This strongly correlates with global average GDP growth and globalization of capitalism: it is obviously much better to do business together than to kill each other. This is a straightforward and very positive learning cycle for an organism that is essentially trained to survive first and foremost, like humans. So very likely this trend will continue. Then, as a next step, we hopefully learn—with the help of the :)$—to appreciate that it is even better to be happy together *and* do business together. I strongly hope that our future proves me right . . .

CASE 12: HACKING THE SYSTEM

Of course, people will try to hack the system. Especially if the :)$ is widely accepted and potentially linked to our monetary system or to the success of companies and politicians during elections. I think it would confirm the success of the system if hacking starts—as in all other digital applications one will face the broad challenge of security. Most important is the security of the primary neurological data and the handling of the :)$. Both challenges can be resolved by currently available double encryption technology, with which only the owner can read out the data and the transmitted :)$ can be tracked based on the underlying blockchain. In more dramatic horror scenarios, one can imagine plantations of slaves being stimulated with a drug cocktail producing :)$, which are subsequently released to a criminal. Scientifically, such a scenario seems unlikely because drug-induced :)$ creation leads to rapid neuronal desensitization. In other words, your "plantation" will have a very poor and declining productivity. Ultimately, we will have to leave the resolution to the law enforcement units.

CASE 13: SELF-ACTUALIZATION AS YOUR HIGHEST LEVEL OF NEED SATISFACTION

Neurologically, it is fine to focus only on your own self-actualization; neurologically, it's fine if you are simply not interested in or satisfied by relationships with others. Everyone can be happy on any of the levels. It all depends on our individual satisfaction vis-à-vis our expectations and ambitions. (Happiness equals reality minus expectations.) Thus, nobody should feel discounted when they are happy on any level of the universal hierarchy.

CASE 14: G-LOVE, THE HAPPINESS *PERPETUUM MOBILE*

Love, in particular G-love, might have the power to continuously create :)$ for two people, even up to the point that the receipt of the :)$ reward creates enough stimulus to directly create more :)$. We end up in a happiness *perpetuum mobile*. This is the best situation you can be in. Stay there as long as possible. Just enjoy it together and enjoy all the :)$ you can create.

CASE 15: WE-ACTUALIZATION CREATING HAPPINESS IN LARGE GROUPS

One of the most powerful settings in which to create massive amounts of :)$ are events that make groups of people happy together. Sharing happiness is the most powerful tool for rewarding system activation and neuroplasticity. I assume that the first :)$ billionaires will be DJs, musicians, and charismatic, purpose-driven leaders of religions, countries, and businesses. And after them, the next :)$ billionaires will be anyone who can create happiness for large groups. In addition, companies that sell happiness-creating products and services—such as

Spotify, Adidas, and Apple—will become very rich in :)$ and in dollars. And if we think about it, they all actually deserve it! In addition, event-created :)$ would be distributed among groups of friends. Indeed, if the :)$ would become the leading currency or reward system, people and companies would focus on joint events that create broad and sustainable happiness, such as sports, music, or other cultural, religious, and social events. Given how well we are trained to accumulate dollars these days, one can imagine a joint push to quickly and effectively accumulate :)$. The largest amount of :)$ you can create is on the level of **We-actualization**.

CASE 16: BEING SUSTAINABLY HAPPY WITHOUT A HAPPINESS TRACKER OR A :)$

First of all, the concept presented here is primarily focused on helping reset our own learning systems—if out of balance—and to open an alternative route to our narrow economic metrics that are insufficient to provide broad happiness to many people. If you are happy—on whichever level of the ultimate happiness hierarchy—then just be happy. Our brains are fully equipped to create and enjoy happiness without any help from an app. Of course, if we are very progressive, we could envision a world where :)$ are the only universal currency, eliminating our freedom *not* to be part of the new system. (To be clear, I prefer freedom.) We will have a closer look at that case in one of the next chapters.

CASE 17: BEING ADDICTED TO BALANCED HAPPINESS THAT DRIVES PROGRESS

Just go for it!

CHAPTER SEVENTEEN

WOULD WE EXCHANGE :)$ FOR US$?

What are new key features of the Happiness dollar system, or :)$ system, that we have created? It is the only system that enables us to quantify happiness in a normalized yet unbiased fashion—the happiness that we keep for ourselves and the happiness we give to others. We can now understand our own happiness, and, if we like, we can manage it. We can also track the ways to best provide happiness to others. Thus, we have created a token of appreciation that everyone around us will recognize because it has been generated by the most important reward systems, the ones that drive us all.

In short, a Happiness dollar, or :)$, is a token of appreciation you may receive for providing happiness to others. Being rich in :)$ shows everyone that you are an awesome person, and very likely this will drive you to trigger more happiness for other people, because recognition in turn makes you—as it makes everyone else—happy. In other words, public recognition for a :)$ billionaire will be fundamentally higher than for a dollar billionaire. We have intentionally designed the :)$ as a currency (or at least as a certificate). It will be recognized and processed by our capitalism-trained reward systems like any other currency. The fundamental difference is that the :)$ is priced unconsciously by our neuronal reward system and not by supply and demand in a conscious market for goods and services.

Finally, and really most importantly to me, in happiness, there is no inequality on the molecular level. That means every human being has the same starting material to be and become happy. From this perspective, all the great phrases in the Charter of the United Nations and most countries' constitutions are finally true: we are all the same. I think that is very fair, and such a re-baselining is long overdue.

To be clear, I am not doubting the dramatic inequality in wealth and money. For me it is just a symptom of the larger issue of insufficient happiness. As long as we refocus on what really matters in life—being happy, not (necessarily) rich—the economic inequality will likely correct itself automatically over time.

From the perspective of happiness, being rich is not necessarily a benefit beyond a certain basic level. As we have learned, the very rich are even more depressed than the poor. From the perspective of a poor person (struggling for food), this seems ridiculous and is very difficult to understand. However, once you take a step back and look at the higher-order needs, it becomes clear that our brain can starve for purpose as much as for food.

On an individual level, the misery created by both kinds of insufficient need satisfaction is very similar. The dimension and type of missing neurotransmitters are pretty much identical, even if two people crave a different kind of need satisfaction. The challenge appears only when you compare yourself with others and miss adjusting the perspective. Just because one poor person craves food does not mean that another person having it should be happy. Just because one rich person is afraid about his kids being kidnapped does not mean that a poorer person without this anxiety should be happy. Happiness is entirely individual—you only can feel and judge your own happiness.

Here comes the problem now: when you are poor in dollars, you better go to work to earn some money to feed your family, right? Don't waste your time bringing happiness to others; the :)$ won't feed you.

Is that actually true?

What can I do with a :)$ in my bank account? What can I buy with it? Or can I exchange it for dollars? Or trade it in for something "real," something material? Can I buy ice cream with a :)$? If I can, should I use a :)$ to buy ice cream?

It is mathematically and logically certain that a link can be made between Happiness dollars and US dollars, or between :)$ and US$. It all depends on how we write our :)$ protocol. Once we establish such a link, either directly or indirectly, it will be possible to buy ice cream with your :)$. Or at least exchange a :)$ for dollars and then buy the ice cream, if there is somebody who is interested in exchanging his or her dollars for :)$. There are other options for buying ice cream with a :)$, even in the absence of a link to our economic system; I will get to this later in this chapter. In essence, we can do whatever we want, depending on how radically we apply the :)$ concept. And on how we code the :)$ cryptocurrency protocol.

Let us remember that we have designed the :)$ to universally cover all drivers that are essential for the positive progress of life from a biological and neuroscientific perspective. Therefore, the happiness universe is substantially larger than the economic universe. First and foremost, we have to decide whether we would like to run the :)$ as a system linked to our current dollar-driven economic system or independent from it. Secondly, we have to decide whether we would like to run the :)$ as a certificate that can be traded once to obtain money or other items of value. Or whether we implement it as a true currency in a way very similar to Bitcoin's original design. In that case, we would first create the :)$ by making other people happy, and then we would use it as a token to trade for other items.

To establish a Capitalism of Happiness we have to overcome a lot of hurdles. Our current economic system based on the capitalist idea is so deeply ingrained in our behaviors and memories that it takes a very open mind to challenge the status quo. The underlying objective is to refocus on what drives our progress as living organisms, both individually and as a species: happiness. In order to tackle this objective, there are various options. We can either aspire to keep but expand our current economic system or ultimately push to disrupt and replace it. Let me introduce four options covering pretty much the entire option space we have.

First, we could utilize the :)$ as a kind of impact certificate that provides a vector for governments, consumers, and investors to guide their investments toward more happiness. These certificates can be linked to our current economic system. I call this first application "*happiness-vector certificates*" (fig. 37, lower left quadrant).

FIGURE 37: HAPPINESS APP LINKED TO OR IN PARALLEL TO OUR CURRENT ECONOMIC SYSTEM

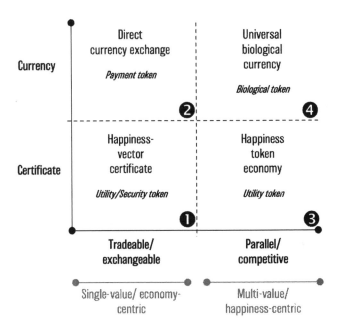

Notes:

❶ Happiness certificates could be connected to and guide taxation, the product/service choices of consumers, and investor decisions.

❷ Temporary or permanent cryptocurrency exchangeable to fiat currency.

❸ Permanent, independent token driving behavior toward more happiness (no exchange to fiat currency).

❹ Permanent, independent, universal currency for every human being on the planet (no exchange to fiat currency), the associated biological token is a novel, yet-to-be-established hybrid version of a utility token (goes beyond digital access to applications or services) and a payment token (goes beyond payment for goods and services) that is based on real biological improvement, such as unconscious happiness.

Second, we could utilize the :)$ as a genuine new cryptocurrency that is exchangeable for US dollars or other fiat currencies. This would create a very strong link to our economic system. Indeed, it would allow everybody to choose what to focus on. We will see later in this chapter that such a real, mathematical link creates a very interesting opportunity for capital growth on the back of happiness growth. We call this second application *direct currency exchange* (fig. 37, upper left quadrant).

Given our deeply ingrained, massive dependency on—yes, even addiction to—consumption and money, there is a serious risk once we link our happiness and economic universes. As with all addictive drugs, there is the risk that our obsession with financial growth will lead to manipulation of our happiness concept in order to just make more money, not more happiness. Such a hostile takeover is a well-known neurological concept called state-dependency. In our case, state-dependency can be avoided if we keep the two systems—economy and happiness—parallel and yet without any link.

Depending on how we design and activate the :)$ system, it is possible, however, that such parallel systems could become competitive. On the one hand, competition is great, because we—as living organisms—love to compete. On the other hand, competition is counterproductive when our economic system still has a huge advantage due to state-dependency. It's like an old heavyweight champion on steroids boxing against a small boy. The fight becomes interesting when the boy is at least grown-up and well trained. That is what we have to consider when establishing a link between the economic system and the happiness system. I will address the risk of state-dependency and some ideas for mitigation in the next chapter.

Third, we could establish a token-based system that drives behavioral change and enables us to enjoy more happiness. We will call this application the *happiness token economy* (fig. 37, lower right quadrant). It can be run entirely parallel to any economic system. Interestingly, this approach has been extremely successful for managing behavioral addictions and drug addictions, such as alcohol, heroin, and cocaine, helping to reinstall functional behavior and long-term abstinence. Actually, it is the most successful approach for reinstalling functional behavior vis-à-vis drug addiction.

Fourth and lastly, I carry on our mind experiment toward a single biological currency. A currency that represents a universal and holistic secondary reinforcer that helps all of us to drive balanced and sustained happiness. And with it our personal progress and the progress of our species. After almost one hundred years running an outdated system, I believe such an update is necessary. We will call this application *universal biological currency* (fig. 37, upper right quadrant). Such a currency would run entirely parallel to our economic system and, because it is much more powerful, would replace it.

It should be noted that the first two applications still hold our monetary system in the center with money being the single value to focus on. There is a theoretical chance that the :)$ becomes the dominant currency but our economic system will continue to drive productivity. In contrast, the last two applications allow a multi-value system that puts our individual happiness as the focus and with it, happiness as a whole.

Let us focus first on applications that would give us a vector to leverage our current economic system toward more happiness. We could use it as a certificate or a currency. Let's start with some ideas of certificates that could help us guide our behavior (fig. 37, lower left quadrant).

CHAPTER EIGHTEEN

HAPPINESS-VECTOR CERTIFICATES

We use the term "vector" here, since any indicator that provides solid and reliable and quantifiable metrics would help to mitigate our economy's sole focus on making money. Indeed, when focusing on happiness, we can even be sure that we will drive repeated revenues, given that our reward system makes us learn and memorize to repeat behavior.

FIGURE 38: HAPPINESS APP: TAX LINK BETWEEN US$ AND :)$

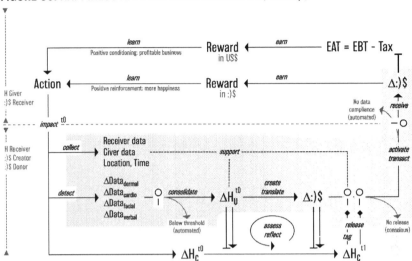

Key: t0: time at start/impact; t1: time after reflection/at release; ΔH_U: Quantitative, Unconscious happiness signal above threshold; $\Delta H_C{}^{t0}$: Conscious happiness before reflection; $\Delta H_C{}^{t1}$: Conscious happiness after reflection; Δ:)$: Created amount of Happiness dollars based on unconscious happiness signal; EAT: Earnings after tax; EBT: Earnings before tax.

Let us apply such happiness-vector certificates to the biggest drivers of economic value: revenues from products/services, financial investments, and taxes. In other words, the certificates could guide our governments to *reduce taxes* for people and companies that provide happiness to society. Or we as consumers could use the certificates to select *happiness-driving products and services* over ones that do not drive happiness. In addition, big investors could use the certificates to *channel investments toward more happiness*. For everyone, the Happiness dollar, or :)$, would provide a reliable metric to show how our actions are channeled and drive financial and happiness growth.

Let's start with *taxes* as a lever for :)$.

The applied tax rate is the biggest negative lever to take earnings away from a business. If we neglect certain special tax constructs for the moment, the tax rates are between 15 and 35 percent, depending on the country or state where you do business. The rate goes up to 40 to 60 percent for the individual tax burden on middle-income and higher-income people, unless you are living in Switzerland or Singapore.

Taxes are justified by most governments in order to have money to provide needed goods and services. The most prominent examples are covering personal safety needs provided by the army, police, fire department, and the health care infrastructure, including general hospitals and public health insurance in some countries. Others provide reliability, freedom, and flexibility through good infrastructure (airports, railways, and roads). In addition, most governments redistribute funds from rich people to poor people through asymmetric tax rates; this is done as a form of a social contract and to provide more material safety for the poorer people.

With respect to the Universal happiness hierarchy, taxes are already a good tool for reallocating happiness—however, taxation mainly acts on the lower levels of the hierarchy. In addition, a large portion of social support to elderly or handicapped people is run by religious organizations. These activities are funded by tithes and other donations, and therefore they are supporting drivers of happiness at the level of interpersonal safety needs.

So through taxes, we already exchange a certain part of the economic value created by individuals and businesses for social equality, and, with it, satisfaction of the lower levels of the Universal happiness hierarchy. However, the biggest limitation of our tax system is that it is perceived negatively by almost everyone, as highly unfair, nontransparent, ineffective, inefficient, and a waste of money for a big central organization instead of a truly useful means of providing well-being for the needy. The main reason why taxes and redistribution systems are so ineffective is the lack of transparency; there is no measure that really indicates what lower-income people need. The only measure we have on hand is their income levels, nothing more. Thus, taxes are the ultimate prototype of negative reinforcement and negative conditioning.

With the transparency we have achieved by examining the created, donated, and received :)$ for each person or business, we could immediately avoid these shortcomings. Looking at the original objective of raising taxes—increase general well-being—we should reward people and businesses that have collected a lot of :)$ over the year, by giving them a lower tax rate on their financial earnings (fig. 38). They have contributed their share to societal happiness already. And the numerical dimension of such a contribution can be quantified by just counting :)$.

In that sense, the :)$ would be used as a kind of certificate for tax breaks. This would have three immediate effects. First, people providing true happiness to society would get relief on their financial income tax—an immediate, substantial reward that should encourage further provision of happiness to others. Given that hands-on activities and physical interaction create substantial :)$, we likely would guide a lot of people to such activities. In all developed countries on this planet, such activities are desperately missing as indicated broadly by dramatically increasing depression numbers due to loneliness.

In addition, using the :)$ as a certificate for tax breaks would provide an immediate upscaling and monetary incentive for the social job sector, which traditionally offers low-salary jobs. Just imagine, nurses in hospitals and retirement homes would earn :)$ from the people they take care of. The :)$ would be created only upon improvement of health or reduction of loneliness, respectively. This would trigger a massive change in how hospitals and retirement homes are run. While the nurses could still be low-salary employees, the quality of service would substantially improve because nurses would be rewarded with :)$. The amount of :)$ created would become a quality label for any hospital and retirement home, attracting more people who would be willing to even pay more dollars. There would be a massive reduction of government cost, due to the reduction of chronic physical and mental illness. By coupling happiness with our economy, you should always get a win-win for everyone participating. The :)$ is the key lever for unleashing such synergistic amplification.

It would further become transparent who is adding the most value to society in terms of happiness. We would also recognize much better who benefits most from the happiness, who is missing out, and even whether there are people who receive happiness and create :)$ but don't release them. Given that information about :)$ is anonymous, we would not violate current data security regulations in obtaining sufficient information to improve our social systems.

Secondly, this approach would orient businesses toward producing goods or services that focus directly or indirectly on providing happiness. Companies could receive :)$ from customers who created and transmitted :)$ to the company after enjoying the company's products. If the products are not triggering happiness, the company would be guided to reflect and explain their contribution to happiness. Alternatively, they could be encouraged to do activities in corporate social responsibility or local social activities driving happiness. This in turn would lead to earned :)$ that could be used as tax deductions if governments would formally make this a part of their tax policy. All of a sudden, corporate social responsibility activities would provide a return on investment for companies—if these activities truly create happiness in people.

Thirdly, the connection of :)$ and dollars through the tax rate leads to an indirect exchange rate for :)$ for dollars and vice versa. If you require more :)$ to reduce your tax rate effectively, it would be economically beneficial to buy :)$ with dollars from other companies or from anyone willing to sell :)$. In other words, you can earn :)$ by providing happiness to others and later exchange your earned :)$ for dollars. All of a sudden, everybody has a choice of whether to focus on return on investment in dollars or on Return on Happiness in :)$. The tax rate becomes the equilibrium factor between the two dimensions and allows the government to moderate between the two forces. Most importantly, such a link would significantly drive acceptance and recognition of true social behaviors that are desperately needed in an aging, increasingly isolated population.

By putting :)$ as the core measure to determine taxation, taxes would—for the first time—become the truly useful levers they were originally intended to be.

At first glance, linking :)$ and dollars through the effective tax rates seems highly compelling, transparent, simple, and likely to be successful. Unfortunately, such a link partly violates a key rule of the :)$ economy. The entire :)$ economy is based exclusively on positive reinforcement. If implemented as a true reduction of today's tax rates, it could perhaps be perceived broadly as positive or neutral. In the long term it would reduce government spending on social jobs and activities as the public and companies would take over. However, in the short term, this would mean a significant reduction of tax revenue for the government. Thus, it's hard to believe that any of the chronically underfunded governments out there would agree to lower their tax rate to reward people who provide happiness. The likely reaction would be to increase the taxes first in order to lower them later by considering the :)$ earnings. From a reinforcement learning perspective, this would be totally detrimental because the :)$ economy would be branded and perceived as an indirect punishment by increasing taxes first ("happiness tax"). A disaster: negative conditioning on all fronts would most likely lead to zero acceptance and adaption rates. Indeed, taxes violate by definition a key rule of the :)$ economy. With the link to taxes, people and businesses who don't want to provide happiness to others are punished by a higher tax rate, which leads to lower return on investment. Punishment does not lead to sustained behavioral change.

In conclusion, I am skeptical whether the :)$ can be successfully introduced as an add-on to taxes. Thanks to our global economy, our well-trained marketing behavior, and our power as consumers, I can imagine a much more powerful lever for the :)$: driving the reputation for companies by providing a real, *relevant impact indicator for products and services.*

Let's anticipate we would just launch the Happiness app to the general public, to consumers like us. We wouldn't care about any mathematical link to dollars by policy makers. If the concept works, it would trigger the creation of a lot of :)$. Some :)$ would be created by activities on the higher levels of the Universal happiness hierarchy. But others would be created by our strong focus on consumption. In other words, a lot of :)$ should be created by simply buying products and services that make us happy.

Initially, we would not be able to release and activate these :)$ because companies whose goods and services trigger our happiness would likely not have :)$ accounts. However, very soon, the companies behind these products would set up their accounts in order to receive :)$. It would be the first and only true closed feedback loop ever received from their customers. It's not "likes" or "dislikes" posted by an anonymous and perhaps manipulated digital crowd. It's also not a market research questionnaire that has been customized and designed for certain answers and therefore lacks all credibility. It's feedback based on true scientific brain data from customers. The immediate next step would be that companies who are leaders in receiving :)$

would publish the amount in their annual report, next to their dollar earnings. It would be the ultimate boost for their credibility and reputation: *"In 2020, our products created REAL happiness worth 1,788,876 :)$ in our consumers!"*

Demonstrating quantitatively that your products provide happiness is the highest value for any consumer company. There is no better advertising campaign for your products. Biologically, you cannot have a better indicator of future repeated product sales—because :)$ indicate healthy and sustained learning and memory.

With this, we have created another indirect but consistent link between return on investment and Return on Happiness (fig. 39).

FIGURE 39: HAPPINESS APP: REPORTING TRANSPARENCY OF US$ AND :)$ EARNINGS

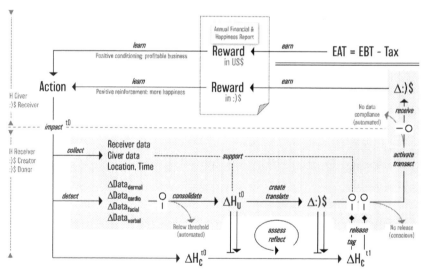

Key: t0: time at start/impact; t1: time after reflection/at release; ΔH_U: Quantitative, Unconscious happiness signal above threshold; ΔH_C^{t0}: Conscious happiness before reflection; ΔH_C^{t1}: Conscious happiness after reflection; Δ:)$: Created amount of Happiness dollars based on Unconscious happiness signal; EAT: Earnings after tax; EBT: Earnings before tax.

Subsequently, other consumer companies would have to also use the Return on Happiness dimension and—most dramatically—the downstream impact on suppliers would be massive. If, from a Return on Happiness perspective, certain behaviors on the part of the suppliers are not acceptable to the buying public, then the companies that sell directly to consumers would be impacted with significantly less :)$ earnings and, thus, less return on investment and Return on Happiness. One could even imagine that future supplier agreements would have a component of :)$ royalties. This would allow the supplier to report their :)$ royalties in their annual report—as a reference for providing happiness to consumers downstream. Reporting of :)$ as the ultimate real value for your products would disrupt entire value chains in a very short time. And rightly so: companies that cannot prove a Return on Happiness with their products should be out of business.

Importantly, the introduction of the :)$ as a reporting item in an "annual financial and happiness report" would also trigger a fundamental change in product development. There would be a much stronger focus on innovative products that trigger measurable stimulation of our happiness reward systems instead of just spending marketing money to consciously and subconsciously influence consumers and make the products addictive. In the development phase, companies would test the effectiveness of their products at creating happiness neurologically. And if the product is not effective enough, it would not be launched, saving marketing and sales investments. The consumer business in general would likely become much more scientific, because a product must earn money *and* must trigger measurable amounts of Unconscious happiness.

The focus on marketing activities would fundamentally change, because our subconscious cannot help creating :)$ in the first place. However, as a repressed form of our consciousness, our subconscious still would play a substantial role when the consumer releases a :)$. Thus, products in a :)$ future would have to provide a real neuroscientific impact on our happiness, *and* the company or brand behind such a product needs enough credibility and recognition to ensure the release of the :)$ to the company.

In the food and beverage industry, all this should drive a fundamental change toward functional products supporting brain health and increasing happiness in the short term, midterm, and long term. Not because a burger would not create :)$ in the first place—indeed, fast food is designed to make you happy immediately. The initial short-term

happiness lasts for only a few hours. Thus, the :)$ would likely be cre-
ated but hardly released after the predefined reflection period (t0-t1)
because the consumer simply feels "overfilled." More dramatically for
the company providing the food, it would become immediately apparent that the product is creating only short-term happiness, not long-
term, which is reflected by a high :)$ creation rate and an insufficient
conscious release rate. Our eating and drinking behavior would likely
substantially improve because there would be a transparent measure
of the Conscious *and* Unconscious happiness potential of a product or
service over a longer period of time.

The obvious limitation is the narrow focus on consumer products and services. So we may get stuck on the lower levels of the needs
hierarchy and still not activate the higher levels. Nevertheless, in the
consumer segment, the introduction of the :)$ would improve prod-
ucts and services fundamentally for more happiness. In the sports,
entertainment, and music industries, joint activities are already now
used frequently to drive brand loyalty. It is primarily seen with joint
running and exercise activities or links between listening to music on
Spotify or Apple and real music events and concerts. The :)$ would
induce a new phase of hyper-growth in these industries with further
improved offerings that truly drive happiness in consumers.

In the entertainment and gaming industry, one would see an even
stronger push toward physical group activities, because you can earn
much more :)$ with them. This would reverse the increasing isolation
and loneliness associated with digital social networks in recent years.
Don't get me wrong, I am not proposing to eliminate digital social networks, tools, and applications. I propose, rather, to expand these tools
from the digital world to real-life, physical group experiences. Because
we know that such group experiences create more :)$ in all partici-
pants. In a sense, our digital tools create an excitement-loaded option
space, while the physical experience with others releases excitement
and triggers the collective creation of :)$.

For example, focusing on just one reward system, testosterone,
applications such as Grindr and Tinder have already proven how well
this can work even with a very primitive concept. Unfortunately, as
with all reward systems that are stimulating only in the short term,
these dating applications have a high risk for behavioral addiction,

which leads to less neuroplasticity in the short term and more depression in the midterm to long term.

In contrast, one of the few end-to-end successful examples of a digital-to-physical crossover is the digital community called Tomorrowland. This digital community is created in preparation for an annual electronic dance music festival in a small Belgian city called Boom. Months in advance, the event organizer creates an online community that prepares the participants for the face-to-face, million-strong festival. Even in the absence of all the recreational drugs likely used during the event, Tomorrowland would probably be one of the biggest creators of :)$ within this community. Burning Man in the US is similar, as are large religious festivals around the world.

Once there are more happy consumers and full transparency regarding consumer happiness, investors will react by refocusing their investments—because impact suddenly will be measurable for any investment fund. And the most relevant impact for us as human beings is sustained happiness.

Thus the :)$ becomes a *quantitative impact indicator for investors.*

Most private, public, and sovereign wealth funds have had defined investment criteria and policies for a very long time. So far, their criteria are qualitative, and they are mainly focused on negative selection instead of positive selection (negative conditioning!). For example, in July 2018, six of the largest sovereign wealth funds— Norway, Abu Dhabi, New Zealand, Saudi Arabia, and Qatar—jointly agreed to a framework to fundamentally consider climate change as one of their investment decision criteria. The according to the One Planet Sovereign Wealth Fund press release, these six funds "reinforce their long-term value creation, improve their risk-return profile and increase long-term portfolio resilience by factoring and integrating climate issues into their decision-making." As you realize from this statement already, it remains unclear what the decision criteria are. It remains opaque whether the funds would invest in companies that merely think about their impact on climate change (while just continuing business as usual) or whether the funds selectively invest in companies that try to actively mitigate climate change. A clear quantitative measure for investment criteria is missing, leaving companies seeking financing rather undirected. In our economic world, leaving such criteria vague is smart. As a fund you have no interest in limiting your freedom to fulfill your first and foremost performance indicator: greater return on investment.

To me, this dichotomy between investors demanding a certain behavior without providing clear metrics for companies to orient toward is a real issue today.

Therefore, in the end, the main focus becomes return on investment metrics for performance again. Because we can measure them so well.

Larry Fink, CEO of BlackRock, one of the largest asset investors worldwide, with $1.7 trillion invested, wrote an open letter recently. He releases such a letter to CEOs once a year. In 2018, the letter requests a fundamental change for companies that want to attract or retain BlackRock as a strategic investor:

> We see many governments failing to prepare for the future [. . .]. As a result, society is increasingly turning to the private sector and asking that companies respond to broader societal challenges. [. . .] Without a sense of purpose, no company, either public or private, can achieve its full potential. It will ultimately lose the license to operate from key stakeholders. [. . .] your company's strategy must articulate a path to achieve financial performance. [. . .] To sustain that performance, however, you must understand the societal impact of your business as well as the ways that broad, structural trends [. . .] affect your potential growth. [. . .] As we enter 2018, BlackRock is eager to participate in discussions about long-term value creation and work to build a better framework for serving all your stakeholders. [. . .] Today, our clients—who are your company's owners—are asking you to demonstrate the leadership and clarity that will drive not only their own investment returns, but also the prosperity and security of their fellow citizens (Fink 2018).

Large investors like BlackRock are desperately looking for a guiding vector toward a higher purpose for their investments and sustainable business growth. On the back of such higher-purpose investments, they anticipate more sustainable growth prospects. A lot of companies reacted to Fink's letter by highlighting the sustainable nature of their products. However, so far nobody has zoomed in on the essential request of Fink's letter: *"to build a better framework for serving all your stakeholders."*

The Universal happiness hierarchy introduced in this book would be the framework of choice to drive the changes Fink is requesting. It's universal to all stakeholders, transparent, objective, and can be measured without manipulation. And it finally provides a new dimension for growth to large institutional investors and asset managers like BlackRock. Happiness is the ultimate driver for repeating a linked behavior, and thus for the progress of mankind.

The mathematical measurement of :)$ would be a welcome element for investors like BlackRock. They obviously will be asked in turn by their investors how they select the companies they invest in for superior impact. By simply asking for transparency in the amount of :)$ received by every company, large investors would have defined inclusion criteria for their investment.

Importantly, Fink is open to investing in activities that focus on "the prosperity and security of your fellow citizens." One way to show that you really care as a company would be to buy :)$ from others who have earned them. The amount of :)$ purchased could also easily be reported in the annual financial and happiness report. These purchased :)$ would indirectly reward people who triggered a lot of happiness by compensating them with dollars. Again, we would have an effective link between dollars and :)$, based on the request of investors to report a certain minimum amount of :)$ on an annual basis (fig. 40).

FIGURE 40: HAPPINESS APP: INFLUENCE BY INVESTORS AND CONSUMERS

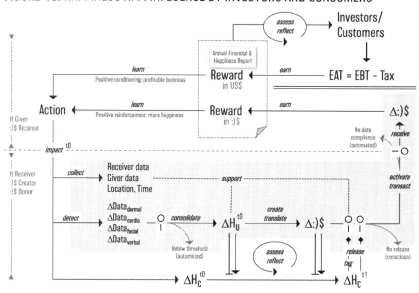

Key: t0: time at start/impact; t1: time after reflection/at release; ΔH_U: Quantitative, unconscious happiness signal above threshold; ΔH_C^{t0}: Conscious happiness before reflection; ΔH_C^{t1}: Conscious happiness after reflection; $\Delta{:})\$$: Created amount of Happiness dollars based on unconscious happiness signal; EAT: Earnings after tax; EBT: Earnings before tax.

This in turn would open up a market between companies—with high dollars and low :)$—and ordinary people—with relatively few dollars and potentially high :)$—leading to a subsequent balance in economic wealth and a positive reputation for companies buying :)$ in return for dollars.

It is this last element in particular that differentiates the lever presented here (investors) from the previous one (consumers and product/service reputation). Whereas the previous lever mainly focuses on products and services, investors may indirectly drive behaviors that just provide happiness to others, by motivating companies to exchange dollars they have earned for :)$ that ordinary people would have created and received based on happiness-making behaviors. As we use blockchain-based cryptocurrency, every company could show whether the :)$ they own were created or exchanged. So either you are a happiness-creating company or you are a socially responsible company—or you are both. Such transparency would provide some highly welcome neutral facts to heated public debates about controversial industries—for example, how much short-term and long-term happiness is really created by the weapons industry.

In the week after Larry Fink's letter, KKR and other large asset management firms released similar statements. Like BlackRock's, these statements also lack a quantitative framework to help companies orient themselves toward new metrics that drive prosperity and security. We have the solution for this dilemma: if the largest ten investors on this planet were to use the Universal happiness hierarchy and the :)$ as the basis to guide their investments, our world's happiness would grow explosively. Exactly what everybody on this planet would like to see.

When looking at the first three levers presented here—taxes, reputation, and investors—we have to recognize that the link between return on investment and Return on Happiness is in the form of a certificate that can be utilized once. In the case of using the effective tax rate as a link, one can use the benefit of :)$ only once. We could imagine that the value of the :)$ is stable for several years, or even forever. However, once utilized as a token, as a certificate for a tax break, it loses its entire value.

Using :)$ as a reporting unit in the company's annual report for reputation purposes is a different story. While this still fulfills the form of a certificate, it would make a lot of sense to show the past four, five, or more years of :)$ earnings development. Even :)$ projections should be possible, given that brain activation can be easily simulated based on historical neurological data, or data extrapolated from products in development. Intriguingly, such projections would be much easier and much more precise than dollar revenue projections in highly uncertain markets. The :)$ would act as a longitudinal certificate indicating the impact value a company has created over a period of time. The same would apply if investors used :)$ as an impact proxy for their investments. Trading such certificates against dollars would therefore be seen as a sale or purchase rather than a currency exchange. In general, that would not be an issue—we would have a mathematical link between Happiness dollars and dollars, or between :)$ and US$.

Having the :)$ as a certificate representing a high value for company reputation and investor recognition is great. And it would be fully sufficient to have a numerical vector for our monetary investments guiding the creation of more happiness. We would have the :)$ be very much in line with other cryptocurrencies that are certificates rather than currencies and are traded at a transparent rate in comparison to the US dollar.

In the world of blockchain and crypto tokens, these happiness certificates would indeed create some additional headaches for finance regulators. We would use the blockchain component only to provide personal data security and consensus. There is no intention to make money with it, but rather to provide guidance on which economic investments have the most impact on happiness.

In the moment when we create a market that allows trading of :)$ to other currencies, we move toward a utility token that provides access to a community of people who create and share happiness. As the :)$ are in essence created by our brains and not by computational calculation, they cannot be used in a pre-sale or pre-financing for a company—in line with the definition of utility tokens. However, if we artificially pre-mint a :)$ for financing purposes, we move the :)$ toward a security token that can be traded only on certified trading platforms. Such a limitation for free trading would defeat the purpose of the :)$. Thus, the :)$ in our three options above can only work as a utility token or not as a token at all. We should never use the :)$ for financing purposes. Doing so would undermine the underlying purpose of the :)$: Our brains unconsciously mine and mint a :)$ upon receiving real happiness. We cannot just create one by consciously applying computational power.

Now . . . could we take this one step further? Could we define the :)$ as a full-fledged, fully functional new cryptocurrency that represents happiness as its core value—a currency that is the numerical unit representing gross global happiness as a novel measure of progress on this planet?

Or a simpler question: What would we have to do to finally buy an ice cream cone with a :)$, just as we can already do with a Bitcoin in certain shops? And more importantly: Would it actually be wise to do this?

CHAPTER NINETEEN

DIRECT CURRENCY EXCHANGE

Let us break the question down into two parts. First, could we technically establish the Happiness dollar, or :)$, as a currency? Secondly, *should* we establish the :)$ as a currency? While I will address the first part of the question now, I have reserved the entire next chapter to answer the second part.

There's an easy answer to part one: yes, we can establish the :)$ as a currency. Bitcoin has shown us it is possible. What differentiates :)$ from Bitcoin is the mining process, or what it takes to "mint" or create a Bitcoin. Bitcoin mining is mathematically defined by the Bitcoin protocol. With that protocol and its rules, mining can be executed on basically any computer. The concept behind the :)$ is very similar. As with the Bitcoin protocol, the underlying neuroscientific "protocol" is identical in everyone's brain. The key difference is that :)$ mining happens not in a computer but in our brains when we produce neurological signals that are captured by an emotion tracker device, which—based on a defined mathematical protocol—translates those signals into :)$. But pulling off this process is much more complex than mining a Bitcoin, isn't it?

Well . . . it depends.

Certified medical devices are crucial tools in health care today. They independently decide to let your heart beat in a healthy rhythm. Or give you an electric shock to make your heart beat again or sustainably control your Parkinson's tremors. Or they precisely tell you your blood sugar in order to adjust your insulin levels. All these devices work universally in patients. Some need a step to normalize or calibrate an individual baseline.

However, as a crucial step they require certification of the production and the precision of the product. That means, when these devices become critical for medical diagnosis and life, such certification has to be provided by an official governmental body like the Food and Drug Administration (FDA) in the United States. For other nonmedical devices, the manufacturer itself provides certificates as a means of product control, accuracy, and liability. Our emotion tracker would need such a certification for sure. In addition, our emotion tracker has to be enabled to communicate with a blockchain-based cryptocurrency: we need consensus between our emotion tracker and the token we mint. Thus we require a chip that individualizes the emotion tracker, so we get the first input for the blockchain from the device. Such chips already exist today, in digital cameras, for example.

Thus, the front end, our emotion tracker, should not be an issue. However, we indeed have a few fundamental questions that theoretically are clear, but still lack experimental proof.

First of all, we do not know how much each individual reward system contributes to the build-out of neuroplasticity, the key biochemical hardware for sustained happiness. It is highly likely that we need a combination of all reward systems being active. But we do not know yet what the "right" balance is and whether such a balance is individually different. While we intuitively tend to believe that we should have substantial individual differences (because we wrongly compare Conscious happiness levels between people), it is rather likely that we'll see few differences between individual *Unconscious happiness* levels and triggers, given that the molecular basis is identical and the link to positive emotions is highly evolutionarily conserved.

To me, this is one of the most exciting experiments to execute. Imagine if the initial signals really are confirmed to be identical, as the molecular and evolutionary foundations suggest? It would finally mean that we are all starting from the same level to be happy and to drive our progress. I would love that. But let us wait until we see the outcome of that experiment. I am sure we will be surprised either way. No doubt, we will have to do a set of experiments to understand these questions better.

Secondly, we do not have any solid scientific data that provide a connection between the Unconscious happiness data we want to measure in the brain and the Conscious happiness that we actually experience. Our concept is based on the assumption that the Unconscious happiness levels detected and measured by the emotion tracker will be used—upon reflection—as behavioral guidance to drive our Conscious happiness, the ultimate target for all of us. The connection is theoretically certain, but experimentally we have no evidence. Thus, we would have to compile a set of experiments that link hard-core neuroscience experiments (like measuring neurotransmitter levels in your brain) with reward system surrogate data (figs. 26, 27) and structured questionnaires addressing Conscious happiness. To my knowledge, nobody has ever even tried such an experiment. The good thing is that substantial work has been done on connecting positive emotions—the ultimate output of happiness—with the underlying reward systems, so we just have to fill in the gaps. Whether we really have to drill down to the molecular level by measuring neurotransmitters in the brain remains to be seen. Very likely this will not be necessary.

Thirdly, we currently have very limited experimental insight into how the short-term happiness primarily detected by our emotion tracker will translate into long-term happiness. If we set it up wrongly, it might well drive addiction in a similar way to other digital applications and games that focus on short-term dopamine satisfaction. We know today that such addictive behaviors are not providing long-term happiness and are detrimental to the build-up of neuroplasticity.

In contrast, based on our existing scientific knowledge, we can be sure that balanced and reflected short-term happiness will drive sustained neuroplasticity and, as such, enables long-term happiness. On that end, the molecular level is totally aligned with the philosophical level—neuroscience corroborates Aristotle. As in any addiction, over-stimulation leads to an unsustainable peak of happiness that leads to a decline in neuroplasticity immediately. As such, addictive behavior should very quickly lead to a reduced output of the rewarding mole-cules our emotion tracker measures indirectly—because the number of interactions decline in line with a decrease in neuroplasticity. Thus, behaviors that are short term oriented only—nonreflected, nonbal-anced—will quickly lead to rapidly declining :)$ signals. Thus, repeti-tion of such nonbalanced activities should be immediately recognized by a declining output of :)$. In addition, our ambition is that the emo-tion tracker will provide sufficient insights into the pattern of reward systems involved and the respective level of overstimulation. So, theo-retically and experimentally, we are very likely already fine.

One key influencing factor we should truly reflect upon: banking regulation. There are two ways to consider regulation: engage very early on with regulators (because they have to understand in all detail what you are planning to do) or just ignore them. Observe what has happened to the crypto-token world in the past year—Bitcoin started as a democratic, revolutionary, anonymous novel currency and has meanwhile reached deep engagement with the finance world, money launderers, and tax regulators.

I personally believe that if we want to establish :)$ as an alternative vector currency for our economic system, we have to cooperate early on with all regulatory bodies. Because we intend to "mint" a currency based on our brain activity. So it should be in our own interest to make sure that the theory is right, robust, and rock-solid.

First, because we started out to create a reliable emotion tracker that drives reflection and creates real happiness—and not an easy way to "print" money. We simply cannot fail on providing the best possible device to guide our happiness. Secondly, because we have to make sure that we get an approved link to the financial system that is controlled by banks and financial regulators. Obviously, they will have some questions on the robustness of our theory and our :)$ protocol and in particular the certification process of our emotion tracker. As finan-cial regulators normally are not top-tier neuroscientists—and vice versa—we can expect some challenges in explaining our :)$ and getting endorsement for it. Thus, we will have to prepare a set of experiments that prove the theory in practice. The good thing is that we can do that rather easily in test groups once we have our device and use some smart learning systems to help us to understand the data we collect. So that challenge should also be resolvable.

In conclusion, I believe that we would be able to create the :)$ as a full-fledged cryptocurrency. There are some technical hurdles and pending scientific questions. However, by combining the existing knowledge around neuroplasticity, medical device certification, and cryptocurrency protocols, the outcome is feasible.

Okay, we are confident that we could get an awesome, robust, scientifically grounded emotion tracker on its feet. So let us start creating and trading our novel happiness currency (fig. 41).

In the world of cryptocurrencies, a lot of new tokens are handled entirely like currencies with different utilities attached via the associated protocols. The creation of virtual markets and trading platforms meanwhile serve a huge crowd of investors exchanging cryptocurrencies into fiat currencies and vice versa in real time. Our underlying economic system has created these marketplaces because trading is possible for everything as long as there is supply and demand, a convincing business case, a speculation goal, or just a promise behind a trade.

FIGURE 41: HAPPINESS APP: EXCHANGE RATE BETWEEN US$ AND :)$

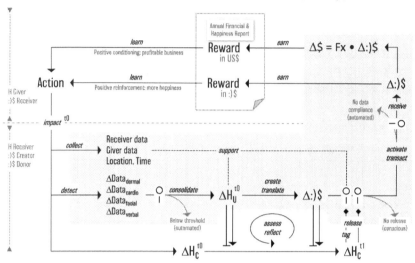

Key: t0: time at start/impact; t1: time after reflection/at release; ΔH_U: Quantitative, Unconscious happiness signal above threshold; ΔH_C^{t0}: Conscious happiness before reflection; ΔH_C^{t1}: Conscious happiness after reflection; Δ:)$: Created amount of Happiness dollars based on Unconscious happiness signal; Fx: currency exchange rate US$/:)$.

The leading example is the Bitcoin itself. In a first step, Bitcoins are created or "mined" by a complex mathematical calculation activity followed by an intense, decentralized validation process. Once created and activated, Bitcoin acts as a normal currency with all the classical features, such as currency exchange transactions on a digital market platform. Several hundred thousand shops now allow consumers to pay for their products or services with Bitcoin.

There is no backing behind it by a country economy or commodity. It is just based on a transparent set of definitions that is perceived worthwhile to invest in or not. First of all, there are all the benefits of cryptocurrencies over fiat currencies, which we discussed in Chapter Twelve. In addition, the most relevant investment argument of the Bitcoin is the transparency of the total number of Bitcoins available in the coming years based on a terminal cap on the total amount and a defined speed and reward for the "mining" of new Bitcoins. These features limit the inflation for Bitcoins to a very low rate at full transparency and certainty for the investors. This is one key reason why some investors exchange dollars into Bitcoins: a hedge against uncertain fiat currency inflation.

As introduced in Chapter Twelve, we have designed the :)$ on the same concept: :)$ are created by a defined molecular signal in the brain and subsequent signal processing. Once released and activated by our conscious transaction to others, it can be used as a cryptocurrency based on the associated blockchain information.

From the perspective of an investor, there are three value propositions for investing in :)$:

The first value proposition is based on the value predictability, impressive value stability, and very limited influence on value manipulation given that we create the value based on unconscious, unbiased scientific data. In contrast to other currencies and investment vehicles, this is unique. We have defined a :)$ as a common measure of a portion of happiness. Once created, such a :)$ is numerically identical for every person. The reason for this identity is the scientific evidence that our neural reward systems are highly identical on a molecular level.

Indeed, scientifically we have to anticipate certain variabilities in response strength and rates. Such variabilities would be driven by epigenetic, post-translational modifications or modifications on an intercellular level. Such modifications are primarily relevant to fine-tune neurological responses and can be different between people. However, for the cryptocurrency definition of the :)$, these changes should be either negligible or can be resolved with a simple normalization, meaning that we individualize the start point for each person to have everyone jump off from the same zero line. In any case, any investor can be sure that a :)$ is numerically identical for every person involved in the currency. Regarding value stability over time, the :)$ protocol is clear: if you don't activate it by rewarding others within twenty-four hours, it devalues completely upon reaching the twenty-four-hour deadline. This mechanism is roughly in line with your neurological happiness levels: if you don't realize (because of conscious suppression) or reflect on your happiness, it will not be well memorized. In addition, if you don't actively work on your happiness, you will not have much to memorize either.

Translated into financial terms, this means it has an extremely high inflation rate: devaluation to zero after twenty-four hours. On the other hand, if you activate the :)$ as a reward to others by transacting it, the value is stable on the side of the receiver forever. This also makes logical and neurological sense, as with any trophy; any reward maintains its value pretty much through reflection and repeated memory, and indeed, can even be enhanced sometimes. These features provide an investor with a scientific and technological certainty of stability across the planet. An activated :)$ will therefore be very stable, as it would be universally accepted.

Now what happens to the :)$ value once activated and transmitted? Neuroscientifically, all experts agreed that you can retain a stable conscious emotional state from a reward over time, depending on how important the memory is and how often you recall it. So there should be no inflation on a :)$. Interestingly, all financial experts assessing the concept were all in favor of having such a systematic inflation rate on the :)$. Their consistent recommendation was to have a transparent, small, but entirely stable inflation rate per design in the :)$ protocol. In their perspective, such an inflation would incentivize people to provide happiness, create :)$, and release them today rather than in the future. The same would apply for exchanging or investing :)$ [if that becomes possible]. The benefits from a financial investor perspective are obvious: we would apply our learned knowledge from other currencies and would provide full transparency and security on the stability of the :)$ cryptocurrency. I think both perspectives are correct in a sense. Nevertheless, we will continue with the neuroscientific idea of having zero inflation rate on a :)$. The good thing is that we can adapt this in the Happiness Dollar protocol underlying the :)$ if we like and learn more in the future.

The second value proposition is based on the promise that a :)$ represents the ultimate token of appreciation and recognition and is an indicator of the progress of life in the future. For purely ROI-focused investors, this might not be enough to invest, so the third value proposition, coming up next, should change their minds. However, for most impact investors, the promise to participate in the ultimate movement driving progress for mankind is definitely compelling. That is why we have defined the :)$ as the ultimate currency of growth and an objective representation of happiness. There is no limit for :)$ creation, and there should not be any cap for the total amount of happiness we can create. In that sense, like the dollar is the unit measuring growth of gross domestic product and gross global product for our economic progress, the :)$ would be the unit measuring gross global happiness, the ultimate performance indicator for us as humans. Using block-chain-based technology for the :)$ will allow us to have digital identity, continuity, and history for every single :)$ created. Early supporters and big supporters will be identified easily—if they choose to be identified [because :)$ are anonymous in the first place]. As :)$ will be the only unbiased quantitative measure on hand, I believe it will be very difficult for any company, any investor, any politician to ignore the power of knowing how many people you—as a person or organization or government—made happy over time. And if you didn't create it directly, at least you can demonstrate how much support you give to the happiness concept by buying :)$ on the secondary market. In our world of global communication, the motivation for ordinary people to use the :)$ should be enormous, because we have designed the system for optimal, sustained learning and memory—our shared evolutionary foundation.

I would like to highlight here again that the vast majority of happiness is created at the interface where people interact positively with each other. Three reward systems have been evolutionarily selected to reward us for activities that are associated with belonging and love: the oxytocin system, the cannabinoid system, and the opioid system. In contrast, products and services—the foundation of today's economy—stimulate only two of the six reward systems, dopamine and serotonin. Not even as a surrogate can they stimulate the remaining ones. Thus products and services create only a minor portion of our happiness. Indeed, with the ongoing satisfaction of the basic physiological and safety needs, most products and services do not contribute any happiness anymore.

The huge growth opportunity for the :)$ lies in activities that are not even part of our economy today. An unlimited growth opportunity through the creation of new Unconscious happiness between people that translates into :)$. Just as productivity raises our gross domestic product (GDP) and stabilizes our fiat currencies, the increase in gross global happiness justifies the increase in :)$ as a reflection of our progress. Thus, the stimulation of our brain by :)$ is several orders of magnitude bigger than its stimulation by dollars. This leads to a self-amplifying positive reinforcement loop: the more :)$ are created and released, the more the entire neural reward system is stimulated—that is, the more we will focus on providing happiness to others. Creation of :)$ becomes a self-fulfilling prophecy, a self-accelerating system for creating more happiness.

Additionally, in contrast to our product and service economy, the creation of happiness by actions is not limited by the marginal cost of labor and raw materials. It is limited only by our biological energy and our motivation to deploy it for happiness. The good thing about using a learning organism for such a task is that evolution has primed us for optimal energy utilization over millions of years—and it has added a motivation system to nudge us in the right direction: the learning triangle of life (fig. 4). In essence, we are already running on the ultimate low-cost production system for happiness, thanks to evolution.

Thus, with the introduction of the :)$, we reboot our brain to strive for the better reward: being happy and giving happiness to other people, instead of becoming richer by ourselves, perhaps even at the cost of other people's happiness. In other words, if you decide to invest in :)$, you invest in and drive gross global happiness, and you will be transparently recognized for it.

Just imagine having a bank account that shows you your money savings and another account that shows how many people you've made happy. Imagine one day *Forbes* magazine publishing the Forbes 100 ranking measured in :)$. I am sure they would do that very quickly once the data is available. And everyone will immediately compete to become the first :)$ billionaire. Thanks to evolution—we all love to compete, remember?

I fully understand that at the moment it seems difficult to believe that the :)$ could evolve into the ultimate secondary reinforcer for recognition, true progress, and We-growth. The good thing is that becoming a :)$ billionaire would mean you created enough happiness value for others that they were willing to say "thank you" by forwarding you a :)$. It does not mean you have made money for yourself. Right now, this is just a promise, like the Bitcoin protocol was a few years ago, and like the first US dollar bills were more than a hundred years ago. The :)$ economy is a promise for growth based on the biological foundations that have driven us toward progress for millions of years. I think that's why it is the ultimate promise, the ultimate investment rationale, actually.

The third value proposition in favor of the :)$ targets our ROI-driven financial investors and is derived from the different importance of money and happiness when moving along the Universal happiness hierarchy from lower to higher levels. We go into more detail about this valuation difference shortly (fig. 42). In accordance with the design of our neurological system, happiness is equally important across all need levels: a :)$ is minted equally whenever an individual need is satisfied. The need defines the price. That could be when we get water to drink after eighteen hours in the desert, or when we receive a Nobel Prize after long years of laboring in obscurity. In contrast, money is critically important on only a few levels—the basic ones—and it is not dependent on our need stage: the price for water is identical for anyone, independent of our thirst level. This need discrepancy creates a dramatic arbitrage opportunity, in both directions, between people on different need levels that can synergistically benefit from each other.

Imagine a group of people who are in a very good mood sitting in a restaurant having fun together. Unfortunately, they are still very hungry and have no money left to buy another meal. At the table nearby, Sarah is sitting alone and sad. Her table is still loaded with food because she has been left behind by friends, who forgot her birthday party. All these people, Sarah and the other group, are likely to be similarly depressed, though for entirely different reasons. The hungry people are missing the satisfaction of a basic need (food) and are craving it (and the associated dopamine reward upon satisfaction). Sarah is missing the satisfaction of her belonging and self-esteem needs (friends celebrating her) and is craving it (and the associated cannabinoid and serotonin reward upon satisfaction).

Sarah holds the key for the hungry people's satisfaction, and the hungry people hold the key to satisfy Sarah's belonging and self-esteem needs. So I am sure after a while the two groups will mingle and have an awesome evening together. Importantly, the dimension of happiness created will likely be similar for all these people even though their satisfaction is associated with different reward systems. They would spend the whole evening creating even more happiness for everyone and likely even spreading this happiness beyond their group. Thanks to the reward systems that are interpersonally triggered, happiness is truly contagious. The hungry group will enjoy a lot of upside once the basic need is satisfied, and the other, higher reward systems will chime in for Sarah thanks to the collective experience. In this thought experiment, the physical proximity and obviousness of the dissatisfaction in the restaurant enables the exchange. In our real world, this is hardly possible, of course, because we miss a connector. Thus, the Happiness app is designed to be the digital connector to match people's complementary needs.

It is therefore of utmost importance to assess the value of :)$ not in isolation, but rather in the context of the value of other classical fiat currencies, such as the US dollar. It's not the value of the :)$ that changes across different need levels. It is actually the value of the classical fiat currencies that changes. Thus, we have to look at the relative value between :)$ and dollars as an indicator. Fortunately, that is also the parameter any currency trader studies when deciding on investments.

Therefore, let us briefly recap what the need levels are where the economic rules fully apply (fig. 24). On the material safety and interpersonal safety level, monetary wealth and happiness correlate nicely. However, monetary wealth becomes less and less important for happiness on the higher levels. The dominance of our current economic system started after World War II, when the fundamental need for build-up was a perfect ground to strive for and provided immediate beneficial impact for a very broad group of people—the people who invested and helped to rebuild (mainly the US) and the people who benefited by the build-up (mainly Europe).

Once we stepped up the hierarchy ladder, we realized that our current economic system is difficult to control and has no means of self-control. And, most importantly, it does not drive our well-being and happiness—but just the accumulation of money and consumption that ultimately leads to depression when we under-stimulate other reward systems.

For example, a single :)$ can be created in connection with many different magnitudes of financial transaction. One dollar could feed someone hungry, or $100,000 could buy a Porsche for someone who has been dreaming of it for thirty years, or $250 million to purchase a yacht to make a multi-billionaire happy. On the highest levels—self-actualization, G-love, and We-actualization—the dollar has lost all its value. You would never sell your loved ones, just as you would never sell your dreams, and no group of people with a passionate goal would quit just for money.

As a consequence, the key investment hypothesis is that, beyond a certain level of monetary wealth, recognition of the ability to make other people happy will be much more valuable than just adding more monetary wealth. In other words, while the :)$ value is very stable and predictable, the dollar value decreases dramatically for an individual trying to satisfy higher-level needs. In a world that is guided only by economic rules, we can be sure that—neuroscientifically and psychologically—we are stuck on the lower levels of the need hierarchy. In case we believe that the world strives for more reward, more happiness in the midterm and long term—which is the biological driver for all living organisms—we can be sure that the dollar value will decrease versus the :)$ from here. Actually, the decrease will be extreme.

Now let us do the thought experiment in detail: say we launch the :)$ as a new cryptocurrency, based on these investment rationales. Would anyone invest? Should we all invest?

By definition, very similar to Bitcoin, we can obtain :)$ in two ways: either creating (mining) it or exchanging it. Creation is primarily achieved by behaviors and actions that provide happiness to other people and subsequent transactions of the :)$ in turn. Alternatively, creation of happiness can be achieved by products and services we develop, manufacture, and sell.

If we want to assess the link between our dollar economy and an orthogonal, novel :)$ economy, we can do that only on the basis of products and services, since we do not have to pay dollars for ordinary, nonmonetized behaviors and actions. Our current economy does not cover such actions—if we pay for it, we effectively convert a behavior or action into a service. Therefore, we will focus first of all on two ways to earn :)$: one, triggering their creation in other people who release them to us after buying our happiness-making products and services, and two, simply exchanging existing :)$ for dollars (fig. 42). We will keep all other sources of creating :)$ as a pure upside right now.

Figure 42A indicates on the y-axis the ratio for the exchange between :)$ and dollars and, on the x-axis, the discrete levels of the Universal happiness hierarchy. The data used here is indicative of and based on our scientific rationale introduced earlier.

FIGURE 42: VALUE CHANGES OF US$ AND :)$ ALONG THE UNIVERSAL HAPPINESS HIERARCHY

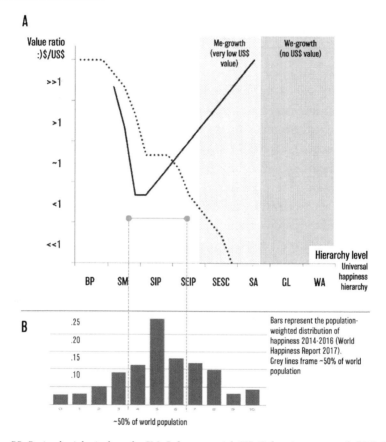

Key: BP: Basic physiological needs; SM: Safety, material; SIP: Safety, interpersonal; SEIP: Self-esteem, interpersonal; SESC: Self-esteem, self-confirmed; SA: Self-actualization; GL: G-love; WA: We-actualization.

Let us look at the dotted line curve first (fig. 42A, dotted line). How expensive would it be to create :)$ by investing financially in products and services that drive happiness? On the lower levels of the hierarchy, very little money is required to create a massive load of happiness. Because these are basic physiological needs—such as food, water, basic health, and shelter—that are very cheap to fulfill but have a massive return in :)$. These products cost little in dollars but create massive :)$ if you are cold, starving, or close to dying of thirst.

When moving up and to the right along the x-y graph in figure 42A, the amount of :)$ for a step-up stays the same. However, creating happiness becomes more expensive in dollars for each created :)$. For example, to provide housing, high-end medical support, and social support on a broader basis becomes more and more expensive. Take health care on a national level: providing it takes almost 20 percent of the GDP in the United States today, a huge amount of money to help sick people and restore their happiness.

Further to the right on the graph in figure 42A, increasing your happiness on the level of self-esteem becomes even more expensive in dollars. For example, we have to pay millions to CEOs to provide them with the necessary self-esteem to function. In addition, even presents that are very expensive in terms of dollars, such as cars, yachts, and jewelry, do not make rich people happy long-term—at least not sustainably. Therefore the ratio between :)$ and dollars falls further when we reach the end of the self-esteem level.

At the far right end of the dotted line curve in figure 42A, it becomes impossible to create :)$ by spending even an insane number of dollars. The area where the dollar can create happiness ends because the dollar is the wrong token for triggering satisfaction at the higher levels of the need hierarchy and in the three higher reward systems. Moving forward toward and into the We-growth area (self-actualization, G-love, We-actualization), we cannot create any more happiness through dollars. As the Beatles famously put it, "Money can't buy me love." Again, no amount of money could entice us to give up the people we really "G-love." Or the other way around: if we ever consider giving up our partner or family for a better job that ensures us with a higher salary, we are clearly on the D-love level, not the G-love level. We are looking for interpersonal safety and interpersonal self-esteem rather than We-growth. Therefore, the dotted line runs against a mathematical limit at the border between self-esteem and self-actualization. Remember Maslow: "Rich people cannot reach the level of self-actualization."

Next, let's look at the solid line curve (fig. 42A). The solid line reflects the hypothetical exchange rate between existing :)$ and dollars. On the level of physiological needs, there is likely no such exchange rate. On that level, people are struggling for their lives, so happiness is very limited, and, in the greater scheme of things, there are likely not sufficient :)$ created. The only focus is on surviving the next few minutes, perhaps hours. In other words, there are simply no existing :)$ that you can buy or exchange for dollars. In addition, people need water, food, and shelter—the most critical primary reinforcers—not money. Therefore, we anticipate that no fluid market for our two currencies would exist on the lowest need levels. Only after our basic physiological needs are satisfied do we have a baseline of happiness; eventually people will have created and activated some :)$ that they are willing to exchange and trade.

From there onward, the ratio between :)$ and dollars falls rapidly, because classical capitalistic wealth creation begins. Satisfaction of material safety needs and interpersonal safety needs drives happiness, and people would be willing to trade some of their :)$ in exchange for dollars for further consumption. In other words, it will be hard to convince a car dealer to give you a car as a present just because you ask very nicely and make him happy. The minimal turning point of the Happiness dollar/monetary dollar exchange rate curve is reached on the hierarchy level of material and interpersonal safety—the center of capitalism. When we move further up the hierarchy, holding more :)$ as a reward token becomes increasingly important for recognition. Therefore, the Happiness dollar/monetary dollar exchange rate should continuously rise. A second key driver for the increase in the Happiness dollar/monetary dollar exchange rate is the reduced importance of economic wealth—counted in dollars—the closer you get to self-actualization. We see the same effect recognized with the :)$-creation curve (dotted line)—once economic wealth is perceived as not important anymore for happiness, the Happiness dollar/monetary dollar exchange rate moves toward infinity. On that level, nobody would readily exchange a :)$ into a dollar. The :)$ substitutes for any other recognition system on that high level of the Universal happiness hierarchy.

To understand where our world population currently stands vis-à-vis the dotted line and the solid one, we have to find a data source that tells us the average position of the world population on the Universal happiness hierarchy. Such data is not available. However, when we overlay the happiness distribution from the latest World Happiness Report with the Universal happiness hierarchy levels, we can observe an interesting correlation. In essence, the key happiness drivers examined by World Happiness Report parallel the Universal happiness hierarchy from the lowest levels up to self-actualization. Essentially, the vast majority of people have met their material and interpersonal safety needs and their interpersonal self-esteem needs (fig. 42B). Remarkably, at these levels, the projected exchange rate between :)$ and dollars is close to its minimum. Given that our current economy works most effectively at these levels, it is no surprise that our world population on average is capped on that happiness hierarchy level.

One thing is for sure: the exchange rate between :)$ and dollars is at an all-time low! Actually, this is a clear recommendation to invest in :)$ if they were available.

However, to make a solid decision about whether we should exchange dollars for :)$ today, let's explore a few future scenarios first.

If we believe there will be an *increase in world happiness* (to the right on the x-axis), we should definitely exchange dollars for :)$ today because it seems to be at an all-time low for half the people on this planet.

If we believe there will be *stagnation of world happiness* (everything staying as it is on average), we should definitely not exchange dollars for :)$, because the exchange rate between :)$ and dollars will likely stay where it is, favoring the dollar. However, we definitely should invest our surplus dollars into areas of the globe where there is a lower level of happiness, where we potentially can find value by creating new :)$. With this move, we would simply switch to the dotted line on our diagram and focus on the upper left in order to address unsatisfied basic physiological and safety needs wherever we find them. If :)$ are then properly created and released, such an investment should provide us with a large amount of newly created :)$ right away and for very few dollars invested.

Interestingly, when we anticipate a dramatic global *decline in happiness* (a move to the left on the x-axis in figure 42A), the data in the graph also suggest exchanging dollars for :)$. However, in a time of total global collapse, the focus would mainly be on the basic physiological and safety needs; I am not sure whether happiness would still play a big role in such a crisis situation and whether one would be sufficiently recognized as someone who exchanges :)$. So I would not recommend exchanging dollars for :)$. And if we anticipate a more diversely distributed local decline, I still would recommend not exchanging but rather investing your dollars in the lower-level happiness pockets on the left side of the graph in order to create happiness and therefore new :)$ for yourself.

In other words, to the left of the intersection between the solid and dotted lines, it is much better to invest your dollars to create or "mine" :)$ instead of exchanging currencies. In contrast, to the right of the intersection, it seems that exchanging your dollars is a better value as you get close to the mathematical limit at the border of self-actualization.

No matter which future scenario we anticipate, the major potential for creating :)$ would be in areas that are very low on the Universal happiness hierarchy. That means wherever misery exists, there is a potential "gold mine" for creating and activating :)$, just by acting to alleviate misery. Every famine or natural disaster would be a potential abundance of :)$. With the :)$ linking individual learning triangles (fig. 34), we have installed an *integrated arbitrage* mechanism and—even more importantly—a happiness *perpetuum mobile*: happiness is missing on both ends of the hierarchy. But both ends working together can make each other whole. At one end, basic physiological and safety needs are not met but can be satisfied with dollars. At the other end, needs for self-actualization and We-actualization are not met, but they could be satisfied with :)$.

Thus, for rich people who are not yet self-actualized, the easiest way to make :)$ is in areas with a lot of misery; in alleviating the misery, this rich person gets :)$ as a reward. But it is necessary to actually go to the area, help people, and make them happy. The interpersonal connection is key to activating the starving higher reward systems. A donation of money will not be sufficient; you have to be active on the ground. Otherwise you would likely not receive the created :)$ from the poor people whose basic physiological and safety needs have just been satisfied. Connected via the Happiness app, both groups would benefit from each other: the poor by a substantial increase in happiness through satisfaction of basic and safety needs, and the rich by substantial, transparent—and, if they prefer, even public—recognition, numerically represented by obtained :)$. The latter can be a core driver toward self-esteem and even self-actualization. The key to making it work is the personal connection between the two groups. This is not new at all. We have known this for a very long time: development aid works well if people involve themselves with money and passion. The happiness arbitrage should hopefully lead to more equality across the economic and happiness metrics. Once the biggest inequalities have been eliminated, we would jointly move on toward the higher need areas. Given the intrinsic, universal interest of every human being to move to higher happiness levels, this should happen automatically, driven by our underlying joint biology.

The higher need areas—self-actualization, G-love, and We-actualization—are largely refractory to the dollar as the ultimate economic performance parameters; instead, they are all dependent on interpersonal activities. That means :)$ will count as the only guiding indicator, the only reward and recognition system for people moving toward higher levels. Therefore, when approaching higher levels, we will see an exponential increase in the exchange rate between :)$ dollars. Your status in such a We-actualized society will be reflected by the amount of :)$ you hold. The :)$ becomes your status symbol. In other words, people on the highest three levels would never exchange their :)$ anymore because dollars have lost their value entirely. For people at and beyond self-actualization, the dollar value is very low. For most people it will be zero.

Remember that the mathematical limit only applies when we use dollars to invest. There are several other options for activities that drive :)$ in the We-growth area, but all of them are nonmonetary. Thus, holistically, there is still a lot of potential for creating fresh :)$ and driving growth even if you are on the highest levels of the Universal happiness hierarchy. One can imagine how massive the economic growth opportunities are. Today, a lot of dollars are not invested in businesses driving returns, but rather are locked in wealth that is not driving any growth. Not dollar growth, not :)$ growth.

In conclusion, we should all definitely invest or exchange in :)$! If we believe that happiness will decline or stagnate, we should invest dollars in defined activities that provide happiness to people in need— at best at very low happiness levels, because we can create and potentially earn a disproportionately high amount of :)$ for very few dollars. In contrast, if we believe that our planet will move toward higher levels of happiness, you can choose: either exchange as many :)$ as you can (they will never be cheaper), or look at areas of need for happiness and invest your dollars there to earn :)$.

In any case, please be aware of the fine but critical difference between exchanging and creating. Exchange does not positively contribute to We-growth. That means average global happiness stays unchanged. In contrast, creating :)$ through investment increases We-growth. This in turn stimulates and drives the entire happiness distribution curve to the right, to higher levels on the Universal happiness hierarchy. As we have seen above, at these levels, the dollar value decreases and the value of the :)$ you hold increases. Therefore, you benefit twice. Of course, if there are only a few people in the :)$ business, the effect will be very small. However, if more people participate, the run will start by the classical investors who have to find more growth for their dollar holdings. Very similar to the latest Bitcoin hype.

But unlike Bitcoin, the fundamental difference is that happiness is the core underlying value for all human life. The introduction of the :)$ drives us to aim for happiness together. Not only for money. And with the huge benefit that happiness does not have a cap on growth.

So far, we have laid the groundwork for the :)$ and the associated Happiness app; the concept seems technically feasible. In addition, as a certificate, but even more so as a currency, the :)$ is a worthwhile investment opportunity—particularly due to the enormous growth potential from arbitrage.

What remains to be assessed is whether the :)$ should indeed be linked to our current economy. The previous pages provide some strong evidence that the :)$ may be the perfect secondary reinforcer we've all been looking for. However, we should not underestimate the strong tendency of our economic system to defend itself against any changes—especially because our population is highly dependent on consumption behaviors we have all been trained to follow by our current economic system. I will address potential routes and mechanisms to escape our current dependencies in the next chapter.

A much easier way to escape any dependency on our current economic system is to not link our :)$ at all and instead run the two systems in parallel. Again, we can do that as a certificate or as a currency (fig. 37, upper and lower right quadrants). Let us start with a very well-known application originally established for addiction management: the token economy.

CHAPTER TWENTY

HAPPINESS TOKEN ECONOMY

Token economies were developed in the mid-1900s as a behavioral therapy based on the principles of operant conditioning. Behaviors that are rewarded are likely to be repeated with increased frequency, intensity, and duration; and behaviors that are punished are likely to be reduced. But such negatively conditioned learning is less effective than positively rewarded learning; and behaviors that are ignored, given no reinforcement, will continuously be reduced until eliminated.

Token economies have been proven successful in children's education and in the military. Interestingly, the most dramatic successes have been seen in the management of learning disorders and deficiencies, drug addictions, and behavioral addictions—in these settings the term *contingency management* is largely used instead of *token* economy. Up to now, contingency management has shown the most sustainable successes for the handling of alcohol, heroin, and cocaine abuse. As I discussed in Chapter Six, cocaine abuse shows a similar pattern to behavioral dependency on work, money, or consumption.

Thus, if we want our society to focus more on happiness instead of on money, it makes sense to try a token economy approach.

The overarching goal of token economies is to teach appropriate behavior and social skills that are critical for personal or group progress. Looking at the Encyclopedia of Mental Disorders definition of a token economy, you will immediately realize that the front end of our happiness tracker is a token economy:

> *A token economy is a form of behavior modification designed to increase desirable behavior and decrease undesirable behavior with the use of tokens. Individuals receive tokens shortly after displaying a desirable behavior. The tokens are collected and can be later exchanged for meaningful objects or privilege or can be kept as a reward for recognition.*

In order to get our happiness token economy going, we would only need a very small adjustment to our Happiness app. We would keep the emotion tracker unchanged and we also would keep the transfer of our token, the :)$, unchanged. However, we would modify our :)$ to be a simple digital token that is disconnected from our economic system. It would be a real, quantified, digital "thank you." This token would still be based on a blockchain, in order to see where it goes and to keep the individual link to the certified emotion tracker.

In addiction management, the stringent process behind a token economy follows seven principles:

1. *Target Behavior.* In addiction management this could be compliance with sessions, working toward sobriety goals, drug-free urine or blood samples, and establishing appropriate relationships. Very clear and simple. In happiness management, this is even simpler: just check your emotion tracker and reflect on what made you happy.

2. *Choice of target population.* In addiction management this is crucial; not everyone needs or wants to participate, given intrinsic motivation levels. The process will be more useful for

clients with poor rates of success in the past. Most important is the free will and drive to participate. In happiness management, this principle applies the same way. Use your emotion tracker only if you want to. And reflect on whether it helps you.

3. *Choice of reinforcer.* The reinforcer is the central success factor in an addiction management program. It is highly individual: what is rewarding for one person might not be rewarding for another. Selection of a desirable reward is the major point of discussion between the therapist and the client. Interestingly, money has shown limited success when applied as a reinforcer in contingency management programs, as it turns quickly to a drug substitute with all the negative withdrawal symptoms. Therefore, nonmonetary reinforcers are used widely and more successfully. In happiness management, the choice of the reinforcer becomes slightly complex. It is very easy when reflecting on the relevant drivers for your own happiness (just look at your emotion tracker, reflect, and enjoy any improvement!). However, the ultimate objective of the Happiness app is to reward people for providing happiness to others. The secondary reinforcer is our happiness token—that's clear. But what is the primary reinforcer we can exchange it for—the thing that makes us happy? Obviously it should not be money. Interestingly, in alcoholism management, the number of tokens representing how long you have been successful in therapy provides the ultimate recognition factor and the energy to continue. With happiness, knowing how many people you made happy would drive you to repeat the behavior that made them happy. That's the goal. Given all the information provided by the blockchain, one could imagine several happiness communities that could be established to collectively drive more :)$.

4. *Incentive magnitude.* Contingency management programs to combat addiction find a balance between what is practical and what is rewarding. Some individuals might need higher levels of reward to stay engaged. In happiness management, incentive magnitude is not an issue. First, the neuroscientific hurdle

will be handled by the certified emotion tracker. Second, we "mint" our :)$ by our brain activity, without any limitation due to our financial budgets.

5. *Frequency of incentive distribution.* In addiction management, the frequency is adjusted so the client receives the greatest benefit. The ideal rate will differ based on the individual's needs. In happiness management, it's easy: as with incentive magnitude, incentive frequency will be handled by the emotion tracker.

6. *Timing of incentive.* In addiction management, the best case is for the reward to be given immediately after a desired behavior or within a short, predefined period of time. This helps to build a strong association between the desired behavior and the reward. In happiness management, this will be slightly different. As outlined in Chapter Five and Six, on the happiness receiving end, we require a period of reflection to enforce sustained learning on who and what made us happy, and why. As a consequence, the happiness token, the :)$, will not be activated until one day later. The good thing is that this relatively short delay also drives repeated reflection, and therefore an amplification by the :)$ when it is activated for release to the happiness giver the next day.

7. *Duration of incentive.* In addiction management, the objective is for sobriety to continue when the rewards are removed. The duration to achieve that objective differs among individuals. The decision to end contingency management coincides with relapse prevention strategies. In happiness management, this can be handled more flexibly. You can stay on the Happiness app in order to climb your way up the Universal happiness hierarchy. Or you can use the Happiness app only until you have reset yourself and gained full awareness again of what makes you really happy; after that, you can continue without the Happiness app. If the Happiness app is used only temporarily, I imagine that the new analog communities will continue outside the app as reward amplifiers because they make

all participants happy. Given that happiness is not physiologically harmful, we can choose whether we use the Happiness app temporarily (to treat) or continuously (to prevent). The true proof would be—as in addiction management—how many people fall back to focusing only on money and consumption after exiting the Happiness app. And find themselves at risk of depression again.

In conclusion, the application of the :)$ in a happiness token economy is the simplest way to improve everyone's happiness and the fastest way to get going. No need to align the :)$ with any tax or financial regulation agency. No need for the emotion tracker to be extremely sophisticated at the beginning (we can refine it as we go). No need for the effort to fundamentally disrupt capitalism. The focus would be solely on creating :)$ and rewarding people for making others happy. A secondary market—as a link to our economic system—is very unlikely to develop. Indeed, we might see a small secondary market where people trade :)$ for dollars—but only if the happiness community allows such secondary access to community events. Likely such a secondary access would defeat the purpose.

On the other hand, the missing link to money and an accepted cryptocurrency reduces our flexibility in obtaining funding to build the first version of the emotion tracker, which would be critical to initiating the happiness token economy. Indeed, the missing link to our highly effective economic system will make it difficult to find investors for ideas that require upfront monetary investments.

What would we have to do to establish the :)$ as the *only* currency on our planet, a universal currency that represents our most important biological heritage: happiness and progress?

CHAPTER TWENTY-ONE

UNIVERSAL BIOLOGICAL CURRENCY

Could we just work with the Happiness dollar, or :)$, as the only currency and forget all other currencies?

In order to go down that route of thinking, we would have to accept that the only reasonable objective for all of us is to sustainably (!) increase our happiness and with it drive progress of life. Progress—as we have defined it in the beginning of the book, as we started the game of life—is focused on staying in the game, adding optionality to counter future uncertainties, and continuously improving. You realize that the definition is continuously forcing a compromise—we all observe that in our lives every day. However, productivity—the leading indicator of progress in our economic system—is obviously insufficient to fulfill our initial definition of progress. Actually, productivity would likely not even be a leading metric to look at anymore. For any psychologist or scientist, in particular evolutionary scientists and neuroscientists, this is easy to imagine—we all were built based on that concept. Done. For most economists, such an idea is simply nonsense.

To bring the two groups together, let me step back one more time and reflect on the objectives of the different systems: classical capitalism and Capitalism of Happiness.

The central objective is to make positive progress in the game of life. Our molecular reward systems—the ones that drive happiness—have been evolutionarily shaped over billions of years to drive the progress of life. Thus, happiness is a robust universal concept to focus on.

In contrast, the central objective of our economic system is based on private ownership of the means of discovering, developing, manufacturing, marketing, and selling, and operating for profit. Productivity is a key measure of success and is expressed as a ratio of output to inputs used across the value chain or within single steps of the value chain. Elevated to the highest level, return on investment is the most holistic performance indicator to look at. Once more, I would like to emphasize that happiness is not considered centrally relevant in the definition of return on investment in our economic system. In a narrow window—when capitalism helps us to focus on the satisfaction of basic psychological needs—a productivity increase correlates with human happiness and progress. Beyond that, however, a productivity increase becomes detrimental to our happiness.

So far, we have perceived money only as linked to capitalism, because it was originally defined as a means to facilitate trade of products and services.

Interestingly, in its general sense, *money is defined as any item or verifiable record that is generally accepted as payment.*

Only in the context of capitalism is money limited to goods and services and repayment of debts—because capitalism is limited to goods, services, and debt. But in general, money can be applied as a tool to facilitate any objective we would like to achieve.

A warning to economists: you probably won't like the next pages. Yes, you are right: this is a neuroscientist rewriting economy. From scratch.

What would happen if we replaced the objectives of our economy with the objectives for happiness and progress while maintaining money as the highly effective tool we all are familiar with to achieve that objective?

In order to guide us, I have graphically displayed the key differences in figure 43 and will stay on a high level to focus on the essentials.

FIGURE 43: ESSENTIAL DIFFERENCES BETWEEN CAPITALISM AND HAPPINESS ECONOMY

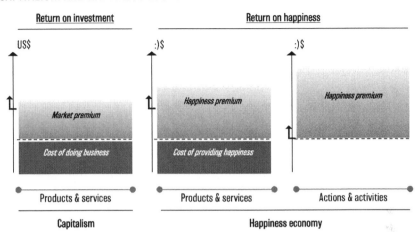

Notes: Ꮻ indicates breakeven for profitable business and positive return on investment and Return on Happiness

Capitalism is productivity focused; it's a seller's market. A buyer can buy only what is produced and sold. Before a company makes any return, all cost of doing business must be compensated by net revenues; only thereafter can a company see a profit. Thus, the key for any profit is to collect a market premium that is based on the customers' willingness to pay more than the cost of doing business. It is remarkable how secretive all players in the market are when it comes to publishing openly about the cost of doing business or the market premiums per product. The consumers as well as the suppliers are kept entirely in the dark about that information. In addition, in capitalism the downstream suppliers normally do not directly participate in the market premium received from the end customer—they are normally paid for raw materials or with a fee for services. It is very important to remember that, in capitalism, raw materials provided by planet Earth basically come for free. We do not consider the future cost for replacement or reparation.

There are two major strategies driving productivity and returns in capitalism: the high turnover of goods, which pushes continuous consumption, and economy of scale, which drives the formation of oligopolies or monopolies. The former is the specialty of marketers who try to establish brand loyalty—or brand addiction, in neurological terms. The latter is the specialty of capitalists reducing fixed costs and reducing competition, which in turn reduces the push to invest in innovation. Both strategies lead to a massive reduction in happiness for an ordinary person: addiction to consumption is a serious mental illness (stress from unemployment is one of the key depression factors on this planet; and less innovation diminishes all our progress and happiness).

The left column of figure 43 shows two additional challenges. First, there is no real incentive for anyone in capitalism to start big, long-term projects. Second, there is no incentive for ensuring sustainability. Both items are fundamental for progress of life and happiness. Thirdly, in capitalism there is not even an intrinsic motivation for deep innovation—only patent law ensures that there is a protection for returns to companies that innovate. These last three realities should immediately show us how flawed the original system truly is.

Now let us look at a world in which progress and associated happiness are central to the economy. A lot of things would be turned upside down. First of all, such a system would be happiness focused and thus become a buyer's market. The receiver of your products, services, and actions provides the returns based on their brain's response, which is translated by the individual emotion tracker.

Let us first focus on products and services in direct comparison to our capitalistic system (fig. 43, left and center column). We would still have the cost of providing happiness, of course. Now—very importantly—these costs are identical to the cost of doing business. It does not matter in what currency or form of money we measure these costs. If :)$ were as widely accepted as dollars, we could simply pay that part directly, use the proceeds to pay for our employees, our suppliers, and raw materials—no difference. In contrast, the premiums between the systems are entirely different. Whereas in our current economy the market premium is a function of desire, limited supply, and limited buying power, the happiness premium is an individual parameter only dependent on a person's psychological need and satisfaction level. The price differences can be huge. Importantly, happiness premiums are paid only upon the creation of :)$ on an individual basis and will be paid repeatedly, very similar to music streaming concepts today.

The associated effect on products and services would be dramatic: it is much more profitable to invent and sell products and services that have sustainable, long-lasting, and repeated effects on happiness, thereby creating deep positive memories. Such products would totally outperform the consumer products that are at the center of today's economy. For example, imagine a mountain bike you purchase in today's economy. At the moment of sale, the producer has collected the premium and there is no economic reason to ensure that you have fun riding the bike or that it is functional beyond the guarantee period. Getting long-lasting happiness from the purchase of a bicycle is economically counterproductive; it is in the sellers' interest to keep you buying new products.

Now imagine you purchase a mountain bike in an economy based on—and rewarded by!—your happiness. Every time you have a great bicycle ride—which creates a :)$—there is the potential of an additional reward to the mountain bike producer, if you release the :)$ to the producer. A consumer product basically becomes a streaming product and returns its true value over time by your customer's happiness. Every time your customer is happy, you earn :)$—not only at the moment of purchase. You can easily imagine how associated services and products would be developed in order to sustain the core product: riding and enjoying your mountain bike. The material good becomes a happiness-making experience. There are a few product classes that are trying to apply such a concept already; however, they focus on extending financial returns. For example, the video game *League of Legends* has built an entire product, service, and experience universe around the original game. Similarly, the makers of the energy drink Red Bull have created an experience universe. A Happiness dollar would drive sustainable products and limit blind consumption. Research and development departments would face a substantial challenge in innovation because suddenly products really have to provide balanced happiness.

All this together would make it very difficult for any player to maintain market dominance based on sheer size. The only way to maintain market leadership would be sustained product and service inventions that really work on our Unconscious happiness. In addition, companies would need a very positive reputation to ensure that people creating :)\$ based on enjoying a given product would be willing to release those :)\$. For the first time, the consumer would really be at the heart of the business ecosystem, rather than an oligopoly of a few big industry players. Companies would focus on people who have a true psychological need for a certain product. In other words, Porsche would focus more on new customers to fetch a lot of :)\$ for the "my-first-Porsche happiness" effect. Companies would focus on real consumer needs instead of maintaining brand addiction. Indeed, any form of addiction would reduce returns immediately, based on the negative effect on neuroplasticity.

In order to entirely focus on the upside, I would strongly advocate being totally transparent about the cost of providing happiness. These costs should be paid up front in :)\$ before the product is consumed—that's the minimum compensation every provider of a product or service should obtain, without question. In a blockchain world, such transparency is possible, and this would allow the participation of all downstream suppliers, all employees, and all raw material in the happiness that the final product or service provides. The downstream value chain obtains a share of the happiness premium. In addition, it would keep the pressure on providing happiness at low cost and would ensure that we can retain a premium segment: only people with a full :)\$ bank account can access that segment. Or in other words, people who made a lot of other people happy should be enabled to enjoy high-cost products, such as a Porsche. If a Porsche still retains its attractiveness as a status symbol (which I actually doubt), for the first time it would encourage the right behavior in people who would also like to drive a Porsche.

As a consequence, we would have a real sharing economy for the first time—not what is called a sharing economy today, where thousands of freelancers without health insurance or pensions support e-commerce concepts that make only a few investors very rich. In a similar way, big expensive projects would be pushed by those with intrinsically high happiness and a high return in :)\$. Importantly, like today, risk-capital owners would still win big-time, but so would all participants in the project, based on their ownership of the underlying token. Everyone would participate and be an owner.

One could even imagine that over time, and, depending on the average happiness progress of a society, the basic cost of providing happiness for food, housing, and health care would be subsidized via a kind of universal basic income. This would be the right move in reflecting the sustainable performance of a society to increase its underlying happiness and level on the Universal happiness hierarchy. Even sustainability would be intrinsically promoted: first, downstream providers of sustainable solutions would be made transparent to the consumer, likely influencing the Unconscious happiness levels and creating an immediate participation of the suppliers and the companies preferring these suppliers.

In such an economy, with the :)$ widely accepted as the proper secondary reinforcer for all our happiness, we can of course buy an ice cream cone with a :)$.

The most substantial benefit of the Happiness economy is the additional pillar of happiness that can be created beyond products and services, by everybody (fig. 43, right column). Indeed, normal activities are already today by far the largest pillar in providing happiness. This is because interpersonal activities and actions stimulate more reward systems than do products and services, which primarily trigger dopamine. Thanks to our addiction to money and consumption, we are feeling the reward less and less, unfortunately. The enormous benefit from a Happiness economy perspective is the cost side. In essence, this biggest chunk of happiness comes at zero cost. (I neglect the rather small biological energy we need to execute these actions and activities—we are the perfect "machines" for creating happiness at a minimal cost in energy.) The cost aspect would be the biggest driver for fundamental behavioral change: we would very quickly move away from satisfaction by consumption because we would realize that hanging out with friends having a good time is much more productive and is self-amplifying; everyone is a happiness receiver and happiness giver at the same time. So much more happiness comes without overproducing the products that are using up natural resources and creating the waste that is destroying our planet.

Before turning to the factors that limit the implementation of such a Happiness economy, let me provide four detailed examples of behavioral change in such a system.

Food and Water. In the desert, the cost of pumping water is very high and cannot be compensated for by a market premium—despite the fact that water is much more expensive in the desert than it is close to a freshwater lake in the French Alps. In a Happiness economy, the cost of pumping water would be the same; however, the happiness premiums would be substantially higher, given the substantially higher psychological need for water. All of a sudden, it would make business sense to sink a well—and not only for NGOs supporting the drilling of wells in the Sahara desert.

The same would apply for shipping food to hungry people. Under today's economic logic, that is not a business, because the shipping costs are much higher than the people consuming the food can afford. In a Happiness economy, the happiness premiums and the :)$ created from people in desperate need of food would outcompete any shipping costs. Actually, I believe such businesses would be the most profitable ones on the planet. If we now turn to a restaurant in a developed country, we would realize that food and water would not create any happiness premium at all. We are simply not hungry and thirsty enough anymore—the basic need for food and water is satisfied. Most probably, we would see a similar business reaction in both economies. Already today, there is a strong push for additional benefits in restaurants. This can be a novel type of food, the food's high quality, a special location, or exclusive entry for certain people only. The restaurant and food industry have already adapted very well to the demand to satisfy higher needs than just hunger and thirst.

Now, I can imagine that in a Happiness economy, restaurants would focus even more on individual needs and desire. Perhaps you get an instant blood test to reveal the nutrients you are missing before the chef prepares your personalized meal. Or a restaurant prepares you a surprise meal based on a few pieces of information. Or restaurants tailor the lighting and sound to certain preferences. Or a restaurant provides shared meals in order to raise the oxytocin levels of all customers—maybe the restaurant even provides a menu of hugs and nurturant kisses, who knows? What sounds extremely expensive from a cost-of-doing-business perspective in our current economy remains very expensive in a Happiness economy. However, one can take that risk to provide more quality and emphasis because the happiness premiums you obtain will be much higher than today's market premiums. Food and water would become associated with self-actualization. What you can see with this example is that on every level, we as a species will stretch the limits to fulfill our needs. We progress as we climb up the Universal happiness hierarchy.

Health Care. Health care has evolved based on the essential need for all of us to stay healthy or—once we get sick—to get healthy again as quickly as possible. Thus, at the center of health care is a human need. Interestingly, over the years a complex industry has evolved. The health care industry is composed of several players. There are the hospitals and health care professionals, such as doctors and nurses, who treat patients. There is the pharmaceutical industry, which develops and provides prescription drugs. There is the consumer health industry, which provides nonprescription drugs, supplements, and medical food. There are regulatory agencies, which control and approve drugs for sale and focus on drug safety. Finally, there are health insurance companies, statutory and private ones, which support patients to pay for their drugs, doctors' costs, and health services—because health care is so expensive that hardly anyone can pay for it out of pocket. The primary objectives of the individual players have evolved further and are interestingly different from the original objective: the main objective of most players in health care is no longer health, but profit. Pharmaceutical companies have to make a return on their investments in order to pay back investors and develop new drugs. The regulatory agencies are paid by the taxpayer in order to ensure that drugs are safe. Finally, the health insurance companies have to stay within their annual budget and try to avoid losses. So if you look at it closely, you realize that the patient and his desire for health—the original centerpiece of medicine—have essentially no role anymore.

Let us take a detailed look at one of the players in the health care system, the pharmaceutical industry. The pharmaceutical industry has been criticized for fleecing patients with unjustifiably high drug prices and with benefits perceived as insufficient. Though there are several reasons for this, an important one is the very high cost to develop and manufacture drugs within the regulatory timeframe. A new drug requires $1.5 to $2 billion in upfront investments before it comes to the market, and the risk of failure along the way is greater than 95 percent.

In addition, there are very high expectations for returns from investors who shared the risk of failure. Whether returns at a level of 40 to 50 percent are justified depends on the perspective. For a gravely ill patient who can't afford a new drug and therefore dies, these returns clearly are not justified. Interestingly, in most developed countries drugs are paid for through insurance plans that are essentially replenished by taxes. So society pays for the medication and realizes every year that health care is essentially too expensive because it takes between 10 and 25 percent of the GDP.

In a Happiness economy, first and foremost the patients and the payers would have transparency about the real cost of doing business. That would likely cut down the cost at the moment of prescriptions by 25 to 50 percent. A huge cost savings for society right there. After a drug is effective and the patient is feeling better, the **Happiness premium** can be expected to be substantial, because health is one of the biggest drivers for happiness. Thus, the pharmaceutical industry would benefit big-time from such a performance-based and happiness-based pricing model.[2] Just imagine, how many :)$ a cancer patient mints who just got cured, just got a pain relief, or just received a supporting smile from a nurse or a doctor. . . . It would be huge, but totally justified profits for the pharmaceutical industry.

In turn, one can imagine that the focus of the research and development units in the pharma industry would change focus entirely—away from providing incrementally better drugs and toward real improvements. And with the huge return upsides, pharmaceutical companies could even afford to invest in difficult, long-term, and riskier projects. In addition, there would be a shift back from small, rare diseases to true public health burdens that have a very big impact on happiness, such as depression (the ultimate disease to address in a Happiness economy), neurodegenerative diseases, and heart disease.

The same effect would drive a much larger focus of pharmaceutical players to provide drugs to developing countries. Today's issue

---

2. A few pharmaceutical players have started to introduce performance-based payment models. However, most of these models request full payment at the beginning with a rebate or payback if the drug does not work as promised. These models help the interface between the health insurers and the pharmaceutical industry, but they do not necessarily help the patient.

that people in these countries cannot afford expensive drugs would go away—simply because happiness premiums upon cure or improvement of the condition would more than compensate for the high cost of drug development. Even more dramatic would be the impact on physicians, other health professionals, and hospitals. First, one would of course have to pay the cost of doing business. This alone would ensure that all the lower-wage service staff get a fair salary. Secondly, the service quality of patient care would jump because being cared for is a key driver of happiness in sick people, second only to direct improvements in their health. The doctor curing a patient from disease or improving their condition would get large premiums from their patients back-loaded. For the first time we would incentivize physicians to provide health instead of just treating sick people without any benefit from the outcome. Further, the doctor's focus would be on the individual patient instead of just rushing through a high volume of patients in order to cover costs. Finally, the best methods for providing health would prevail in real life—if it is a surgery, let's go for the surgery. If it is a drug treatment or psychotherapy, choose those treatments. Every physician would be interested in making the patient healthy again, independent of which approach is used—the physician would use the approach that has proven to be the best. Finally, health insurance would pay only the cost of doing business to all providers in the health care sector. The upside—the Happiness premium—is paid by the patient. Over time, as a society moves to higher levels of the Universal happiness hierarchy, I would expect health insurance to be totally covered by the country or state and not by the patient or the employer.

Work. Today we have a substantial discrepancy in access to high-quality jobs and good salaries. All this is driven by the classic capitalist logic of supply and demand. In addition, at a certain rank in the company, participation in the value of the company is a tool for retaining higher management and founders. This lever is dramatic and the main driver of inequality in our economy. Access to these levels is usually enabled by inherited wealth—hardly anyone makes it from zero to very high income levels where they have the ability to invest in and participate in company success.

In a Happiness economy, this upside for risk-taking and investing by individuals should remain—I am even fine if it becomes bigger. And

I would expect it to increase, given the substantially bigger market for happiness than for financial returns. The basic salary for all workers should not change, given that the cost of doing business is assumed to be the same. That would also mean that the debate on the minimum wage and outsourcing to low-cost countries would continue. However, there would be a big shift: everyone in the value chain—everyone who had a part in the product's success—would earn :)$ because they provided happiness. It would turn employees into owners. In addition, it would put massive pressure on companies to provide top-level products and services that sustainably drive happiness. Because that is the only way to retain talent—the better your products or services, the more participation for the employees, the higher is the attractiveness for talent to join your company. Again, everyone participates in that economy.

Investments and Investors. Just as you need money to start a business in the traditional dollar economy, you need money to start a business in the Happiness economy. The token would now be a :)$ and not a dollar, but still you have to earn it first to invest it later. The good thing is that you can source :)$ from more places than dollars. While the dollar is largely restricted to people who are rich by birth, have built a profitable business, or investors managing other people's money, :)$ can be created outside of products and services. So you can fund a small business based on :)$ created when you helped your mother in the kitchen, for example. Thus, a Happiness economy based on :)$ would enable many more people to build small businesses. Medium to large business investments will still need large investors. The good thing is, however, that these investors own their wealth because they previously made other people happy. We can be sure that such investors are much nicer people than the investors hoping for a quick return in dollars from buying low and selling high.

Heritage. In contrast to US dollars, :)$ cannot be inherited. Everyone has to make their own effort to make other people happy. In a world where we have only one currency—the :)$—we will have introduced a fundamental rebalancing act for wealth. As we should. In a world with two types of currencies—the :)$ and fiat currencies—we would expect that aging people who are rich in :)$ would likely start exchanging their :)$ for dollars. However, I believe—anticipating the character of people rich in :)\$—that they would donate or bequeath that money to social organizations and not to their children, or only partly to their children. Because they know that on the path to becoming financially rich there is much more to be learned and :)\$ to be made instead of starting from being rich.

All these examples look very positive. However, what would happen to the banking sector (including central banks)? And what would happen to governments and their tax departments?

First of all, we can be sure that we will continue to pay taxes. Taxes will never go away. Interestingly, if the government would like to make returns on their taxes, they would obviously invest them in the happiness of their people—that's the easiest way to make a return in :)\$. Now before doing that, the government should ensure the maintenance of the current happiness levels. Such maintenance investments would not create a return in :)\$, and that is important. People who are used to a certain level of comfort are not triggered to create :)\$ by the mere fact of enjoying the same standard they already have. The need level is already satisfied. In other words, a public swimming pool will have to be maintained just to keep the happiness baseline. Now, under normal circumstances one would expect an increase in taxes year on year. This in turn should enable any government to increase the average happiness level and thus obtain returns on their tax investments. The Happiness dollar will make paying taxes a rational act. For the first time ever.

I would hope that central banks disappear—because I strongly believe, along with Hayek, that money should be with the people, not with a central institution. With the :)\$, the money is clearly not with a banking system; it's in everyone's brain. I further believe that the role of banks would change. With one single cryptocurrency, the transactional contributions of banks should be very minimal. However, on the investment side, the banking sector would have to change to an entirely different position, given that now money could also be created by activities.

I would further predict that there will be a large decentralized organization that secures the blockchain's integrity, security, and consensus in return for :)\$, which we are all happy to pay them. The :)\$ would need something more sophisticated than Bitcoin's current blockchain network. Mining of new Bitcoins is directly linked to guaranteeing the security and integrity of the underlying blockchain network. In the :)$ concept, these two steps are decoupled. We create the :)$ based on our reward system activity (above a certain threshold) in our brain. Only thereafter do we infuse the :)$ into the blockchain network. Thus, we have to make securing the :)$ blockchain network an attractive business for coders. The most logical way would be to share a certain portion of every :)$ created with the community of coders who secure the network. In essence we provide a quantitative "thank you!" to them for securing our entire economic base. Thus they too become a creator of happiness.

We have assessed the potential of four possible applications for the Happiness dollar:

+ a happiness-vector certificate
+ a direct currency exchange
+ a happiness token economy
+ a universal biological currency

The first two, the happiness-vector certificate and the direct currency exchange, have a rather tight link to our current economic system. The second two applications would run in parallel with—or even compete against—our current economic system.

I think I have sufficiently explained why it is fundamentally important to all of us to shift our system objective from return on investment to Return on Happiness. We further have learned that all these applications are theoretically feasible and scientifically robust. One possible path—the happiness token economy—would be very simple to implement. Others—like the direct currency exchange—would carry substantial implementation hurdles.

So we have answered one of the key questions. Yes, we can create and implement a new economy that is centered on happiness.

However, there is an even more important question. Should we actually do it?

CHAPTER TWENTY-TWO

STATE-DEPENDENCY

The book in front of you is one I originally wrote just for me—mainly as a brain teaser. I had always been very suspicious of whether our current economic system is fully aligned with our biological drivers. For two years, I did not even think that the concept could be implemented.

Until I encountered an unintentional small case study featuring Lisa, five years old, and Marie, seven. My two kids. At the time, we had the mandatory ritual of a bedtime story before they went to sleep. But my genetic defect is that I am bored when I have to tell a story twice. As a consequence, I invented a new story every night. It was a very intensive time of storytelling, and after half a year and over a hundred stories, I simply blanked on further ideas. Both kids were disappointed. Until Marie asked me what I was writing every night until late. I hesitated at first to disclose the story about the Happiness dollar. But finally, the two little girls persuaded me to tell them the story. It saved me almost two weeks of inventing new stories, before we moved back to the usual stories of girl pirates and dance competitions.

Three months later, I was sitting with my two little ladies at the dinner table: steak with potato croquettes. As always, Lisa and Marie each had the same number of croquettes on their plates. As always,

Marie was eating very fast while Lisa was eating very slowly. And as always, Marie ended up staring down at her own empty plate and stealing glances at Lisa's full one. Under normal conditions, Marie would ask whether she could have some of Lisa's, and Lisa would refuse to give her any—even though she never ate up all her croquettes.

This evening, however, the play ended differently. As always, Marie asked for some of Lisa's croquettes and—big surprise—Lisa calmly gave Marie three croquettes. Marie was totally amazed and happy—caught by surprise. Right after dinner, Marie walked over to the table where the girls had been drawing. She grabbed a bold black pen. She drew a 2-cm circle with a :) inside, and then she cut out the first ever Happiness dollar bill. She walked back and gave it to Lisa—I will never forget Lisa's smile as Marie said, "Just like the story Daddy told us a few months ago!" After that, we never had trouble with Lisa having leftover croquettes and Marie unhappy and hungry. From that day on, Lisa gave up her croquettes while receiving a paper Happiness dollar in return.

I know the story is too good to be true—but actually it gets even better. I did not realize for another month how the game had evolved. One day, I went into Lisa and Marie's room to grab their linen for laundry. And I found roughly forty paper Happiness dollars under Lisa's bed and almost the same number under Marie's bed. Interestingly, their paper Happiness dollars had two colors. Marie had a few green and the majority in red, while Lisa had the reverse. I was amazed that apparently the number of paper Happiness dollars was similar for each girl.

However, I could not make any rational sense of the colors and in particular why they were not equally distributed. When the two girls came back from school, I asked them directly. Marie's answer was stunning: "Oh Daddy, that is easy, Lisa has the green happiness coins, I have the red ones. When Lisa makes me happy, I give her some of my red ones. If I make Lisa happy, she gives me some of her green ones." I still didn't understand why there were more red than green ones with Marie and more green than red ones with Lisa. Marie's answer: "Oh Daddy, that's easy—whenever we play together we both take a happiness coin."

I realized that when they were playing happily together, they would each take a happiness coin—but apparently, they did not exchange those, they just kept their own color. So I could now see that they created many, many more happiness coins by playing together—and having fun together—than by just one girl making the other happy by giving her croquettes, for example. In less than a month, they had realized that the most happiness coins can be made when actively playing together. In addition, intentionally or unintentionally, they ensured that their happiness—and with it the number of happiness coins—was equally distributed. All this happened intuitively, unconsciously, based on the natural, still unspoiled "emotion tracker" in their brains.

That was the moment I realized that perhaps the Happiness dollar concept could really work and I should put real effort into completing the book.

Of course, the story of my two little girls is cool and very illustrative. However, it just provides repeated proof of an old experiment done in the mid-1900s, which showed the effectiveness of tokens when associated with an objective (make Lisa happy, or make Marie happy). I just observed a classical contingency management experiment—in the absence of any understanding of money and definitely in the absence of addiction to money.

In the course of the next year, a lot of people provided amazing input. However, one issue consistently came up. While everyone agreed that this could be implemented, there was broad uncertainty about whether the Happiness dollar, or :)$, should be really created as a currency that is exchangeable for financial currencies like the dollar.

When my friend Steffen read an earlier version of the manuscript, one that proposed pushing for a direct exchange between dollars and :)$, he said that I fundamentally underestimated the state-dependency capitalism has created in all of us—in particular over the past hundred years. Because of that deeply rooted dependency, he believed, I would doom mankind when "unleashing" the :)$. Not because it would not work, but because our capitalist state-dependency would immediately abuse the :)$ for its own underlying purpose: making money.

State-dependency is a neurological feature of the retrieval of stored information, one of the most critical aspects of learning and memory. Retrieval is most effective when it occurs in the same context in which initial learning has occurred. In other words, everything we have learned over the past hundred years has been learned in the context of our capitalistic system. Essentially, escaping that state-dependency on capitalism seems impossible, from a neurological perspective. Steffen raised the fundamental concern that state-dependency on capitalism would easily and quickly reverse the intention of the :)$: Instead of being a secondary reinforcer driving real biological happiness, it would be immediately abused to make . . . money. We would not learn how to become happier; instead, we would learn how to fake happiness in order to trigger the emotion tracker to create :)$. With the objective of quickly exchanging them for dollars.

We would have created the worst of all systems, one that—again— cannot be controlled and has no control over itself. But now without leaving any escape, because all reward systems would be connected to the :)$ system. We would all fade away while continuously faking our own happiness to trick the emotion tracker. The ultimate nightmare.

I have to admit that I followed his concerns, but I was less worried. To me, it all was dependent on how robustly the emotion tracker would work in detecting Unconscious happiness. In addition, I had a strong belief that the interpersonal reward systems would be very hard to fake. Of course, I did not have any scientific proof for my assumptions and—indeed—Steffen's worst-case scenario is a really bad one.

Now the problem is that Steffen is theoretically right. And I am theoretically right too.

Disrupting state-dependency has been proven to be extremely difficult in addiction. That is why the biggest risk for any substance addict is the sight, the smell, the sound where the respective addictive substance was consumed the first time; these sense perceptions are paired with very positive memories. The most effective support for an addict in getting off the abused drug is to move them to a new environment completely detached from the one where the addiction began. When we apply this scientific evidence to the state-dependency we face in our world of consumption and money, it seems pretty clear that we simply cannot escape into a new environment. State-dependency on capitalism is deeply ingrained in all of us. Everywhere, all the time. Unless we move to Mars or a very isolated island and start completely fresh. It is almost impossible.

Now on the other side, the :)$ concept is based on the strong scientific evidence that addictions can indeed be overcome—even in the presence of strong state-dependency—if new stimuli appear that deliver a superior reward. For example, deep social or familiar stimuli—a baby or a child for instance—apparently are strong enough to get heavily addicted people off their drug. These observations confirm what we have observed when looking at our reward systems: the systems triggered by interpersonal and social stimuli—such as the oxytocin and cannabinoid system—are very strongly rewarding.

In conclusion, it is likely that a universal :)$ could indeed be powerful enough to overcome the addiction to money and consumption that is exclusively driven by dopamine and serotonin. As we know, these two systems are insufficient to provide broad and sustained happiness. Furthermore, it seems difficult to believe that interpersonal rewards can be manipulated on a molecular level in the brain. The sensory detectors triggering these interpersonal rewards are very sophisticated. For example, just consider the difference in hugging your baby and hugging a stranger—obviously a totally different dimension for experiencing happiness.

So who is right? Steffen or Axel? Well . . . most likely still both of us. It just depends on one's assumptions about what will happen in the future. But we will not know how it works out in real life unless we try. Steffen's recommendation was: don't even try it, too dangerous. My recommendation would be: experiment with it carefully and learn—and most importantly, consider the power of state-dependency right from the start.

Under the assumption that Unconscious happiness cannot be manipulated, we have to assume that our current economic state-dependency would likely drive us to consciously trick the emotion tracker whenever we can to "mint" money, not happiness, in our brain. Over time, if successful, such conscious adaption would influence our behavior and promote faking of the emotion tracker. We would get stuck again satisfying only our lower need levels. Whether faking happiness could over time change our Unconscious happiness creation is not clear today. Whatever we do, such an addictive escape has to be prevented. This is fundamentally critical because we can imagine that artificial abuse and addiction to :)$ would be almost impossible to overcome, given the design of :)$.

Theoretically, there are three ways to achieve such prevention.

First, we could make the :)$ available for a limited time only. The time limitation could be mathematically represented in the :)$ protocol for full transparency. The :)$ would then act as a temporary substitute for our money addiction in order to make us learn again how good and happy we feel when we fully leverage all six reward systems—and not only the consumption-triggered and money-triggered dopamine and serotonin systems. The :)$ would be a kind of curative treatment that would reset our neuroscientific, psychological, and behavioral systems for full leverage. The obvious limitation would be that after the specified period of time, we might fall back into our ROI-driven behavior, just as before. However, the people really benefiting would make more of an effort to stay on the path of happiness, because being happy is addictive by itself—that's the basis of life. This way would be a temporary variant of the second application, direct currency exchange, described earlier.

Secondly, we could leave the availability of the :)$ open-ended but introduce it as a cryptocurrency in a controlled manner. It would be similar to how an antidepressant medicine would be introduced and how novel currencies like the euro were introduced over time. By limiting the audience utilizing the :)$, we can learn how different people use it and how neuroscientific data and behavioral data connect. Or in other words, whether Unconscious happiness data is really closely linked to Conscious happiness and whether we can confirm the connection between short-term and long-term happiness in such an experiment.

In addition, we would discover a reasonable threshold for creating a :)$ in the first place. Most likely, we would put that threshold at a very high level, to filter out and learn about our most important drivers of happiness first. Exchange between :)$ and dollars would be controlled by providing a predefined pool of real dollars that can be exchanged exclusively at a "central happiness bank." With such an approach, we would be able to leverage the full potential of the :)$—if it is safe, we can be sure that happiness is indeed stronger than state-dependency on capitalism. If it's not safe, we just stop the experiment before any broader rollout or stop it from being a currency altogether. To test new ideas in controlled environments is standard and—of course—bears the remaining risk that you miss the behavior of those people not covered in your test population. Or you simply don't foresee what people will develop out of an idea over time as they learn and adapt.

As a scientist, I can only recommend running the test in a controlled environment and seeing what we learn. I have no doubt that reflection on the results and the prompted broader discussion will already, by themselves, dramatically improve worldwide happiness. I would not be overly worried about the addictive escape, actually. The recent developments around the Bitcoin show me that whenever fiat currencies and central banks get into the game, regulation is fierce. In particular, tax regulation. From a revolution of free, anonymous, and democratic money exchange, Bitcoin has just been turned into another currency. But let's not speculate—let's run the tests and see. And learn. To be clear, this option would come with the possibility of losing control to state-dependency on capitalism. It is clearly the riskiest option and would be a permanent, but stepwise implementation of the direct currency exchange.

Thirdly, we could establish the :)$ in parallel to our economic system, to avoid any exchange in the first place. We have shown and described two of these variants earlier already: the happiness token economy and the universal biological currency (fig. 37, right quadrants). I actually like this third way the most.

We need to avoid distorting the whole point of the :)$ by letting state-dependency on capitalism take over. To do so, I propose a stepwise approach (fig. 44):

FIGURE 44: ESCAPING CAPITALISM STATE-DEPENDENCY THROUGH THE HAPPINESS ECONOMY

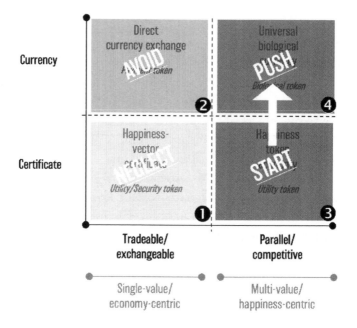

Notes:

❶ Happiness certificates could be connected to and guide taxation, the product/service choices of consumers, and investor decisions.

❷ Temporary or permanent cryptocurrency exchangeable to fiat currency.

❸ Permanent, independent token driving behavior toward more happiness (no exchange to fiat currency).

❹ Permanent, independent, universal currency for every human being on the planet (no exchange to fiat currency), the associated biological token is a novel, yet-to-be-established hybrid version of a utility token (goes beyond digital access to applications or services) and a payment token (goes beyond payment for goods and services) that is based on real biological improvement, such as Unconscious happiness and increased neuroplasticity.

1. Let us start with a happiness token economy (figs. 37 and 44, lower right quadrant) that focuses only on activities, not at all on exchanging the tokens into consumable products or services. The benefit of starting there is to enjoy the pure happiness upside from activities that cannot be purchased with

money. Based on scientific evidence about addiction treatment, we can also be sure that it will help us focus more on things that make us happy holistically—with a primary focus on the top three reward systems: the oxytocin, cannabinoid, and opioid systems. That first step is perfectly suited to develop and test the emotion tracker without any early interference from regulators—because we are not treating disease, nor are we entering the finance market.

2. The next step is to evolve the :)$ into a cryptocurrency that can be used to reward activities that make others happy. With this step, we stay entirely separate from the product and service economy. So there is no chance for state-dependency on capitalism. We can establish the entire cryptocurrency system in that stage and limit all tests to small groups and societies. We essentially create a local/regional happiness currency that at first has a narrow use, but has the features to later be expanded to goods and services. With this activation route, we avoid any interference from state-dependency on capitalism while educating everyone about the huge benefits of interpersonal activities for our holistic happiness. The point is to create a healthy tendency to turn away from consumption—and we would create this without even touching our current economic system or waking up banking or tax regulators. Given the vast surplus of happiness created from interpersonal activities, one could even assume that this refocus should be fully sufficient to recalibrate our reward systems, and to overcome our consumption and money addiction.

3. Applying a functional emotion tracker to really understand the happiness characteristics of products and services is very tempting for almost all players in today's economy. I therefore do not believe that it is possible to avoid using the emotion tracker as an indicator of product and service impact on happiness. For me, such a link—as a certificate, basically—could be still acceptable, because it would do a lot to improve the quality and sustainability of all our products and services.

Investors and tax authorities would obviously come next to apply the emotion tracker for their needs. We should not push such a direct link to our economy, but indeed, I feel that by simply ignoring such developments we would still have enough time to establish the :)$ as our universal biological currency.

4. By all means, one would have to avoid, for as long as possible, establishing the :)$ as a currency that can be exchanged for fiat currency. Otherwise we can be fairly sure that the :)$ would end up in the same dead end as the Bitcoin. Unfortunately, with a much more powerful token than the Bitcoin negatively impacting all of us. The original idea of the Bitcoin as an anonymous, democratic currency was amazing—there was no need at all to make it exchangeable for dollars. But all the interference from the classical players had to come—money laundering, tax regulations, and financing regulations castrated the idea of a revolution for everybody. We have to do everything to prevent that from happening to the :)$. Let the :)$ be our tool to measure our progress. And our happiness.

To be clear, the full power of the :)$ to advance the world for the better (or for the happier) happens only when we have a true currency exchange between :)$ and dollars (fig. 44, upper left quadrant). Only then can we leverage the happiness arbitrage all along the Universal happiness hierarchy. People at the lower end of the hierarchy would see their basic needs met, and people at the higher end would attain self-esteem, love, and actualization. The world's happiness would increase for everyone—the perfect synergy. Leveraging the arbitrage first in an area that today's economy does not cover—personal and interpersonal actions and activities—we have enough time to learn again how much more happiness such actions provide in contrast to pure product and service consumption. At that point we will have to pause and have a look at the situation. Because today's regulation, finance, and tax authorities will block us to handle the :)$ as a full currency anyway. I hope that there is an evolution of a limited "gray" :)$ market that allows all of us to observe what happens in a size-limited real-life scenario. If the available neuroplasticity evidence holds true, both systems should continue to work in parallel, providing a vector for each other.

In conclusion, the concept presented here should not stay on a theoretical level; it has the power to be implemented in real life. I am fully aware that the concept today is still rough and holds a few hypotheses that still need to be scientifically proven. However, I agree with Franz Kafka's words of wisdom: *"Wege entstehen dadurch, dass man sie geht,"* meaning, "Paths are formed by walking them." And I agree strongly with a stepwise and tightly controlled approach so we can avoid my friend Steffen's worst-case scenario: capitalistic state-dependency reverses the intention of the :)$. Avoiding that scenario is critical. Otherwise we have trapped our happiness on the lower levels of the Universal happiness hierarchy forever.

Yes, the level of ambition portrayed here is radical. However, to have a chance of moving the idea from theory to practice, I don't see a path other than thinking big. And just going for it.

Even the first step on the path to more happiness will change the world. How? I will explain in the next chapter.

CHAPTER TWENTY-THREE

CHANGING THE WORLD

How would today's world change if we embarked on this journey toward more happiness?

First, already with the first step, we would create immediate change. Actually the two of us have already done so: I by writing this book and you by reading it to this point. I truly hope it triggered your reflection on happiness in a more general sense, as it did for me when I was writing it. Depending on how far we advance on the Universal happiness hierarchy together, the happiness accumulates and with it, all our optionality for progress.

Let me slice our journey into five stages in order to dissect the impact each stage would have on us. And on the world.

1. Basic education about happiness
2. Understanding our Conscious happiness
3. The emotion tracker: understanding our Unconscious happiness
4. The Happiness app: an interactive, honest reward network
5. The Happiness dollar: creating a new economy

1. BASIC EDUCATION ABOUT HAPPINESS

Isn't it frightening that everything you've read about happiness in this book so far—information you need to live a happy life—is not taught at school?

We teach math, history, natural sciences, and languages, but the fundamental basics on how we function, what it takes to cooperate and live together, and why we are here—these are not taught. To me, the school subject that should be emphasized from the first to the last school grade should be happiness. It is the ultimate objective for all of us. We can start with the overall concept, not diving deep into neuroscience, psychology, and behavioral biology. However, to understand the overarching concept, how progress works, and how rewarding happiness influences that progress, should be central even when you are a kid—learning experiments would be so easy to compile and would stick in our memory as we learn together and with all senses.

Focusing on your own happiness is the first critical step; it is critical to explain this in any happiness education. The next step is to strive for joint happiness—because it provides you with even more happiness. It is critical to teach children about the boost of happiness that appears if you work hard and persistently on an objective for long time—because the path to happiness is a part of it, given that it builds your neuroplasticity. As you move on to higher school grades, the philosophy, psychology, and neuroscience of happiness can be introduced. I would see ten essential elements that everyone on this planet should know and understand—basically the **Ten Commandments of Happiness**:

I.   The answer to the uncertainty of life is to create *optionality* for yourself and others.

II.   *Collaboration* is evolutionarily more successful (and much more fun) than competition.

III.   Keep your *learning triangle* in balance (functional reward systems, functional behaviors, satisfied needs).

IV.   *Reflection* is the key for neuroplasticity. And for taking *responsibility* for your life.

V.   *Short-term happiness* is the fuel for survival. The learning on your path to *long-term happiness* is the fuel for flourishing.

VI.   Dopamine, testosterone, and serotonin are essential for our *basic happiness*. And they are a secure path to addiction and depression if not kept in balance. (Money and consumption will never make you happy.)

VII.   Real interaction with other people—triggering the oxytocin, cannabinoid, and opioid systems—is essential for sustained and *ultimate happiness*.

VIII.   Ultimate love: take the challenge to work and advance from Deficiency-love (D-love) to Growth-love, *G-love*.

IX.   *Have fun together.*

X.   Create and participate in as many We-actualization moments as you can.

I truly hope that the book gives you sufficient motivation to try keeping these ten commandments.

2. UNDERSTANDING OUR CONSCIOUS HAPPINESS

Understanding, self-awareness, and reflection on what drives our own happiness is fundamental. Based on all we know about psychology and neurology, understanding our Conscious happiness would fundamentally change the way we live. We would realize how much more happy we are when we're physically active, how much we gain from really interacting with people, and how much we learn from trying new things. We would realize how little happiness we obtain from bullying others and how much happiness we obtain from truly taking care of others. We would realize to what a large extent dopamine and serotonin are driving our happiness, and how much this limits our happiness.

I don't believe we would all change our perspective toward addictive drugs and behaviors, but I strongly believe we would understand earlier when we lose control—by just learning how true Unconscious happiness declines as we move into addiction. We can start today, learning to better understand our happiness. Just take ten minutes before you go to sleep (or when you wake up) to write down who and what made you happy in the past twenty-four hours, and review this information every month, reflect on it, and take action to change if needed. We all keep business calendars to organize our workdays. Some of us keep training diaries to improve our physical fitness. But hardly anyone tries to take note of and act to gain more happiness.

We can start such a "happiness diary" immediately—and it will have a fundamental impact on our own happiness and health. And an even deeper impact on the people around us, whom we will make happy because we are happier. Such a diary is just a qualitative write-up of observations. There is no need to dissect our observations and attach them to certain reward systems—that is very difficult anyway. However, if we would like more sophistication, we can start trying to allocate our observations to the ten key positive emotions: enthusiasm, sexual desire, pride, contentment, nurturant love, attachment love, amusement, liking/pleasure, gratitude, and awe. You can then roughly dial back to the underlying reward systems, as indicated in figures 26 and 27. This will provide you with huge insight on what drives your happiness. Or what is desperately missing or out of balance.

3. THE EMOTION TRACKER: UNDERSTANDING OUR UNCONSCIOUS HAPPINESS

The emotion tracker introduced in this book is not available (yet). However, let us assume for a moment that it is.

First of all, we would understand for the first time what we miss on a daily basis due to repression of Unconscious happiness. This alone would make us much more conscious of embracing happy-making moments. Secondly, we would have quantitative metrics that help us to better steer and to improve. Quantitative metrics are great to feed our dopamine system and create enthusiasm. I strongly believe that we would start to compare our happiness levels very quickly, very much as we compare our physical fitness and our appearance. In contrast to the rather superficial appearance, competing on happiness is immediately and sustainably healthy. If our emotion tracker works well, we would not have any route to move toward a short-term happiness addiction or faking the emotion tracker—we would immediately realize it. The emotion tracker detects the bullshit. All this should fundamentally improve mental health on average across all income levels. The biggest positive impact of that self-awareness would come from an early feedback on addiction and the early prevention of clinically relevant depression. Already medium depression is very difficult to revert. The emotion tracker would provide us early on with an indication if we move too long down the path to mild and later more severe depression. The impact on preventing physical and mental health declines would be huge.

In hindsight, the emotion tracker would have helped me avoid three fundamental crises in my life: first, it would have given me transparency on my key anxieties as a teenager about interacting with others, which took me almost ten years to understand; second, it would have given me a warning when I was going down my first path to burnout by working too much; third, it would have given me insight into the crisis I was going through before the family got destroyed. I don't really believe these insights would have ultimately prevented the things I went through. However, such insights would have allowed me to reflect much more and gotten me back to progressing instead of searching blindly for an exit for a very long time. In essence, not having the emotion tracker as a guide cost me fifteen years of my life. I learned a lot on that path, of course. But as an organism with a very limited time span, it took too long to leverage that knowledge for my progress and the progress of the people around me.

The emotion tracker, together with a ten-minute reflection on our Conscious and Unconscious happiness every evening (or every morning), would fundamentally improve our lives. And very likely the lives of those around us. Remember, happiness is highly contagious.

4. THE HAPPINESS APP: AN INTERACTIVE, HONEST REWARD NETWORK

Up to this point, we have focused on our own happiness. If we stopped here, we could assume that other people around us would like to benefit from something we'll call collateral happiness improvement. The lever—our increased happiness—will obviously be very limited on a global scale. Even if everyone on the planet used the emotion tracker, we would just randomly see benefits to the network of human beings because we have not systematically guided our society toward happiness. Not yet.

With the Happiness app, we create a new global language. A language that allows us to send a reward to whoever made us happy; a language that is universally accepted as something very positive—talking about positive events, providing real thanks, rewarding others, and providing positive feedback. We would learn that the highest, most complete levels of happiness are driven by making others happy, working together with other people for a higher purpose. We would deprioritize time spent on purposeless activities and instead focus on what creates a return on providing happiness.

The Happiness app is fundamental to releasing the *perpetuum mobile* of happiness. Creating happiness for others becomes a self-fulfilling prophecy because it also makes us happy. Positive feedback—a reward—via the Happiness app will just amplify our happiness-making behaviors.

The Happiness app would fundamentally change behavior in our society, particularly in smaller communities, perhaps on a nationwide level. However, it would not directly mitigate the weaknesses of our economic system, and we would still have difficulties addressing the huge inequalities in happiness and wealth build-up. Collaterally, I believe some changes would appear as products, services, and investments would be assessed via the Happiness app. However, capitalism in today's form would likely not move much. Primarily because we have actively excluded investors from monetary participation in happiness so far.

To unleash this ultimate power, we have to finally create a new, universal currency, the Happiness dollar, or :)$.

5. THE HAPPINESS DOLLAR: CREATING A NEW ECONOMY

The moment we translate happiness into a currency, we activate a new superorganism. All of us together as *one* species. Suddenly we can leverage the arbitrage of happiness along the Universal happiness hierarchy by our novel economic system. Driven by their lead metric, return on investment, the few rich people on our planet would lead the effort to create happiness for others. On the back of all these investments targeting, first, areas of sustained misery, happiness would explode. For the first time, an economic system would truly create broad well-being.

This last step would exponentially improve happiness and would engage all leading structures, organizations, and countries in the most important objective for mankind: happiness.

As I have elaborated in the previous two chapters, the timing of the switch to the :)$ as a currency is critical. The network utilizing the Happiness app has to be big enough and sustained enough before we enable the :)$ to be traded in our financial world. Personally, I do not care whether we end up with one universal currency focusing only on Return on Happiness, or with two—the :)$ and the fiat currencies ensuring productivity and return on investment for happy-making activities, products, and services. To jump-start the Capitalism of Happiness on our planet, two currencies would likely be an accelerator. We all like competition, remember?

And this time, the competition will be a highly collaborative one. This time, it will focus on everyone's progress.

The good news is, we have started the journey already—with you finishing the book in front of you.

Let progress begin.

EPILOGUE

What does it take to make the Capitalism of Happiness work—in particular starting from where the world stands today? And would it really translate so we can find *ultimate progress*, the aim of the game of life?

The :)\$ is intentionally based on positive reinforcement alone. Thus far this book hasn't discussed the cost of unhappiness for an individual, for society, or even for the progress of life. So what do we lose today by silently accepting all the unhappiness out there? And what do we lose by fighting each other instead of cooperating?

We lose genetic variability, diversity in thinking, and brilliant minds too early due to wars, hunger, criminality, suicide, and disease. The long list of traumatic ills for millions of people include humiliation, bullying, rape, physical abuse, addiction, insufficient education, and missed opportunity. It is important to note that people don't necessarily die of missed opportunity; most of them fight their whole life and live on with relatively low levels of happiness.

Unhappiness is the ultimate infectious disease. It replicates much more effectively than any virus. It spreads silently, physically, and digitally; one unhappy person can even infect millions at the same time. So unhappiness is heavily contagious within a generation. In addition, unhappy people can still reproduce, in contrast to people with a severe disease. Thus they unconsciously ensure the next generation will be unhappy too, surrounded by their parents' misery. Statistics confirm that emerging from an unhappy environment makes it extremely challenging, if not impossible, for the following generation to live a happy life.

As indicated in the opening chapters, the latest data indicate that almost 50 percent of all humans on this planet struggle with an addiction. In addition, on average 50 percent of the global population face more than one period of severe depression in their lifetime. Obviously that is already dramatic—both for the individuals facing addiction and depression, and for everyone around them, who are collaterally impacted. As discussed, depression and addiction are disproportionately impacting middle-income and high-income people. And their families and communities.

Now, just take a minute to digest the following fundamental data on the next generation's situation. I focus only on the lowest level of psychological needs in order to provide an indication of what the next generation is facing. On top of the addiction and depression we already experience in the developed world, there are the following social ills:

- 19.5 percent or 387 million children live in extreme poverty, which means below $1.90 per day—this number has increased in the past years.
- 63 million primary school–age children and 61 million secondary school–age children are not going to school, excluding them from basic education right from the start. There has not been any improvement in these numbers for the last ten years, effectively.
- Worldwide, three-quarters of children aged two to four—close to 300 million children—are regularly subjected to violent discipline (physical punishment and/or psychological aggression) by their parents or other caregivers at home, and around 6 in 10 (250 million) are subjected to physical punishment.
- Bullying is experienced by close to 130 million students aged thirteen to fifteen worldwide.
- 9 million girls aged fifteen to nineteen years old were forced into sexual intercourse last year.

I stop here, because the pain of seeing the numbers of today's misery and imagining the impact on our future is so frustrating . . .

All these issues affect not only the individuals in question, not only their families and surrounding communities. As a broader consequence, we all lose when so many people are not "productive" in the sense of providing happiness to others. If you yourself are not happy, there is no energy left to make other people happy. There is not even energy left to be economically productive. If we add up all the numbers, we probably miss the contributions of more than 70 percent of all humans, people who could otherwise add productively to the world's happiness. And in losing their contributions, we lose out on the optionality we all will require to continue to play the game of life. We need every single brain, gene, knowledge, and network on this planet to fortify ourselves for all the uncertainties coming our way. In particular, the big and ugly ones coming toward us.

We need to fundamentally change how we leverage who we are as a species. We are falling short of our full potential, big-time. The only way to initiate this change is to make all of us experience again how much fun we can actually have building things together. Without striving for money, without fully manifested drug addictions, without having a dopamine rush because we have won a small fight against ourselves or other people. But by just activating the other reward systems as well as we currently do with dopamine.

And we have to actively take care of those who have been hurt, humiliated, and traumatized. If we don't show them that it is worthwhile to live on and seek happiness, the disease of depression will continue to spread and exponentially increase in the generations to come. Of course we can just pretend that we don't care, since we will all be dead by then. Based on what I have outlined here, I believe we should care. Not for the others, actually; no, for our own happiness. Life is just more fun together if you take care of yourself and of others.

The key question is whether we should deter or punish people who deliberately and continually provide unhappiness to others. How much can the :)$ support this effort?

On the one hand, it should be easier in the future to convince governments to invest in violence prevention programs and criminal rehabilitation programs, even though they are expensive in dollars. The amount of happiness created and the :)$ earned as a secondary effect will be huge and will easily justify such activities. On the other hand, given the harm that criminal offenders inflict on their victims, it seems intuitively correct to punish such people substantially. Even more so if we anticipate the impact beyond the current generation. Looking at the Return on Happiness dimension, child abuse or bullying becomes exponentially more severe compared to today, when we obviously react with disgust that we can't quantify.

I would project that over time, we would see a change in how we handle criminality and punishment. First, we would likely be much more drastic with punishment and transparently make people learn what it means to damage the happiness of other people today and in the future, in this generation and potentially in the ones to come. (Attention: negative conditioning never works!) However, secondly, we would positively intervene much earlier given that such people are underserved in experiencing happiness by themselves in the first place.

Some people will support these efforts because they are just good human beings. However, all of us—including our governments—will be supportive because there are massive amounts of :)$ to be earned. I am a strong believer that there are very few—if any!—criminals or bad people only by genetic predisposition. Like Maslow, I strongly believe it is a lack of happiness, a lack of satisfying essential psychological needs, in particular in early childhood. That's where the lever is for all of us: Educate our children so they understand and experience all six reward systems. Once they know, their memories will always remind them how awesome it is to be happy together. Our children will be the generation equipped to drive progress. Not for us. Not for them. But for our whole future.

The obvious challenge of this observation is . . . time. In education, it normally takes three full generations with pretty bold persistence to change something. The main reason is that our education is decentralized during the most critical years. How will a person who has known no other reward system but active dopamine educate their own children? How will our teachers educate our children if they are fighting for their basic safety needs due to too low of a salary? How will our universities educate our students for happiness if the professors know it is all about the next research grant and every exam is designed to separate the good from the not-so-good in order to prepare them for a good job later? How can the world believe that happiness is really possible if all leaders steer their countries based on fear? Fear of unemployment, economic crisis, refugees, terrorists, insufficient health care.

The introduction of a currency that rewards people for providing happiness is only a first step. But it is a very good first step, given how well we all have been trained in the past two generations by money and our economic system. The :)$ is an advanced "substitute drug" to get rid of our behaviors that focus purely on money, stuff that money can buy, or surrogates that money pretends to represent. The real benefit is that the :)$ has been designed to be the best substitute drug so far invented: it makes you reflect on the benefits of the original drug—the dollar—while providing you much more happiness! In addition, the :)$ takes away the negative health impacts. The :)$ is the most effective drug, and—on top of that—it drives brain health. Thus, I believe the new token of appreciation—the :)$—will be more attractive than anything else we have had before as a species. For the first time we will utilize our learning potential in its entirety—from a psychological perspective *and* from a neuroscientific perspective.

The ultimate success of the introduction of the :)$ would be more people reaching the upper three levels of the Universal happiness hierarchy: self-actualization, G-love, and We-actualization.

We-actualization and G-love go beyond our individual growth needs. These levels expand self-actualization to a couple, family, or group of people looking toward a joint objective, a joint purpose, and working on it together. On that level, neurologically, there is no interpersonal competition anymore. It is pure cooperation. Neuroplasticity and happiness explode when we work together for a higher purpose, when we grow together, when we cooperate. In particular, when we cooperate and enjoy progress together in order to overcome big challenges. In essence, three of our six reward systems are primarily there to support cooperation and drive We-actualization. From a neuroscientific perspective, the level of We-actualization especially drives exponential, collective happiness: "herd happiness," if you will.

How does this actually work? How will the :)$ drive cooperation and ultimately We-actualization?

In order to address this question, we have to go back to the start of this book. The evolution of life is based on genetic mutation, natural selection, and cooperation. On the one hand, evolution is based on competition and therefore drives selfish behavior and success at the expense of competitors. On the other hand, cooperation is fundamental for the stepwise changes of evolution, like new levels of organizations that outcompete single building blocks. In essence, while competition is the evolutionary driver, collaboration is the best strategy for winning, and, as such, is the key lever for progress of life. Without cooperation, there is no breakthrough progress.

The challenge for cooperation is that without any supportive mechanism for the evolution of cooperation, natural selection on the lower level (within groups) favors being selfish—the direct opposite of cooperation. Interestingly, on a group level, pure cooperator groups grow faster and outcompete pure competitor groups. In contrast, in mixed groups defectors grow faster than cooperators, ultimately destroying cooperation and driving such groups to lose against groups with strong intrinsic cooperation.

Since Darwin, biologists and, later, mathematicians have tried to explain selective altruism and cooperative behavior among individuals within a species and between species. Several supporting mechanisms driving cooperation have been identified in theoretical mathematical models. In general, all models heavily depend on the cost-benefit ratio for altruistic behavior. The fundamental challenge for cooperative behavior is the phasing difference of benefit and cost and the associated uncertainty. While the costs are incurred immediately and with high certainty, the benefits are highly uncertain and will be borne out only in the future.

Most models are too narrow to allow for relevant applications in real-life settings. Either because they focus only on relatives (kin selection) or look at a limited number of interactions (direct reciprocity, network reciprocity) or highly simplified natural selection (group selection). Thus, we will not look at these theories here.

However, I would like to test the potential impact of the :)$ on positive selection for cooperative behavior in two more sophisticated theories: *indirect reciprocity* and *green-beard selection*.

Reciprocity is a term from evolutionary biology and social psychology. It describes a behavior in relationships that responds to positive actions with a positive feedback. In addition, negative or hostile actions will provoke other negative actions, sometimes even worse than the original one. Direct reciprocity takes only direct interpersonal interactions into account: my response to you considers only how you treat me. In contrast, indirect reciprocity considers what you have done to me *and* what you have done to others. Reciprocity is not altruism. Altruism does not expect or hope for a future positive response when we act. Reciprocity does.

Therefore, direct reciprocity is widely applied in our economy. Basically everywhere. Primarily as a marketing tool to drive product sales, such as giveaways of free samples in order to trigger real future purchases. The free cheese samples given in the supermarket likely drive the purchase of a bigger piece after people tried the sample for free—or at least some other cheese. It also works in elevating returns on providing above-average service: tip somebody who serves you. A cool or funny waiter likely gets more tips than a grumpy one. In direct reciprocity, money helps us to guide the dimension of our response. We rarely give a thousand-dollar tip to a waiter who serves us a twenty-dollar meal, but perhaps two to four dollars. If reciprocity gets out of balance or is abused, we move toward bribery. Importantly, reciprocity does not really work anymore if the positive response is predefined, such as the informal minimum 20 percent tip rule in San Francisco or the zero-tip policy in Singapore.

Indirect reciprocity has become fundamental to our behaviors in our world of deep global analog networks and digital networks and social media, and it is therefore accepted today as the best model to mimic real-world relationships. Indirect reciprocity requires social intelligence in order to monitor and interpret the interactions of others—interactions of others directly with me and interactions of others among themselves. We have to embrace the concept of reputation in order to reflect on possible consequences for our own reputation based on how we act and how people perceive us. Bad acts diminish a person's reputation while good acts improve it. Thus, the shaping (or faking) of our digital profiles is doing nothing else: promoting my positive behaviors, actions, and attributes while hiding the negative ones.

In addition, we like to learn from the experience of others. Spreading the learning of indirect reciprocity requires sophisticated language to explain details on facts and emotions. There is strongly supporting evidence that indirect reciprocity has provided substantial natural selection pressure for human language, social intelligence, morality, and social norms. Indirect reciprocity is a central mechanism to drive evolution on the individual and on the group level toward or away from cooperative behavior.

The assessment of indirect reciprocity is difficult, but one decisive factor promoting cooperation has been clearly identified: social acquaintanceship. In other words, the better we know the reputation of a person represented by their social acquaintanceship, the better we can assess whether we should interact with that person and in which form in order to optimize our benefit in the future.

In mathematical terms, cooperation behavior is evolutionarily favored if our benefit in the future (b) divided by the cost today (c) is larger than the multiplicative inverse of social acquaintanceship (q), or:

$$\frac{b \ (\text{future})}{c \ (\text{present})} > \frac{1}{q}$$

This simple formula indicates the key challenge in today's world: we have hardly any clue about q, the social acquaintanceship of the people we interact with; q is highly uncertain. So our future benefit is highly uncertain, while the cost we have to incur today is pretty certain—we know pretty much what we have to invest into a relationship today with respect to time, money, and emotions. The uncertainty around social acquaintanceship has dramatically increased with the advent of social media and the internet. While available information has massively increased (which is good), the reliability of evidence about that information has basically collapsed.

There is hardly any objective measure to indicate reliability or trustworthiness or social acquaintanceship of a person we interact with and potentially would like to cooperate with. Most of the time we trust our gut feeling or rely on references, both entirely subjective measures. In a :)$ economy, we would have the ultimate unbiased numerical indicator to assess q, social acquaintanceship. The amount of :)$ a person owns is a very good proxy for cooperativeness, simply by providing an indication of how much happiness that person has provided to others. If we decide to cooperate, we will prefer to cooperate with a person who has a rich :)$ account.

The other key challenge is the delay until the benefits readout for a cooperative person. The future benefits are highly uncertain at the moment when the decision to cooperate must be made. Only much later, in the far future, does the cooperative person get confirmation on whether the altruistic behavior was worthwhile. In the time until the readout, behavior adjustments are hardly possible, because there is no measurable feedback to review. With the :)$ we now have an objective feedback loop that provides pretty immediate certainty on our benefits.

In conclusion, application of the :)$ fundamentally drives selection of cooperation over competition in indirect reciprocity. First by substantially reducing the uncertainty around social acquaintanceship. Second, by substantially reducing the uncertainty around future benefits for the person engaging in cooperation. The :)$ fundamentally drives cooperation and We-growth.

Next, the evolutionary thought experiment of green-beard selection was originally proposed by legendary biologist William Hamilton in 1964. The experiment later got its name from a quotation by evolutionary biologist and author Richard Dawkins in 1976: "I have a green beard and I will be altruistic to anyone else with a green beard." The concept emerged in order to resolve the paradox that genes driving altruistic behavior are not naturally selected, in accordance with the basic evolutionary rules of mutation and natural selection. In essence, a gene for behavioral altruism will be positively selected only if the altruism is primarily directed at other individuals who share the gene—and benefit from the selection. In theory a "green-beard selection" can occur when a single gene or a set of genes produce three effects: a phenotypical trait (the green beard); recognition of this trait by others; and strongly cooperative treatment of individuals with the trait.

Over the years, biologists have debated the validity of green beard genes and green-beard selection. Indeed, recently a few examples of such genes have been identified in fire ants, lizards, and mice. In addition, the biological and cultural aspects of language selection have been linked to green-beard selection recently.

I never believed that cooperative behavior was based purely on individual genes—I was always skeptical of the hunt for green beard genes. Cooperative behavior goes way beyond our genetic makeup; it is strongly influenced by culture, education, knowledge, and learning. Instead, I believe that certain behaviors—partly inherited, partly learned—are essential to enable cooperation. From that perspective, winning cooperative strategies tend to be generous, positively risk-taking, and forgiving. These three items are related: if I am generous, it is easier for me to forgive and to take some risks cooperating with a new partner in a positive sense.

The missing element that would fundamentally select cooperation is an indicator of generous, positively risk-taking, and forgiving people. Such an indicator does not have to be a phenotypical expression and representation of a gene or a set of genes. It just has to be an objective indicator of behavior. In essence, I don't care about the individual genes underlying the behavior as long as the associated genes working together are there. The behavior drives the selection for cooperation—and the genes enabling such behavior come with it.

With the introduction of the :)$ we resolve this issue. The :)$ becomes the transparent indicator—the green beard. With the :)$, people can recognize those who like to provide happiness to others. Because the highest returns can be achieved by cooperating with each other, the :)$ becomes a direct surrogate for cooperative behaviors. The :)$ keeps its role as a secondary reinforcer. It's not a gene, nor does it link to a single gene or gene cluster. However, it represents various combinations of selective traits that drive people to provide happiness to others.

Based on mathematical models applied in experiments so far, the :)$—our green beard—will rapidly drive evolutionary selection of people genuinely willing to provide happiness to others and to cooperate; and this will happen in a highly accelerated manner, after an estimated two or three generations. The :)$ provides an upfront "seal of approval" for cooperative behaviors that should ultimately drive successful cultural reproduction and—along with that—genetic reproduction. The :)$ serves as a universal, highly reliable indicator today for benefits in the future. A group composed of such cooperative members who are driven by the most effective biological reward—happiness—is simply unbeatable in any selection challenge that happens on a group level. Defectors can't penetrate such cooperative groups.

In these groups, winners don't punish—because in cooperation, there are no individual winners; we only win all together. The joint experience of success is one of the key hallmarks of We-actualization, the ultimate driver for the progress of life.

Putting it all together, I think it is time for an update of our current economic system, amazing though it is. We should enhance it to include happiness at its core. Happiness is the ultimate leap for mankind. But this one I believe we should enjoy together.

We-actualization FOREVER! ☺☺☺.

ACKNOWLEDGMENTS

There are a number of people I would like to recognize and thank for making this book possible. Foremost, I'd like to thank Mark Boutros, Ben Goldhirsh, Steffen and Anne Weitzdörfer for hours and days reading through immature concepts, providing fundamental feedback and amazing discussions. I'm ever grateful to Said Francis, Ciaran Lawlor, and Eric Huang for legendary nights in Boston debating and testing the concept of a happiness dollar. My gratitude to Natalia Brzezinski and Daniel Ek for the opportunity to present at Brilliant Minds in Stockholm 2018, and to the Brilliant Minds community for pushing me to publish my thoughts. I'd like to thank Kira Peikoff for hours of editing work combined with brilliant input and ideas, and the Girl Friday Production team for successfully and patiently guiding me through the publishing jungle. Most of all, I would like to thank Marie, Lisa, Sandra and Paul—my family and closest friends—who ultimately ensured that I did not lose myself over endless night shifts in the past years. Finally, I would like to thank Berlin, the best city in the world, and Lilly, the girl from Amsterdam who, without intending it, set me on this journey five years ago.

REFERENCES

Adler, N. E., T. Boyce, M. Chesney, S. Cohen, S. Folkman, R. Kahn, and S. Syme. 1994. "Socioeconomic Status and Health: The Challenge of the Gradient." *American Psychologist* 49: 15–24.

Advameg, Inc.; Encyclopedia of Mental Disorders: http://www .minddisorders.com.

Alderfer, Clayton P. 1972. *Existence, Relatedness and Growth: Human Needs in Organizational Settings.* New York: The Free Press.

Algoe, Sara B., and Jonathan Haidt. 2009. "Witnessing Excellence in Action: The 'Other-Praising' Emotions of Elevation, Gratitude, and Admiration." *The Journal of Positive Psychology* 4: 105–127.

Algoe, Sara B. 2012. "Find, Remind, and Bind: The Social Functions of Gratitude in Everyday Relationships." *Social and Personality Psychology Compass* 6: 455–469.

Andersen I., K. Thielen, P. Bech, E. Nygaard, and F. Diderichsen. 2011. "Increasing Prevalence of Depression from 2000 to 2006." *The Scandinavian Journal of Public Health* 39: 857–863.

Aristotle. 1893. *Nicomachean Ethics*. 5th ed. Translated by F. H. Peters. London: Kegan Paul, Trench, Trübner & Co.

Alexander, Richard D. 1987. *The Biology of Moral Systems*. New York: Aldine de Gruyter.

American Psychiatric Association. 2013. *Diagnostic and Statistical Manual of Mental Disorders (DSM-5)*. Arlington, VA: American Psychiatric Association.

Bartlett, M. Y., and D. DeSteno. 2006. "Gratitude and Prosocial Behavior: Helping When It Costs You." *Psychological Science* 17: 319–325.

Brandt, H, and K. Sigmund. 2004. "The Logic of Reprobation: Assessment and Action Rules for Indirect Reciprocation." *The Journal of Theoretical Biology* 231: 475–486.

Brem, A-K., K. Ran, and A. Pascual-Leone. 2013. "Learning and Memory." *Handbook of Clinical Neurology* 116: 693–737.

Buettner, Dan. 2008. *The Blue Zones: 9 Lessons for Living Longer from the People Who've Lived the Longest*. Washington, DC: National Geographic Books.

Cacioppo, S., J. T. Cacioppo, and J. P. Capitanio. 2014. "Towards a Neurology of Loneliness." *Psychological Bulletin* 140: 1464–1504.

Campos, B., M. N. Shiota, D. Keltner, G. C. Gonzaga, and J. L. Goetz. 2013. "What Is Shared, What Is Different? Core Relational Themes and Expressive Displays of Eight Positive Emotions." *Cognition and Emotion* 27: 37–52.

Compton, WM. et al. 2006. "Changes in Prevalence of Major Depression and Comorbid Substance Use Disorders in the United States between 1991–1992 and 2001–2002." *The American Journal of Psychiatry* 163: 2141–2147.

Darwin, Charles. 1859. *On the Origin of Species by Means of Natural Selection, or the Preservation of Favoured Races in the Struggle for Life.* London: John Murray, Albemarle Street.

———. 1871. *The Descent of Man, and Selection in Relation to Sex.* London: John Murray, Albemarle Street.

———. 1872. *The Expression of the Emotions in Man and Animals.* London: John Murray, Albemarle Street.

Dawkins, Richard. 1976. *The Selfish Gene.* Oxford: Oxford University Press.

Davidson, R. J., and B. S. McEwen. 2013. "Social Influence on Neuroplasticity: Stress and Intervention to Promote Well-Being." *Nature Neuroscience* 15: 689–695.

Diener, E., P. Kesebir, and R. Lucas. 2008. "Benefits of Accounts of Well-Being, for Societies and for Psychological Science." *Applied Psychology* 57: 37–53.

Diener, E., and L. Tay. 2011. "Needs and Subjective Well-Being around the World." *The Journal of Personality and Social Psychology* 101: 354–365.

DeSteno, D., Y. Li, L. Dickens, and J. S. Lerner. 2014. "Gratitude: A Tool for Reducing Economic Impatience." *Psychological Science* 25: 1262–1267.

Diamond, L. M. 2003. "What Does Sexual Orientation Orient? A Biobehavioral Model Distinguishing Romantic Love and Sexual Desire." *Psychological Review* 110: 173–192.

Eriksson, K., I. Vartanova, P. Strimling, and B. Simpson. 2018. "Generosity Pays: Selfish People Have Fewer Children and Earn Less Money." *Journal of Personality and Social Psychology* Advance online publication. http://dx.doi.org/10.1037/pspp0000213.

Evans, M. K., J. M. Lepkowski, N. R. Powe, T. LaVeist, M. F. Kuczmarski, and A. B. Zonderman. 2010. "Healthy Aging in Neighborhoods of Diversity across the Life Span (HANDLS): Overcoming Barriers to Implementing a Longitudinal, Epidemiologic, Urban Study of Health, Race, and Socioeconomic Status." *Ethnicity & Disease* 20, no. 3 (Summer): 267–275.

Fink, Larry. 2018. "Larry Fink's Letter to CEOs: A Sense of Purpose." https://www.blackrock.com/corporate/investor-relations/2018 -larry-fink-ceo-letter.

Fromm, Erik. 1956. *The Art of Loving.* New York: Harper & Brothers.

Gershman, S. J., and N. D. Daw. 2017. "Reinforcement Learning and Episodic Memory in Humans and Animals: An Integrative Framework." *Annual Reviews of Psychology* 68: 101–128.

Global Burden of Disease 2016. The Lancet (September 2016): https:// www.thelancet.com/gbd/2016.

Gonzaga, G. C., R. A. Turner, D. Keltner, B. Campos, and M. Altemus. 2006. "Romantic Love and Sexual Desire in Close Relationships." *Emotion* 6: 163–179.

Gordon, A. M., E. A. Impett, A. Kogan, C. Oveis, and D. Keltner. 2012. "To Have and to Hold: Gratitude Promotes Relationship Maintenance in Intimate Bonds." *Journal of Personality and Social Psychology* 103: 257–274.

Griskevicius, V., M. N. Shiota, and S. L. Neufeld. 2010. "Influence of Different Positive Emotions on Persuasion Processing: A Functional Evolutionary Approach." *Emotion* 10: 190–206.

Güsewell, A., and W. Ruch. 2012. "Are Only Emotional Strengths Emotional? Character Strengths and Disposition to Positive Emotions." *Applied Psychology: Health and Well-Being* 4: 218–239.

Hagnell O., L. Ojesjö, L. Otterbeck, and B. Rorsman. 1994. "Prevalence of Mental Disorders, Personality Traits and Mental Complaints in the Lundby Study." *The Scandinavian Journal of Social Medicine* 50: 1–77.

Hamilton, W. D. 1964. "The Genetical Evolution of Social Behavior." *The Journal of Theoretical Biology* 7: 1–16.

Hanauer, Nick. February 8, 2015. "Stock Buybacks Are Killing the American Economy." *The Atlantic.*

Hayek, Friedrich August von. 1976. *The Denationalization of Money.* London: Institute of Economic Affairs.

Helliwell, John F., Richard Layard, and Jeffrey Sachs. 2012. *World Happiness Report 2012.* New York: UN Sustainable Development Solutions Network.

———. 2016. *World Happiness Report 2016.* New York: Sustainable Development Solutions Network.

———. 2017. *World Happiness Report 2017.* New York: Sustainable Development Solutions Network.

———. 2019. *World Happiness Report 2019.* New York: Sustainable Development Solutions Network.

Hertenstein, M. J., D. Keltner, B. App, B. A. Bulleit, and A. R. Jaskolka. 2006. "Touch Communicates Distinct Emotions." *Emotion* 6: 528–533.

Hidaka, B. H. 2012. "Depression as Disease of Modernity: Explanations for Increasing Prevalence." *The Journal of Affective Disorders* 140: 205–214.

Hunt, A. 2014. "Expanding the Biopsychological Model: The Active Reinforcement Model for Addiction." *The Graduate Student Journal of Psychology* 15: 57–69.

Ito, Joi. February 1, 2018. "The Big ICO Swindle." *Wired.* https://www .wired.com/story/ico-cryptocurrency-irresponsibility/.

Jia, L., L. N. Li, and E. M. W. Tong. 2015. "Gratitude Facilitates Behavioral Mimicry." *Emotion* 15: 134–138.

Kandel, E. R., J. H. Schwartz, and T. M. Jessel. 2000. *Principles of Neuroscience.* 4th ed. McGraw-Hill Medical.

Kuppens, P., A. Realo, and E. Diener. 2008. "The Role of Positive and Negative Emotions in Life Satisfaction Judgment across Nations." *The Journal of Personality and Social Psychology* 95: 66–75.

Lindenfors, P. 2013. "The Green Beards of Language." *Ecology and Evolution* 3: 1104–1112.

Loonen, A. J. M., and S. A. Ivanova. 2016. "Circuits Regulating Pleasure and Happiness—Mechanism of Depression." *Frontiers of Human Neuroscience* 17, 10: 1–25.

Lustig, R. 2017. *The Hacking of the American Mind.* New York: Avery Publishing.

Marcus S. C., and M. Olfson. 2010. "National Trends in the Treatment of Depression." *Archives of General Psychiatry* 67: 1265–1273.

Maslow, Abraham H. 1954. *Motivation and Personality.* New York: Harper and Row.

———. 1968. *Toward a Psychology of Being.* New York: Van Nostrand Company.

————. 1971. *The Farther Reaches of Human Nature*. New York: The Viking Press.

Martin, R. A. 2010. *The Psychology of Humor: An Integrative Approach*. Burlington, MA: Elsevier Academic Press.

Marx, Karl, and Friedrich Engels. 1867. *Das Kapital*, Volume I. Hamburg: Verlag von Otto Meisner.

Marx, Karl. 1885. *Das Kapital* Volume II. Hamburg: Verlag von Otto Meisner.

————. 1894. *Das Kapital* Volume III. Hamburg: Verlag von Otto Meisner.

McCullough, M. E., S. D. Kilpatrick, R. A. Emmons, and D. B. Larson. 2001. "Is Gratitude a Moral Affect?" *Psychological Bulletin* 127: 249–266.

Mortillaro, M., M. Mehu, and K. R. Scherer. 2011. "Subtly Different Positive Emotions Can Be Distinguished by Their Facial Expressions." *Social Psychological and Personality Science* 2: 262–271.

Muise, A., E. A. Impett, and S. Desmarais. 2013. "Getting It On Versus Getting It Over With: Sexual Motivation, Desire, and Satisfaction in Intimate Bonds." *Personality and Social Psychology Bulletin* 39: 1320–1332.

National Institute on Drug Abuse: https://www.drugabuse.gov.

Nowak, M. A., and K. Sigmund. 2005. "Evolution of Indirect Reciprocity." *Nature* 437:1291.

Nowak, M. A. 2006. "Five Rules for the Evolution of Cooperation." *Science* 31: 1560–1573.

———. 2008. "Generosity: A Winner's Advice." *Nature* 456: 579.

Ohtsuki, H., and Y. Iwasa. 2004. "How Should We Define Goodness? Reputation Dynamics in Indirect Reciprocity." *The Journal of Theoretical Biology* 231: 107–120.

Olfson, M. et al. 2002. "National Trends in the Outpatient Treatment of Depression." *JAMA* 287: 203–209.

Olds, J., and P. Milner. 1954. "Positive Reinforcement Produced by Electrical Stimulation of the Septal Area and Other Regions of Rat Brain." *The Journal of Comparative Psychology* 47:419–27.

One Planet Sovereign Wealth Fund, press release, June 28, 2018: https://oneplanetswfs.org.

Oxfam Davos Report 2018. https://www.oxfam.org/en/pressroom/pressreleases/2018-01-22/richest-1-percent-bagged-82-percent-wealth-created-last-year.

Postman, Neil. 1985. *Amusing Ourselves to Death: Public Discourse in the Age of Show Business.* New York: Viking Penguin.

Piff, P. K., P. Dietze, M. Feinberg, D. M. Stancato, and D. Keltner. 2015. "Awe, the Small Self, and Prosocial Behavior." *Journal of Personality and Social Psychology* 108: 883–899.

Rasmussen, Dennis C. June 9, 2016. "The Problem with Inequality, According to Adam Smith." *The Atlantic.*

Riolo, R. L., M. D. Cohen, and R. Axelrod. 2001. "Evolution of Cooperation without Reciprocity." *Nature* 414: 441–443.

Roseman, I. J. 1996. "Appraisal Determinants of Emotions: Constructing a More Accurate and Comprehensive Theory." *Cognition and Emotion* 10: 241–278.

Ruch, W. 1993. "Exhilaration and Humor." In *The Handbook of Emotion*, edited by M. Lewis and J. M. Haviland, 605–616. New York: Guilford Press Publications.

Sauter, D. A., and S. K. Scott. 2007. "More Than One Kind of Happiness: Can We Recognize Vocal Expressions of Different Positive States?" *Motivation and Emotion* 31: 192–199.

Shiota, M. N., B. Campos, D. Keltner, and M. J. Hertenstein. 2004. "Positive Emotion and the Regulation of Interpersonal Relationships." In *The Regulation of Emotion*, edited by P. Philippot and R. S. Feldman, 127–155. Mahwah, NJ: Erlbaum.

Shiota, M. N., D. Keltner, and A. Mossman. 2007. "The Nature of Awe: Elicitors, Appraisals, and Effects on Self-Concept." *Cognition and Emotion* 21: 944–963.

Shiota, M. N., S. L. Neufeld, W. H. Yeung, S. E. Moser, and E. F. Perea. 2011. "Feeling Good: Autonomic Nervous System Responding in Five Positive Emotions." *Emotion* 11 : 1368–1378.

Shiota M. N., B. Campos, C. Oveis, B. Campus, M. J. Hertenstein, E. Simon-Thomas, and D. Keltner. 2017. "Beyond Happiness: Building a Science of Discrete Positive Emotions." *American Psychologist* 72, no. 7: 617–643.

Skinner, B. F. 1938. *The Behavior of Organisms: An Experimental Analysis*. New York: Appleton-Century-Crofts.

———. 1953. *Science and Human Behavior*. New York: MacMillan.

Smith, Adam. 1759. *The Theory of Moral Sentiments*. Edinburgh: Andrew Millar in the Strand and Alexander Kincaid and J. Bell.

———. 1776. *The Wealth of Nations*. London: W. Strahan and T. Cadell.

Span, P. December 30, 2016. "Loneliness Can Be Deadly for Elders; Friends Are the Antidote." *New York Times.*

Sussman, S., N. Lisha, and M. Griffith. 2011. "Prevalence of the Addiction: A Problem of the Majority or the Minority." *Evaluation and the Health Professions* 34: 3–56.

Tracy, J. L., and R.W. Robins. 2007. "The Prototypical Pride Expression: Development of a Nonverbal Behavior Coding System." *Emotion* 7: 789–801.

Tracy, J. L., A. F. Shariff, W. Zhao, and J. Henrich. 2013. "Cross-Cultural Evidence That the Nonverbal Expression of Pride Is an Automatic Status Signal." *Journal of Experimental Psychology: General* 142: 163–180.

Twenge, J. M. et al. 2010. "Birth Cohort Increases in Psychopathology among Young Americans 1938–2007: A Cross-Temporal Meta-Analysis of the MMPI." *Clinical Psychology Review* 30: 145–154.

United Nations Office on Drugs and Crime. 2010. *World Drug Report 2010.* New York: United Nations.

———. 2016. *World Drug Report 2016.* New York: United Nations.

———. 2017. *World Drug Report 2017.* New York: United Nations.

Watson, J. B. 1930. *Behaviorism.* New York: W. W. Norton and Company.

———. 1913 "Psychology as the Behaviorist Views It." *Psychological Review* 20: 158–177.

Watson, J. B., and R. Rayner. 1920. "Conditioned Emotional Reactions." *Journal of Experimental Psychology* 3: 1–14.

Williams, L. A., and D. DeSteno. 2008. "Pride and Perseverance: The Motivational Role of Pride." *Journal of Personality and Social Psychology* 94: 1007–1017.

White, Norman M. 2011. "Reward: What Is It? How Can It Be Inferred from Behavior?" In *Neurobiology of Sensation and Reward*, chapter 3. Boca Raton, Florida: CRC/Taylor & Francis.

Wood, Graeme. April 2011. "Secret Fears of the Super-Rich" *Atlantic Monthly*.

INDEX

Note: Bold page numbers refer to figures.

H

ABOUT THE AUTHOR

Photo credit: Gene Glover, Berlin 2017

Axel Bouchon is a biochemist, neuroscientist, and serial entrepreneur. He holds a doctorate degree in biochemistry. After years spent studying the immune system, the brain, and how we learn, his personal and professional passion turned toward finding fundamental breakthroughs for mankind in the area of bioscience and technology. After a presentation at the Brilliant Minds Conference in 2018 in Stockholm, the audience inspired him to publish his vision for a new economic world order. *Capitalism of Happiness* is his first book. He lives in Berlin and enjoys a modern family life with his two daughters, his ex-wife, and a lot of wonderful friends.

Made in the USA
Middletown, DE
08 November 2019